"Marilyn Watson and Laura Ecken show us the power and the many heartwarming pleasures of creating a caring classroom. This book is profoundly inspirational."
—Eric Schaps, president, Developmental Studies Center, Oakland, California

"Combining great wisdom, extensive knowledge of research and theory, and years of practical experience, Marilyn Watson compellingly presents an evidence-based model for educating all children more effectively. She provides powerful stories and insightful analyses of student-teacher interactions that engage students, and offers practical strategies and techniques to motivate students to be and do their best. This book will renew the optimism and resolve of educators who sometimes feel frustration and doubt about promoting successful outcomes with challenging students and classrooms. Watson describes approaches and perspectives that can prepare teachers to become the educators that parents want their children to have and that students remember for a lifetime. Watson's views and suggestions will energize and excite readers about the potential positive effects of high-quality education. At CASEL, we are often asked to recommend books for teachers, administrators, and parents about integrated academic, social, and emotional learning. *Learning to Trust* is at the top of our list."
—Roger P. Weissberg, executive director, Collaborative for Academic, Social, and Emotional Learning (CASEL), professor of psychology and education, University of Illinois at Chicago

"I regard this book as a wonderful gift. It is quite unusual to find a book that is so well grounded both in research-based theory and in classroom practice. I want the content of *Learning to Trust* to be known by all the participants in the teacher preparation program I direct—student teachers, master teachers, supervisors, and course instructors."
—Paul Ammon, Professor of Education and director of the Developmental Teacher Education Program, University of California, Berkeley

"I kept seeing myself and my students in this book. As recognizable negative situations arose I kept thinking, 'How in the world is she going to get out of this one?' Over and over, Laura showed how to turn negative situations around so that the students weren't cornered, but were empowered in a positive way."
—Sandi Turner, teacher, Mariemont School, Sacramento, California

"In this book, Marilyn Watson has taken years of experience, wedded it to a deep understanding of child development, and applied a powerful ability to listen and interpret the experience of one remarkable and courageous teacher, Laura Ecken. Together, Marilyn and Laura show us all a more enlightened way to work with challenging children in schools. The unique application of attachment theory to classroom management and discipline offers all educators a new vision for fostering healthy classrooms and children of character."
—Marvin W. Berkowitz, Sanford N. McDonnell Professor of Character Education, College of Education, University of Missouri-St. Louis

"*Learning to Trust* provides powerful and thought-provoking insights that will act as a springboard for discussion for educators wrestling with the challenge of effective classroom discipline. This book will make you want to talk."
—Shelia Koshewa, resource teacher and Child Development Project coordinator, Jefferson County Public Schools, Louisville, Kentucky

"The Child Development Project is a remarkable R&D effort that works to promote positive social values in elementary school classrooms throughout the country. The author shows how this project works by writing about her partnership with this inner city teacher, as Laura learns, teaches, inspires, encourages, and builds classroom community. This dynamic view of the conditions that are developed over time to provide for students' basic needs to belong, to care for one another and to be competent, will help teachers and parents see what they have to do to participate in creating these conditions."
—Ann Lieberman, senior scholar, the Carnegie Foundation for the Advancement of Teaching and visiting professor, Stanford University

"At last! A real teacher's voice and feelings revealed! This accessible book about the daily doings of a dedicated, intelligent, caring classroom teacher, her challenging and challenged students, and her equally committed critical friend left my student teachers inspired to find ways to better serve their students."
—Karen Benson, associate professor, California State University, Sacramento

"Why didn't I have this book last semester? It would have supported me through my challenges and led me to meaningful ways of working with my students."
—Alicia Ellsworth, student teacher, California State University, Sacramento

"*Learning to Trust* is a powerful resource for teachers looking for ways to help all children become good learners and good people. Watson brings the theory and the philosophy of developmental discipline to life by documenting the compelling and recognizable experience of a real teacher and her students."
—Pamela Siegle, executive director, Open Circle Programs, The Stone Center, Wellesley College

"With this fine, in-depth case study, Marilyn Watson shows convincingly the importance of relationships in the classroom. This is an intellectually persuasive account that packs a terrific emotional wallop."
—Nel Noddings, Lee Jacks Professor of Education Emerita, Stanford University

LEARNING TO TRUST

LEARNING TO TRUST

Transforming Difficult Elementary Classrooms Through Developmental Discipline

Marilyn Watson

in collaboration with

Laura Ecken

o

Foreword by

Alfie Kohn

JOSSEY-BASS
A Wiley Imprint
www.josseybass.com

Published by Jossey-Bass
A Wiley Imprint
989 Market Street, San Francisco, CA 94103-1741 www.josseybass.com

Jossey-Bass books and products are available through most bookstores. To contact Jossey-Bass directly call our Customer Care Department within the U.S. at 800-956-7739, outside the U.S. at 317-572-3986 or fax 317-572-4002.

Jossey-Bass also publishes its books in a variety of electronic formats. Some content that appears in print may not be available in electronic books.

Library of Congress Cataloging-in-Publication Data

Watson, Marilyn, 1937-
Learning to trust : transforming difficult elementary classrooms through developmental discipline / Marilyn Watson, Laura Ecken ; foreword, Alfie Kohn.— 1st ed.
p. cm. — (The Jossey-Bass education series)
Includes bibliographical references and index.
ISBN 978-0-7879-6650-8 (alk. paper)
1. Classroom management. 2. School discipline. 3. Teacher-student relationships. I. Ecken, Laura. II. Title. III. Series.
LB3013.W382 2003
372.1102'4—dc21 2002156566

FIRST EDITION

The Jossey-Bass
Education Series

To Laura Ecken and her hard-working students.
May some of them be for future children
the kind of teacher Laura was for them.

CONTENTS

FOREWORD

Alfie Kohn

IN WHAT WOULD SEEM to be a deliberate attempt to test the upper limits of my blood pressure, people who are familiar with my views about discipline enjoy regaling me with descriptions of particularly horrible programs they've heard about. By phone or e-mail, in letters or even in person, they feel obliged to fill me in on how a specific school (often the one attended by their own children) has come up with a uniquely diabolical punishment for malefactors or a particularly patronizing system to reward students for their obedience. By now, I'd like to think I've heard all the variations on behavior management that are out there, from cutesy to sadistic, but the sad truth is I probably haven't.

One father, for example, called me to describe how his son's first-grade teacher rates the children's behavior every day on a four-point scale. The boy explained to him how the system works: a 1, the lowest possible rating, is very rare; a 2 is essentially a punishment for any action frowned on by the teacher; and a 3 signifies that the child has followed the rules. "What about a 4?" asked the father. "Well," replied the boy, seeming awed by the mere mention of this number, "to get a 4, you'd have to be a statue!"

Even a very young child realizes that such policies are not intended to foster curiosity or creativity or compassion; they are primarily designed to elicit mindless compliance, the ideal evidently being a student who resembles an inanimate object. Some techniques are not quite so crude, and some commercial discipline programs cloak themselves in progressive rhetoric, but at the end of the school day, the objective is still to control children.

I've come to believe that everything turns on the fundamental questions that drive classroom practice, even if these questions are not posed explicitly. What some teachers and administrators want to know is this: "*How can we get these kids to obey?* What practical strategies can you offer that will make students show up, sit down, and do what they're told?" But other educators begin from an entirely different point of departure. They ask, "*What do these kids need,* and how can we meet those needs?" The more I visit classrooms, talk with teachers, and read the literature, the more I believe that you can predict what a school will look like and feel like just from knowing which set of questions is more salient for the adults. You don't even have to know the answers they've found (which tactics will be used to secure compliance, in the first case; what children are thought to need, in the second). What matters are the questions.

Most of us need help to create a classroom or school that is genuinely defined by children's needs. Ideally, that help comes from supportive colleagues and administrators. Failing that—or, better, in addition to that—one looks to people who have thought deeply about these issues, whose thinking is rooted in theory and research but also in experiences with many different kinds of classrooms. If you win the lottery, as Laura Ecken did, you get extensive personal coaching from Marilyn Watson. Otherwise, you derive those benefits secondhand by reading a book like this one.

Actually, I should say, "by reading this book," not "a book like this one." There are no other books quite like this one, in large part because there are no other thinkers quite like Marilyn. Long before she got around to collecting her thoughts between two covers, she was the program director for a school change effort called the Child Development Project, based in northern California, where I had the good fortune to meet her in the late 1980s. I immediately noticed that her head and hands were always in motion; she used up calories just sitting and talking. She was always running behind schedule because she had trouble tearing herself away from whatever she was doing.

What she was doing was figuring out how to help teachers work with their students to transform classrooms and schools into caring communities. She showed me some of the results and also helped me understand the significance of what I was seeing by taking me to visit classrooms where teachers relied on behavior management programs. In effect, she gave me a filter through which to see—and to recoil from—conventional practices. In the years that followed, she graciously allowed me to interview her for articles and lectures I was preparing about family discipline, assertiveness, grades, fear of spoiling kids, human nature, and other topics. In the process, I came to be influenced by her as much as by any other single person in the field. Mind you, that doesn't mean she's responsible for, or necessarily agrees with, everything I say. It just means I owe her quite a lot, and I'm thrilled that you, too, now have the chance to learn from her, thanks to *Learning to Trust.*

I have suggested that where we end up is directly related to where we begin and, specifically, whether we ask, "How can these kids be made to obey?" as opposed to "What do these kids need?" Marilyn constructs a profound defense of starting with the latter question, as well as a reasonable answer to it that is based on a branch of psychology known as attachment theory. Then she proceeds to demonstrate, precisely and engagingly, just what it means to ask that question—and give that answer—in a real classroom with real children. She offers not merely a polemic seasoned with short illustrations but a detailed description of how one teacher labored to put these precepts into practice (with her help). This book explains a model by telling a story. As if all of these features are not sufficiently unusual and refreshing, the teacher in question works with low-income children whose family situations and resultant attitudes present the hardest possible case for those who oppose control-based management methods. If progress is possible here—and it is—it is possible anywhere.

Those of us who share Marilyn's skepticism about the value of punishments and rewards, as well as her optimism about the usefulness of an alternative approach, will of course welcome her testimony. But the real value of this book derives from what it has to say to practicing teachers and administrators, particularly those who have reluctantly adopted one or another traditional discipline strategy because they assume they have no choice. This book gives such educators permission to try something they already may have found more intuitively appealing, and it offers them a wealth of concrete suggestions for putting that alternative into practice.

Even with tough kids, Marilyn tells us—and, more important, shows us—the teacher's job is not to demand obedience but to build relationships, to understand the students' aching need to be cared about. It is a radically liberating notion that aggression and other disturbing actions can be attributed to kids' lack of skills or ability to trust rather than to their being bad. Everything follows from that perceptual shift, and Marilyn lays out in considerable detail the sorts of interventions that do follow, along with Laura Ecken's struggle to make them work. This book once and for all dispels the myth that we simply must resort to bribes ("positive reinforcement"), threats ("consequences"), and other instruments of coercion in order to deal with angry, resistant students. That alone is reason to buy it, read it, read it again, and then buy more copies to hand out to one's colleagues. Almost anyone who is still open to learning about children will find in *Learning to Trust* not only practical strategies but a different way of seeing, of understanding, of thinking about classrooms and the people who live in them. Her approach can be energizing for teachers and subversive to the status quo in schools. More important, it can make an enduring difference in the lives of students.

Alfie Kohn is the author of eight books about education and human behavior, including *Beyond Discipline: From Compliance to Community* (Association for Supervision and Curriculum Development [ASCD], 1996) and *What to Look for in a Classroom . . . and Other Essays* (Jossey-Bass, 1998). He lives (actually) in Belmont, Massachusetts, and (virtually) at www.alfiekohn.org.

PREFACE

We should educate all our children not only for competence but also for caring. Our aim should be to encourage the growth of competent, caring, loving, and lovable people.
—Nel Noddings, in *The Challenge to Care in Schools* (1992, p. iv)

NEL NODDINGS and her focus on caring have long influenced my thinking about what is most important in educating our children. Over the years, as I worked with schools where qualities of caring were high on the agenda for children as well as teachers, my convictions about the role of caring only deepened. I saw that when children felt cared for, their competence grew and they were able to reciprocate caring to those around them.

The schools I worked with and the classrooms I visited over two decades were those collaborating with the Child Development Project (CDP), which purposefully integrates children's social and ethical development into daily classroom life. CDP has been the subject of dozens of research studies. It is one of the research-based school reform models endorsed by the federal government through the Comprehensive School Reform Demonstration (CSRD), or Obey–Porter legislation.

Research about CDP has found it to be effective in promoting students' concern and respect for others, their intrinsic academic motivation, and their positive social values and skills. It is most effective when students experience their classrooms and schools as caring communities (Battistich, Solomon, Watson, and Schaps, 1997).

In reflecting on the conditions for CDP's successes, I came to believe that Developmental Discipline, the most ambitious component of the CDP program, is key to succeeding with all students. Developmental Discipline is not "discipline as usual." It is discipline that derives its power from the quality of the teacher–student relationship and its efficacy from the caring quality of the total classroom environment. Unlike most of the familiar approaches to classroom discipline that focus on controlling children, Developmental Discipline focuses on building a caring classroom community and a nurturing, trusting partnership with each student. These partnerships do not eliminate the need for adult control, but more frequently they involve teaching the social, emotional, and moral skills and understandings that children have not yet developed.

Because Developmental Discipline touches almost every aspect of classroom life and is a radical departure from discipline as usual, it has been difficult to satisfactorily answer the most basic question of all: What does Developmental Discipline look like in the classroom? I hope this book provides an answer by example. It follows the actions, outcomes, and reflections of one inner-city teacher, Laura Ecken, as she works across two years to build caring and trusting relationships, meet her students' and her own needs, and inspire her students to care about learning, one another, and the world outside the classroom door. It is the result of a long and deep collaboration between Laura and me, as we worked together to more fully understand the implications of attachment theory and what it means when Developmental Discipline structures daily classroom life.

The children in this story are gloriously and sometimes heartbreakingly real. Their stories and words are true, but their identities and those of Laura's colleagues have been changed to protect their privacy. I wish I could report that every one of Laura's students is thriving—and, despite great odds, many are. But thriving or not, they will all remember this remarkable teacher who cared about them.

February 2003
Vacaville, Calif.

Marilyn Sheehan Watson

ACKNOWLEDGMENTS

MANY PEOPLE have contributed in a variety of ways to this book. Eric Schaps, president of Developmental Studies Center, and Judy Kingsley, the former managing director, graciously provided me the time I needed to get a good start on the writing. They, together with many wonderful colleagues at Developmental Studies Center, helped sharpen my thinking and supported my efforts to shape Developmental Discipline into a coherent and workable approach. In particular, I would like to thank Vic Battistitch, Stefan Dasho, Catherine Lewis, and two cherished and valuable colleagues who did not live to see this book finished, Sylvia Kendzior and Dan Solomon. Although we did not always agree, having the privilege to work and talk with them challenged, supported, and expanded my thinking. I also owe a debt of gratitude to the many teachers and principals who were part of the Child Development Project and the teacher educators involved in DSC's Preservice Project.

Several people directly contributed to the book by reading earlier versions of the manuscript and offering both critical and encouraging comments. I want to thank Karen Benson and Lana Daley, of California State University at Sacramento, and the teachers from Mariemont School who were part of Karen and Lana's Intrinsic Motivation Project, Gayanne Leachman, Deanna Victor, Joan Wulff, Kalei Kahumoku, and Sandi Turner. I also want to thank Jennifer Dieken-Buchek, a teacher and administrative intern at Tillman Elementary School, and Karen Smith, principal of Mark Twain Elementary School, both doctoral students in Marvin Berkowitz's character education class at the University of Missouri-St. Louis who, along with Marvin, provided many helpful comments. I owe a special debt of gratitude to Paul Ammon, Erick Hesse, Alfie Kohn, Mary Main, and Nel Noddings for their inspiring work, collegial conversations, and insightful and helpful comments on the manuscript.

Three former colleagues at Developmental Studies Center were particularly important in the creation of this book: Cindy Littman, who helped me comb through thousands of pages of transcript to find the vignettes to tell the story, Peter Swartz, who worked with Laura and me throughout the period of data collection, and Lynn Murphy, who edited this book with love and painstaking care. Throughout the writing, Lynn provided constant encouragement as well as critical feedback and graceful editing.

My children, Joie and Sean, contributed to this book in ways that they do not really know. It was they who first sent me searching for alternatives to rewards and punishments. My husband, John, contributed in ways that he knows all too well. Whether reading early drafts, discussing the fine points of psychological theory and research, or engaging in what seemed like an endless search for a title, his patience, knowledge, logic, and good judgment made invaluable contributions. My mother, Lucille Sheehan, provided a model of trust and trustworthiness that shaped my earliest understandings of what it means to care.

Thanks also to the editors at Jossey-Bass, Mark Kerr for his efforts to get the manuscript into production in a timely fashion, and Naomi Lucks-Siegel for a final round of careful and creative editing.

And last, I thank Laura Ecken. I was indeed fortunate to find a teacher so naturally in tune with the underlying principles of Developmental Discipline and so willing to work openly and collaboratively to craft workable classroom strategies from those principles. I also thank Laura and her students for the classroom artwork that appears in each chapter. Quite simply, without Laura and her students this book would not have been possible.

Marilyn Sheehan Watson

LEARNING TO TRUST

INTRODUCTION: A CLASSROOM WHERE EVERYONE BELONGS

I know why young people join gangs: to belong, to be cared for, and to be embraced. I hope we can create a community that fulfills these longings, so young people won't have to sacrifice their lives to be loved and valued in this world.
—Luis Rodriguez in *It Doesn't Have to Be This Way: A Barrio Story* (1999, p. 3)

DANNY WAS one of those children teachers warn each other about. He was already known as a terror early in kindergarten. In first grade his reputation only grew worse. By the time he was seven years old, Danny did not like school or his classmates, and his classmates did not like him. It was then that Danny became a student in Laura Ecken's ungraded primary class. In describing her feelings about being his teacher, Laura does not minimize the problems Danny causes, but she accepts them as a challenge rather than an opportunity to write him off.

> At first Danny was very, very active. Even his eyes would constantly be shifting from side to side, like he was watching everything you did. He had a lot of trouble staying in his seat. He wanted to touch everything. He'd bang the pencils, the heating vents. He'd rock back and forth in his chair. He shared a work table with three other kids, and he liked to lift the table a few inches off the floor and then let it drop. Or when everyone was supposed to be writing, he'd shake the table to mess the other kids up.
>
> With his own writing work, by the time he got finished it would be just destroyed. It wasn't even on purpose. As he was working, somehow the paper would get ripped and smudged and crumpled and wadded up into a little ball until it practically disappeared. It was really strange.
>
> He would make noises when I was teaching. Sometimes he would bark like a dog and just make all kinds of noises when I was talking or

> trying to give instruction. It was almost like he had Tourette's Syndrome, except that he wouldn't do that stuff unless I was trying to give instruction or talk to the class. It seemed very deliberate to me. The other kids didn't want to be friends with him, didn't want to be around him. They seemed a little bit afraid of him.
>
> I remember when his teacher from the previous year came to warn me about Danny. She told me about the weird things he did, like I should watch out, be ready to get in his face. I made up my mind right then that he wasn't going to have a bad time in my room, at my hands, that I was going to do everything I could to help him fit in and settle down and be part of the class. Already I was thinking, "When he does all that, I'm just going to talk to him and explain why I really need him to stop. I'm not going to make a big deal about it, and I'm not going to interrupt the class a lot. And I'm not going to punish him.

Because Laura knew Danny would be a challenge, she consciously set out to build a nurturing relationship with him and to help him make friends. Her resolve was tested daily. Over and over, for months, Laura had to stop Danny from disrupting the class. At the same time, over and over, she tried to reassure him that she cared about him.

In late November, Laura set up individual mailboxes for everyone, including herself, and the class used letter writing as a way to make personal connections. This is the first letter Danny wrote:

> Mrs. Ecken
> Doo you lik me
> Danny

Although Laura felt that she had consistently treated Danny with patience and respect, Danny worried about whether she liked him, whether she really cared about him.

The next time Danny acted up, Laura decided to be more direct with him.

> I just sat down with him, and I said, "You know what, I really, really like you. You can keep doing all this stuff and it's not going to change my mind. It seems to me that you are trying to get me to dislike you, but it's not going to work. I'm not ever going to do that. If you really need to do this stuff all the time, I can deal with it. I'm going to stop you. I'm going to talk to you about it and explain to you why you need to stop it, but it's never going to change the way I feel about you. I'm just letting you know."

> It was after that, and I'm not saying immediately, that his disruptive behaviors started to decrease.

Laura's experience with Danny illustrates two main themes of this book. The first is that even though most teachers care about their students, it can be a challenge to form caring relationships with students who are difficult. And second, these children often find it hard to believe that their teachers really care about them, despite the evidence that they do.

However, the book also shows that when teachers have a framework that allows them to believe that even their most disruptive and disrespectful students want, deep down in their hearts, to be liked and respected, it will be possible to engage all students as partners who need assurances that they are worthy of care, as well as guidance and support, in their struggle to become competent members of the classroom community. It's important to be patient. Creating a classroom in which students and teacher alike feel trusted and cared for takes time. But it is that atmosphere of mutual trust and care that will lead to a naturally well-managed and disciplined classroom.

Incorporating a Developmental Approach to Discipline

When Danny entered Laura's classroom, Laura's whole school was involved with the Child Development Project (CDP). A core assumption of this project is that the more teachers and others are able to create caring classroom and school communities, the more likely students are to become good people as well as good learners. This assumption derives from everything we know about evolution, especially the fact that human beings are biologically prepared, or wired, to acquire the skills and values of their communities. In a school or classroom community, if our values are clear and if we meet children's basic human needs for autonomy, belonging, and competence, then our values will become their values.[1]

However, with children like Danny who constantly disrupt the classroom, it is difficult to meet the misbehaving child's needs for autonomy, belonging, and competence and also maintain a safe and productive classroom. Laura and just about all the teachers in her school had been trained in Assertive Discipline. This approach, which relies on rewards to encourage good behavior and punishments to discourage bad behavior, had not worked with Danny. Children like Danny, who enter the classroom prone to misbehave, are bound to feel coerced and alienated when their teachers try to curb their unacceptable behavior with punishments.

In contrast to coercion, CDP advocates an approach to classroom management called Developmental Discipline, which stresses that teachers

- Form warm and supportive relationships with and among their students
- Help their students understand the reasons behind classroom rules and expectations
- Teach any relevant skills the students might be lacking
- Engage students in a collaborative, problem-solving process aimed at stopping misbehavior
- Use nonpunitive ways to externally control student behavior when necessary

The CDP approach to discipline made sense to Laura, and she embraced it.

> When CDP came to my school, I had been teaching four years and I was feeling really uncomfortable about the job I was doing. I had kids who were acting up, and I wasn't dealing with them very well. My discipline program was Assertive Discipline. I think it made me a control freak. If somebody was talking or if somebody acted up or whatever, I'd put their name up on the board. If they got three check marks, they'd get a note to take home to their parents. And if they got four checks, they'd get kicked out of the room. Lots of times I felt like a zombie following a script: "Just go over to the board, and don't even stop teaching, just have the chalk in your hand and put that check mark on the board, and don't even break stride, just keep on doing what you're doing."
>
> I had really started thinking that maybe teaching wasn't the job for me.
>
> Anyway, CDP came along, and they started talking about how some kids really don't know how to do school and how to be and that they need to be taught, they need to be talked to, they need someone to sit down and talk situations over with them. All of a sudden, as I'm sitting there hearing this, it just became clear to me why I was feeling so bad about the job I was doing. I was humiliating those kids. I was just walking over and putting a check by their names. And if the whole class was talking, I'd just pick out somebody and put a check by their name, and you can be sure that I picked out the same kids all the time—the kids I had problems with.

> When I started as a teacher, I was so busy trying to learn how to teach and how to do the curriculum that I really didn't stop to think about what I was doing with the discipline. I had a plan that I was taught, and I used it. I didn't think much about another way. I was too busy thinking about how to teach division or how to teach comprehension skills. I was running a curriculum, not even thinking that I had little people in the room who needed to learn much more than the history of Kentucky and how to do math.
>
> So when CDP came in talking about kids and what they need, it made sense to me: kids need to belong. They need to feel competent, to learn things, and to know that they can do them well. And they need to make decisions and be part of what's going on in the classroom. It was basic stuff that, quite frankly, I hadn't had time to sit down and think about.
>
> But when I heard the CDP philosophy and the research about what kids need, I knew that I could teach that way and that I really wanted to. So I embraced the project. I just threw myself into it.

Laura didn't feel successful with Danny until January. It took that long for Danny to stop most of his disruptive and hurtful behaviors and to feel that he was connected to Laura and to his class. Even while Laura worked to build her relationship with Danny and to help him make friends with his classmates, she frequently doubted the wisdom of her approach. This new approach took time. Developmental Discipline involved lots of talking with Danny, as well as other misbehaving students, about their actions; it meant engaging students in problem solving and specific activities to help them get to know and like each other; and it called for class meetings to build shared values and goals. Laura worried that she might be giving short shrift to her students' academic development. And she worried that students would take her new, "softer" approach to discipline to mean that their misbehaviors weren't really serious.

However, because in her heart she believed that her students were good people who needed her help and because Laura herself was supported by CDP staff and surrounded by many colleagues who shared her beliefs, she persevered and she succeeded.

Not only did Laura succeed but a number of teachers working with CDP persevered with Developmental Discipline and succeeded. For those who did, Developmental Discipline became the heart of their practice—a way of being that they felt they could never abandon. But a number of other teachers rejected Developmental Discipline without even trying it, and a number tried it briefly and then gave up.

As the person primarily responsible for defining and pushing for CDP's Developmental Discipline approach, I struggled with why Developmental Discipline was so difficult to implement and why so many teachers discounted it or gave up on it too quickly. Why, I worried, did it take so long for teachers using Developmental Discipline to feel successful?

While still wrestling with these questions, I began teaching a class in social and ethical development to first-year graduate students in the Developmental Teacher Education Program at the University of California at Berkeley. Many of these students, who were well grounded in a Piagetian, constructivist perspective to teaching and learning, were attracted to Developmental Discipline, seeing it as an approach to classroom management that would help children construct their social and ethical understanding. However, most found Developmental Discipline difficult to apply in the classrooms where they were doing their student teaching. The videotapes I showed them that documented what Developmental Discipline looks like in a well-functioning classroom didn't really apply to their situations. What, they wanted to know, did it look like in the beginning? What did the first week of school look like? What did the teacher do when students refused to comply with her requests?

How This Book Began

Although it had always been clear to me that Developmental Discipline was more like a philosophy than a set of techniques, my preservice students' questions made me realize that beginning teachers, at least, would need many concrete examples and maybe even a set of techniques before they would be able to apply this philosophical perspective in their own classrooms. I decided to collect many such examples, focused on a single classroom where the teacher was successfully applying Developmental Discipline. My plan was to begin with the first week of school and follow this classroom over two years. I hoped in this way to create a series of vignettes that showed the classroom evolution, or development, of Developmental Discipline.

To do this, I needed not just a teacher who was committed to Developmental Discipline but someone who could make it work in a classroom that other teachers wouldn't automatically dismiss as too middle-class or racially homogeneous or without students with special needs. Laura Ecken seemed ideal. She was determined to make Developmental Discipline work, and she taught in an inner-city school that shared a formidable chain-link fence with the largest housing project in Louisville, Kentucky. The children were poor. Their community and many of their parents were stressed. Racially, the school was about equally mixed African American and European American. Laura's classroom of approximately twenty-six seven- and eight-year-olds was also a full-inclusion classroom. At different times, between four and six of Laura's students were identified as having special needs. So I asked Laura if she would be willing to open her class to me. She agreed; she was enthusiastic about the potential to help others and the chance to improve her own practice.

> I guess the main reason I said okay was because I really felt that it would be helpful. I wanted people to see that Developmental Discipline can be done and that it can be done with very difficult children—kids who bring a lot of issues to the classroom. I thought that if teachers could have a model of someone dealing with very difficult kids and could see the things you can do to make the classroom feel safe for everybody, then maybe other teachers, particularly new teachers, wouldn't become disillusioned with teaching in the way I had.

I talked with Laura by phone almost every week for two years. Without either of us realizing it, these weekly conversations, conceived to help others understand Developmental Discipline, became important for us. They became a source of support and encouragement for Laura, and they helped both of us deepen our own understanding of Developmental Discipline. Our weekly conversations helped answer the questions I had been struggling with.

As we spoke, I began to appreciate the difficulty teachers face when trying to implement research and theory that did not originate in classroom settings. Although it makes intuitive sense (and is borne out by research) for teachers to provide students with the same motivational and developmental support that nurturing parents provide their children, the classroom presents a very different context for development. Approaches to socialization and discipline that might arise naturally in the context of the family and that depend on strong relationships between adults and children are more difficult to implement in the classroom. As teachers, we are building relationships with other people's children—lots of them at once. I came to see that it's not always intuitively obvious how we should go about building relationships in the classroom.

A particular concern for teachers may be the "gestation" period required for building trusting relationships with some children. Laura had to persevere for months with Danny before she saw clear, positive results. And as hard as Laura tried to make her classroom a caring community for all her students, some students remained untrusting and uncooperative throughout the entire year. It took a great deal of stamina and trust for Laura to continue to believe that even the most defiant children inherently wanted to learn and wanted to be contributing members of the classroom community.

My weekly conversations with Laura began the year following her experience with Danny. We hoped that the students entering her class that fall would be able to stay with her for two years, thus enhancing conditions for building successful relationships and making the success of Developmental Discipline more likely. During those two years, Laura had no students who were more dramatically responsive to Developmental Discipline than Danny, but she had lots of students who made substantial progress. For some of them, however, this progress wasn't evident until the second year, and most teachers keep their students for just one year.

Working with Laura and seeing how long some children remained uncooperative helped me to realize that, for many teachers, belief in the ultimate goodwill of their misbehaving students was as unsupported by their personal experience as belief that the earth goes around the sun. I came to feel that, just as knowing the Copernican theory of the universe is important for sustaining our belief in the workings of the solar system, understanding attachment theory is important for sustaining our belief in the ultimate goodwill of chronically misbehaving children.

All of us have powerful belief systems that shape the way we see the world. We build these belief systems out of the experiences of our daily lives, the content of our formal education and reading, and the general beliefs that are part of the culture in which we live. In American culture, two powerful theories about human nature—learning theory and Freudian theory—have strongly influenced our conscious and unconscious beliefs about children and even how scientists of human behavior frame their research. Both theories begin with the premise that children are isolated individuals focused on seeking personal pleasure and avoiding pain. In both learning theory and Freudian theory, it is necessary to tame children's pleasure seeking in order to socialize them to become productive members of society. When children behave in antisocial ways, it is assumed that they are succumbing to their selfish desires and failing to control themselves.

With such a belief system, it is natural to see frequently misbehaving children as selfish and responsible for their own unacceptable behavior. And so it becomes very difficult to like the children who frequently misbehave, especially if they aren't our own. And if we cannot like them—if we can't unconditionally accept and value them—while we work to control their unacceptable behavior they will feel emotionally distant from us and less able to learn from us. Yet this is how American education has been structured to respond to misbehaving children for the past century.

Attachment theory, based on psychological theory and research on children's relationships with their primary caregivers, offers an alternative to the selfish, individualistic view of children that we have inherited. Attachment theory assumes that children are socially oriented from birth. They depend on the care and support of their caretakers for their survival and development. If their primary caretakers are sensitive to their physical and psychological needs, children will enter a collaborative relationship with their caregivers and strive to maintain that relationship. Socialization from the perspective of attachment theory is a collaborative process between child and adult rather than a coercive one. Attachment theory also explains why some children do not respond appropriately to our caring and, perhaps more important, offers workable suggestions for ways to break through their resistance.

It became clear to me that if teachers did not understand the theories and evidence supporting a belief in children's basic social orientation, their experience would lead them to fall back on theories that view children as being primarily self-interested and needing to be controlled by rewards and punishments. In listening to Laura describe children who seemed particularly resistant to her help, I came to realize how helpful it would be for teachers both to understand attachment theory and to see how learning theory and Freudian theory influence their views and thinking about children.

It also became clear that for most teachers to accept Developmental Discipline, they would need to consciously reject long-held beliefs that children, although lovable, are basically motivated by self-interest. Teachers would instead need to understand the basis for believing that children are naturally motivated to learn and to be empathic and cooperative in a caring and nurturing environment. In other words, teachers would need to understand attachment theory. Because attachment theory views children and their development so differently from the views that have shaped mainstream education, it will take time to fully understand it and its implications for your classroom.

The brief summary of the major tenets of attachment theory that follows is meant to provide a start. A fuller description of the theory, its origins, and supporting research is in Appendix 1. If you are not already familiar with attachment theory, please read the fuller description. The more you understand the theory, the better you will understand Laura and the relationships she forges with even the most challenging children in her class.

Understanding Attachment Theory

According to attachment theory, children's development and socialization are products of the relationship between children and their caregivers. If all goes well, the child and caregiver enter into a cooperative relationship in which the adult helps the child accomplish the tasks of development. In the context of this cooperative relationship, the child develops basic trust—a positive expectation not only toward the caregiver but toward relationships in general. The child's capacity for empathy and tendency to comply with a caregiver's requests—an evolutionary predisposition to be collaborative and prosocial—emerge from the child's secure attachment relationship (Stayton, Hogan, and Ainsworth, 1971).

The adult-child partnership that supports the child's healthy development begins in infancy. For example, if the infant's emotions are raging out of control, the nurturing adult helps the infant achieve calm. Gradually, with maturation and support from their nurturing caregivers, children learn to regulate their emotions on their own. But for a long time it is a collaborative process. If the child is afraid to walk, the nurturing adult supports the child until he or she can walk alone. If a child cannot share toys with a playmate, the nurturing caregiver adjusts the situation, perhaps joining in the play or providing two of the same toy so the child can successfully share. If a child cannot fit the pieces into a puzzle, the nurturing caregiver provides hints or guides the child's hand to enable the child to achieve success. Children, through these dyadic processes with their caregivers, gradually engage their prosocial orientation and develop a sense of autonomy and the ability to regulate their emotions and behavior.

Children with a history of responsive and sensitive caregiving tend to be cooperative and prosocial. In our classrooms, they do not need to be enticed with rewards or coerced with punishments. They may need help acquiring the understanding and skills needed to be kind or helpful in particular situations, especially when their wants are in conflict with the wants of others, but they usually want to be cooperative and to respond with empathy and care toward others. That desire arises from secure attachment relationships with caregivers.

Attachment Theory and "Difficult" Children

For some children, early socialization and attachment do not go well. Some caregivers, for a variety of reasons, are not able to provide their children with reasonably consistent, sensitive, and responsive care (Ainsworth, Blehar,

Waters, and Wall, 1978). Because all children need the attention and nurturance of their caregivers, these children nonetheless strive to build and maintain relationships with them. However, because they cannot rely on their caregivers to meet their needs, their attachment relationships are built on mistrust.

These children have low self-esteem, little or no trust that others can be relied upon to care for them, and a belief that relationships are conflictual in nature. They are likely to be either anxious, withdrawn, and passive or angry, aggressive, and controlling as they strive to make their way in the world. In classrooms, these children need help building trust in our care for them. We must help them learn how to be cooperative and prosocial, as well as gain the desire to be so—a desire based, at first, on the strength of their relationships with us.

Attachment Theory and Classroom Discipline

Socialization approaches based in learning theory or in Freudian theory hold that the motivation or desire to be "good" needs to be instilled in the child from the outside by some kind of controlling or taming process. Attachment theory presents a very different picture. From this perspective, children are biologically predisposed to acquire the desire to be cooperative and prosocial as a result of experiencing sensitive and responsive care.

The majority of children in most classrooms have had the benefit of secure attachment relationships. We can assume the cooperative and prosocial orientation of these children and concentrate on helping them acquire the additional understanding and skills they need to be cooperative and prosocial in school. Still, some may have a difficult time in the classroom. For a variety of reasons, even securely attached children may find the environment of the classroom unresponsive to their needs. We need to pay close attention to the match between the opportunities and demands of the classroom and the needs and characteristics of the children, but if we make the needed adjustments, these children will be ready to enter into a collaborative relationship with us.

Children with a history of insecure attachment to their caregivers, however, build "working models" of relationships as coercive and of themselves as unworthy of care.[2] These children are apt to withdraw from social relationships or become focused on satisfying their own needs through dependency, control, or aggression. They look for ways to test our caring, often by refusing to comply with our most reasonable requests, and they fully expect us to fail their tests. They fail to appropriately receive our care and to believe in our care, and we frequently feel at a loss as to how to achieve a mutual or cooperative relationship with them.

If we try to teach these children to want to be cooperative and prosocial by rewarding their good behavior and punishing or controlling their unacceptable behavior, we will only succeed in confirming their view of relationships as coercive and encourage their tendency to be self-focused. If we become angry and withdraw our affections, we will further alienate them and reinforce their negative view of themselves. If, instead, we do nothing and simply let them withdraw from learning activities or behave inappropriately, we will likely grow to resent or dislike them and fail to help them develop cognitively, socially, or ethically. To help these children, we need to find a way to keep their negative working models of themselves and of relationships from becoming self-fulfilling prophesies.

From the perspective of attachment theory, to build the desire of these children to be cooperative and prosocial, we need to build a responsive and nurturing relationship with them; by so doing, we help them change their working models of themselves and of relationships. The building of caring and trusting relationships becomes the most important goal in the socialization of these children. Of course, while we are building these relationships, we must find nonpunitive ways to prevent the children who are aggressive and controlling from harming others and to encourage self-reliance and confidence in those who are withdrawn or dependent. How does a teacher do all this in the demanding real world of the classroom?

This book explores Laura's day-to-day experiences as she tries to build relationships and manage a classroom community from the perspective of attachment theory. I hope as you read these chapters your understanding will grow and change, just as Laura's and mine did as we worked, thought, and talked together.

Laura's experiences are examples of one teacher's use of Developmental Discipline and attachment theory, in one context, with one group of children. They are examples only. They are meant to help you build your understanding of attachment theory and Developmental Discipline and your faith in the possibility and necessity of building trusting and nurturing relationships in the classroom. In forming such relationships with children, it is not the specific behaviors or specific techniques that matter but the general principles inherent in approaching children as partners in support of their development. Laura's teaching is offered as a way to clarify these principles so that you will be more able to apply them in your way, in your context, with your children.

Laura Ecken's Challenges

Laura Ecken set out to create a classroom where everyone belonged—a community where her students would feel that they were not only cared for and embraced but safe. To accomplish this, she had to find ways to negotiate the tensions between her vision for the classroom and the reality of her students' lives outside school.

Laura was naïve about what her students' lives were like. She and her students lived in the same city but in very different worlds. Laura had grown up in Louisville as the daughter of a successful drugstore owner. She was European American. She now lived with her husband and children in a comfortable house in a quiet middle-class neighborhood. Most of her students were growing up in Louisville's largest and toughest housing project. More than half were African American; all were poor, with 88 percent qualifying for free or reduced-price lunch.

In the morning meetings that began each classroom day, kids sometimes talked about their lives at home and in the neighborhood. Laura was often reminded of how much she took for granted in her own life. One of these meetings began with an exploration of parents' role in defending their children and went on to reveal just how dangerous life felt, even to the most "hard-boiled" of these six-, seven-, and eight-year-olds.

> In the morning meeting, Leonard was describing a confrontation with Yolanda's father.
>
> He said, "I went over to Yolanda's and she was skating and I told her it looked like she got her skates from the DAV." That stands for Disabled American Veterans—they have shops where they sell things cheap, like the Goodwill.
>
> Leonard said, "Her dad came out and said to me, 'It looks like the shoes you got on came from the DAV.'"
>
> "I told my dad and he said if he ever says another thing to me, my dad's going over there and beat him up."
>
> I said, "Leonard, I don't understand this. You were at Yolanda's home and you were making fun of her and the daddy comes out and he's defending his child? And you're going to have your father come over and beat him up? It seems to me that you started this and the dad was just protecting his daughter.
>
> Denise didn't miss a beat, "It's none of Yolanda's dad's business. Yolanda can take care of herself."
>
> Right then, I stopped. I said, "Listen, guys, if somebody came into our house and started making fun of Mary Beth [Laura's daughter],

Tim [Laura's husband] would make them leave. He wouldn't allow them to come to our house and hurt our children. What do you all think of that?"

They started talking about how parents have no right to say anything to anybody else's child.

Janice told me, "You don't understand the projects. You kick somebody out of your house, you might get killed. You're just going to cause a big old fight because parents come over and fight other parents all the time because they've done something to the kids."

You know, I have to admit I was surprised. I mean, everyone knows the projects are full of violence, but many of these little children already have to put out an attitude like, "We take care of ourselves and no adult needs to step in."

I said to them, "Okay, I want you to think about your own kids. Think about when you have kids. Don't you want to be able to protect them and keep people from making fun of them?"

Yolanda said, "Miss Ecken, when I get old I hope I have a husband like Tim that'll keep my children safe. And I don't want to live over in the projects where there's all that writing on the walls."

Martin said, "I'm going to tell my kids to fight and take it like a man. Even girls can give kicks and punches. They can fight just like the boys. I'm going to tell my girls to fight too."

Brian disagreed. "I don't want to get my kids to fight because somebody tried to beat me up and I ran."

Denise said, "Miss Ecken, we've got so much trouble over there, there's so many gangs and people are putting up all these signs now with their hands, and they walk along and this is the Blood sign and this is the Crip sign. Or they say kill or chill. People are getting beat up now because they're giving these signs."

I said, "Do you have to give those signs? Do you have to walk around and put the signs up?"

And Leonard's like, "Yeah!"

But when I asked him why, he said, "I don't know. You just got to show what you belong to and what you're with."

John said, "When I get old I'm going to move out of the projects with my kids, and I'm going to have a house with a yard and four dogs to chase those people off."

Everybody was saying how they'd like to move and get out and raise their kids differently and not have all that stuff around.

Denise said, "I'm leaving. I'm getting my kids out of this whole country."

Even Martin, after crowing about teaching his kids to fight, said, "I'm going to take my kids and live somewhere else too. I'm not living in Louisville because there's too many shootings, too many killings, and too many knifings."

Then Leonard said, "Why should I move? All my friends are here, I'm not moving, I'm not leaving. And if my kids get into a fight, I'm going to tell them to fight."

Leonard's uncle was beaten by some gang members, and he's still in a coma. So I said, "Well, Leonard, think about your uncle."

All of a sudden, when we started talking about his uncle, he said, "You know what, Miss Ecken? I could move with my kids, but then I could go back and visit, couldn't I?"

I said, "Leonard, that's something that you could do—get yourself in a safe environment when you get older and then, if you do have friends here, you could visit."

Martin, Denise, Kenny, and Tyrone all said that they knew people who have been killed for fighting or being involved with gangs. John said his big cousin almost got shot once when he was with him.

Well, just then Betty Adams [a member of the school staff whom the children don't know very well] walked in. It was the strangest thing. I said to her, "We're just sitting here talking about how dangerous it is and thinking about what we want to do when we get older."

And before I could say another word, Martin said, "I like where I live just fine and I'm not leaving anywhere."

Denise was sitting right next to me, and she added, "Neither am I. I'm staying right here. I'm living right where I live." Then Leonard said the same thing.

As soon as Betty walked in, those three just immediately went into their "not safe" mode. It was like the spell of dreaming about a different life was broken, and those kids knew it was just too dangerous to let anyone think you were scared of your own neighborhood. It was just unbelievable.

That particular morning meeting was a real eye-opener for me into how unsafe their world feels and their sense that they have to fend for themselves. It sure made me think about how difficult it must be to come into the classroom and be able to trust somebody. Really, I was just shocked.

Laura had two overriding challenges in creating a classroom where collaboration was part of everything students did, where problems were solved by talking, and where discipline was not synonymous with punishment.

First, she had to be respectful of her students' families and cultures when their values diverged from hers. And second, she had to be careful not to deprive the children of the skills to survive in a world that she knew little about. She hoped that life in her classroom would help her students learn to value a peaceful and just world and give them the skills to create such a world for themselves.

In the chapters that follow, you will see how Laura strived to create a caring community of what she and the kids referred to as "serious" learners. Drawing on attachment theory and Developmental Discipline, she worked across two academic years to build nurturing relationships with her students—relationships that met their needs for belonging, autonomy, and competence and taught the Kentucky state curriculum as well.

Laura's Classroom

Laura taught in a K–5 elementary school with about six hundred students. The building might be called a classic. It had two stories of solid brick construction with high ceilings and wide locker-lined halls, generous many-paned windows, and lots of pale green paint. It was clean and well maintained but old. Her classroom was a large, bright, corner room with windows along two exterior walls.

In Laura's classroom, her desk and a supply cabinet were to the left of the entrance; a sink and small computer station were to the right. Five round tables, each large enough to comfortably accommodate four children, occupied the center of the room. Beyond the tables, the far right corner of the room was carpeted and partially enclosed by low bookcases. This corner also held two beanbag chairs and was a cozy place for listening to stories and conducting class meetings, as well as a quiet place for students to work in partnerships.

In the far left corner, adjacent to the carpeted area, a large work table and some chairs were partially enclosed by low bookcases. This was where Mack Thatcher, the special education teacher, worked with students who had special needs. It also served as a quiet spot where students could work individually or in partnerships.

Under the windows along the wall between her desk and the work table, Laura had made a "couch" for students by adding cushions and pillows to the top of a long, low cabinet. The room was packed with lots of books in the bookcases all around, but at the beginning of each year the walls were practically bare. Gradually, as the year progressed, student work filled and then overflowed the walls, reminding everyone whose room this was.

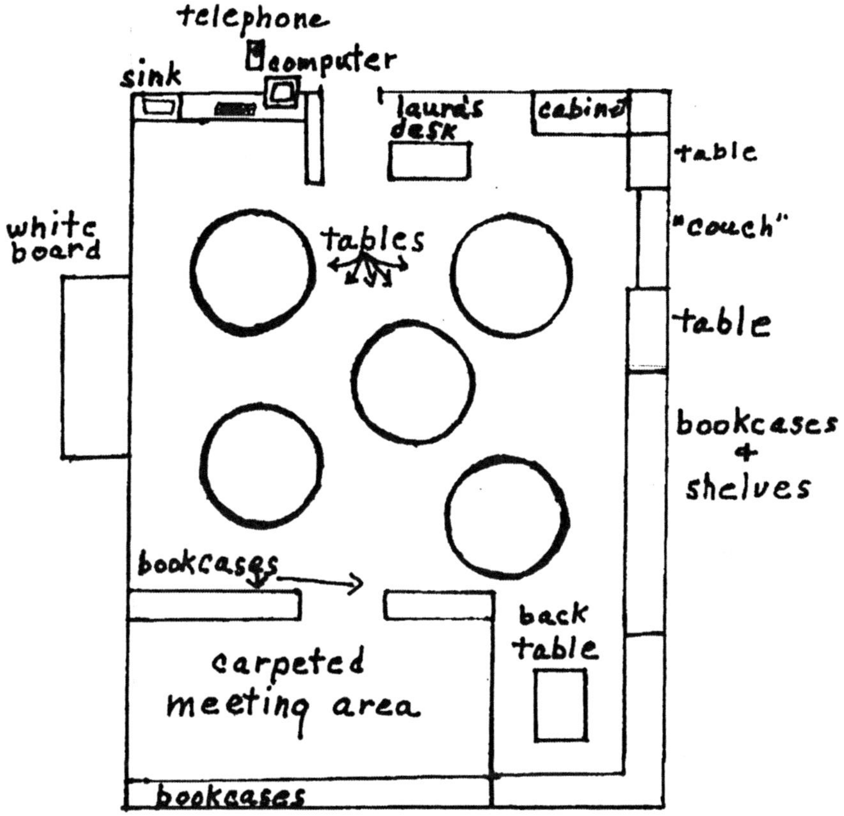

Laura's Students

Laura's class was a full-inclusion, ungraded primary class. At the beginning of the first year, it was roughly equivalent to a combination second–third grade. At the beginning of the second year, it was still a combination second–third grade but later stretched up to grade four to accommodate a particular student.

As in most inner-city schools, many students transferred in and out during a year, but between eighteen to twenty students were usually assigned to the class. Generally, ten students were African American and seven were European American. Two biracial students were class members both years; one was African American and European American, and one was Vietnamese and European American. Laura started the first year with eighteen students in the class. Over the course of the year, two students left; one left and later rejoined the class. Four new students joined for varying amounts of time. Sixteen students were part of the class for the entire school year. As it turned out, this was one of the most difficult classes that Laura had ever taught. Many of her students had learning or behavior problems, or both. Laura knew immediately that this class would be full of challenges.

> This class was very different from any class I ever had. They were very needy. At the beginning, it was like they each wanted me all the time. If I would sit down and talk to somebody, somebody else, on the other side of the room, would start doing something so that I would have to go and be with them. It was like they were worried that if I paid attention to someone else it meant I loved that person and not them. It was very hard for them to share my attention.
>
> Also, it was very hard for them to get along with each other. Several kids in the class constantly teased and put down the others, and several were constantly upset at being teased or messed with in some way. Whenever we would get together as a group, some kids would just start messing with people. Just as a small for-instance, if I said to Louise, "Louise, please don't talk when somebody else is talking because people can't hear what they're saying," then probably five or six kids would try to get Louise's eye and kind of "Ha-Ha" in her face. And then, of course, Louise would be furious. At the beginning I had a whole bunch of that kind of stuff going on, and it was very, very difficult because there was so much to deal with.
>
> But on the other hand, I had a class that was interested in learning. And you could tell right from the start that they wanted to learn. But they just, at that point, didn't have the skills that were necessary to pull it together as a class.

As in any class, individual students stood out in various ways. Three who thought of themselves as streetwise and tough claimed much of Laura's energy. Their skill in intimidating their classmates made it possible for them to act as leaders either for good or ill. Laura describes them here: Leonard, Martin, and Denise.

> Leonard turned out to be a decent, nice kid, but he didn't have a lot of self-control. He was the oldest one in the room. He hadn't passed third grade the year before. I didn't make an issue of that; I just said that we had a second-, third-, and fourth-grade class. He liked to keep up this image that "I'm tough, I'm not going to be pushed around." He's not someone you can do a lot of talking to. You just have to tell him what you think about what's going on and walk away. I didn't know how to

back off at first. I would say, "Leonard you need to stop that," and instead of walking away, I'd try to wait 'til he stopped or keep on talking with him. We'd both get ourselves into such a frenzy. He'd be yelling, "Suspend me. Kick me out." And I'd be saying, "If you don't stop that I'm going to kick you out of here." He and Martin played off each other a lot. If one of them started laughing or making fun of another child, the other would kind of join in. Although Leonard had a reading and writing disability, he was very intelligent. He was very verbal and able to talk about things and so, once he saw that we were getting into some serious learning, he did try and was pretty serious about school.

Martin, at the start of the year, was just six years old. He wanted to be a very powerful person in the class. He really messed with everybody—made fun of them, took their things. He did a lot of complaining with just about every activity. He would mumble and shake his head, and he would have the angriest look on his face. He really upset me and I had to get over that. I was just so sick of him carrying on like that. I had to come above the way I was feeling and just be very supportive and kind. A lot of times he would refuse to do what I asked. He would bully others, especially in the line, always wanting to be first. He was very argumentative and also really into humiliating people—just yelling and screaming stuff out about people's parents and their families. He also was a kid who could read very fluently. He did have some comprehension problems when it came to understanding why characters did what they did or why certain things happened in the story, but he was proud of the fact that he was very fluent in his reading. I think he was serious about learning, but he just couldn't get past the issues of how to deal with all the other kids in the class. He was constantly competing with them for my attention and my affection. If we'd go to sit on the carpeting, he might knock five people over to get back there to sit right beside me. He was just so needy. He needed me to be there to talk to him and to have my arm around him.

Denise was so angry. She had gotten a raw deal in life, and she was smart enough to know it. Both her parents were in prison, and she was living with a very sickly aunt and basically having to take care of the aunt, her younger brother, and herself. She was especially angry at white people because she had watched the white police officer beat up her mother when they arrested her. She had some real issues there with me trying to tell her what to do. She was very intelligent, but she really didn't know how to get along with people. Yet she was streetwise and smart about

> the ways of the street and how to defend herself against Martin and Leonard when they'd make fun of her. She had such a difficult life, yet she couldn't handle disappointment. Like if I said we were going to do something and then things changed and we didn't, she couldn't shake that. She was very talented artistically. I made sure she had a lot of outlets for that in the classroom.

Most of Laura's students had difficulty handling disappointment, and some would respond to almost any kind of stress by crying, throwing things, or even throwing themselves on the floor. Some students, like Kenny and Tyrone, seemed to lack self-confidence and self-control, whereas others, like Jennifer and Janice, responded to conflict or disappointment by taking total control—withdrawing and refusing to move or be part of the class.

Next, Laura describes Tyrone and Jennifer and their two very different ways of responding to difficulties.

> Tyrone, to me, was like a little lost soul. His mom was in serious trouble with drugs, and his dad was in jail. He had trouble reading and writing and also had some motor skills problems. But he was very quick to catch on to new math concepts. In the beginning, he had a hard time staying focused on his work; he played around a lot, and it seemed difficult for him not to move around. And he was little—the smallest child in the class. He talked in a different way. I don't know how to describe it, but it was sort of like he was talking to himself at the same time he was trying to talk to you. He just used words in a different way, so at first people assumed that he didn't have much to offer. He was very insecure about whether people liked him and whether he could do the work. He'd cry a lot and literally just throw fits and start screaming, "I'm not doing this," and just get himself worked up about things. Yet Tyrone also was a serious learner. If I was reading aloud or we were discussing things, he'd be right with us and had some really good things to say if you could sort them out. Thank goodness the children were perceptive, and after a little while they could understand him and were more respectful.

> Jennifer came from a home where her mother was abused by her father. She was easily upset, would clam up very quickly, and was just a very emotional kid. Jennifer could read and write like a million dollars, and she was proud of that. But then again she was quiet and just kind of watched a lot of what went on in the class. She was another one who couldn't deal well with disappointment. She had trouble working with

> people in a partnership. If there were any rough spots, she'd put her head down and stop working. If she was upset and I asked her to come to the table or to move from where she was, she'd just freeze and flat out wouldn't do anything. She was a fairly well-respected child in the class and got along with the kids unless something didn't go well; then she didn't have a lot of skills for handling conflict.

A number of Laura's students had difficulties with reading. William was nearly blind and needed special books and help to be able to read at all. Approximately half the class was reading below grade level, and five students (Rebecca, Tralin, Yolanda, Kenny, and Tyrone) couldn't read the very easy readers that Laura was accustomed to using for partner reading. For some students, the inability to read was compounded by being especially vulnerable to teasing.

> Rebecca couldn't read. I mean she literally knew very few words. I think at the beginning she didn't want to be found out. When things got difficult for her, she would shake her head, fold her arms, and refuse to participate. And Rebecca also got very upset when people teased her. So the people who liked to mess with others really liked to mess with Rebecca. She would throw fits and stomp her feet and just do things that they would love. She had a lot of trouble at first.

> My first impression of Tralin was here's a kid who knows about life. I'd start talking about how we want to be and how we want to act in the classroom, and Tralin was right with me on that. But she had a whole lot of trouble reading and writing, and actually she had a language problem, too. It was difficult for her to make us understand her thoughts—what she was thinking and feeling. She had a difficult time getting the words out. When it was time to do partner reading, she would do things to disrupt the class, I guess because she was so nervous about being with a partner and not able to read the words. And, like Rebecca, she would get very upset when people messed with her. So some of the kids messed with her a lot because she'd get real loud and real pouty about it. They just loved to see her reactions; they got a charge out of them. And so she was difficult and had a lot of trouble at first.

Of all the children in the class, none was more frequently subjected to teasing than Louise.

> Louise had already had a lot of trouble in first grade. I could tell that by the way the other kids treated her and talked to her and the way she

> reacted to them. She was very sneaky. She would say and do stuff to them when I wasn't looking, and then they'd do stuff back and I'd be all over them, thinking that they were picking on poor Louise. It took me a little while to realize that she was starting a lot of the stuff. She just didn't know how to make friends or to be friends. She was very mistrustful of me; she really thought that I was not going to like her. Also, she was very sensitive to any kind of correction. And she did a lot of stuff, so I was constantly trying to talk things over with her to help her see the trouble she was causing. When I had to conference with her about her behavior, she would kind of mope and pout. And she'd get really upset if I spent time with other kids. At the beginning, she didn't have many skills as far as getting along with people and being part of the class.

Several of Laura's students looked for every opportunity to tease or make fun of their classmates, frequently laughing at them or calling them names. Martin, Leonard, Yolanda, and Shereka often instigated teasing or name calling, but they were often joined by Denise, Rebecca, Tralin, and Louise—some of the same students most victimized themselves.

Not all of Laura's students had difficulty at the beginning of the year. Several were easygoing and capable. Although they would sometimes misbehave—sometimes seriously—Cindy, Rachel, John, and Nina got along well with the other kids and generally did as Laura asked, willingly engaging in the class activities. Brian, although he struggled academically, was also cooperative and friendly.

Shereka and Leonard left the class in November, and Nina left in January; Leonard returned in February. The new children who entered the class after the start of the year—Shawn, Wilma, Tangela, and Joe—all had some kind of learning or behavioral disorder. Of these, only Tangela stayed through the year (see Table I.1).

Tangela was diagnosed as having attention deficit hyperactivity disorder and, indeed, she had a very hard time sitting in her seat or focusing on the work for very long. When Tangela entered the class, her mother warned Laura that she needed to watch Tangela or else "she will steal you blind." Tangela did have a problem with stealing, and she had a difficult time getting along with the other students. She frequently engaged in taunting and name calling and initially refused to work with anyone who was assigned to be her partner.

As the year progressed, so did Laura's students. The class made slow-but-steady progress toward becoming a caring community. At the end of the first year, Laura felt that she and they had come a long way—and that they still had a long way to go. She kept all her second-grade students for another year. William, Janice, and Yolanda went on to fourth-grade classrooms, and Denise did not return to school in Louisville. Because the principal believed that the class had too many children with serious learning and behavior problems, one student, Kenny, was moved to a different class. At the start of the second year, eight new children joined the class: Mary, Gabrielle, Ella, Paul, Tom, Tara, Chantelle, and Lana. Mary, Paul, Tom, Tara, and Lana quickly formed positive relationships with Laura and the other students. Gabrielle struggled. Like many of Laura's students from the first year, she couldn't handle disappointment and had a hard time learning to trust Laura. Two of the new students, Ella and Chantelle, had a very difficult time in the beginning; it took Laura months to build positive relationships with them and to begin helping them build positive relationships with their classmates.

o

In the second year, even though Laura and her new and old students had to struggle hard to become a caring community of serious learners, progress was much faster than during the first year. Several factors contributed to this progress. Laura was clearer about her goals and about her role in keeping the classroom safe, and she created more structure in order to reduce the demands on her students' self-control. Also the students from the first year had themselves made considerable progress, and they helped Laura bring the new students into their community. At the start of the second year, Laura was able to build on the already strong relationships she had built with her returning students. The existence of these relationships helped her establish trust more quickly with her new students. This phenomenon was not unique to Laura; teachers often report better relationships with their students and fewer discipline problems when they keep students for more than one year (Flinders and Noddings, 2001).

In the rest of this book, you will see how Laura worked with her class across the two years. These chapters do not tell the story of Laura's classroom chronologically. Each chapter focuses on a particular teaching goal, such as teaching students to be friends, and describes some of the ways Laura accomplished that goal and some of the ways her students responded. Vignettes from across both years appear in each chapter, and they are arranged to illustrate how the class and the children changed through time with respect to a particular goal.

The chapters, like children's needs, begin with belonging.

Table I.1. Class Enrollment in Years 1 and 2

Year 1 Students							Year 2 Students		
Started Year 1	Entered during Year 1	Left during Year 1	Returned during Year 1	Moved away over the summer	Trans-ferred to a different class for Year 2	Went up to fourth grade classrooms for Year 2	Started Year 2	Entered during Year 2	Left during Year 2
Leonard		Leonard	Leonard				Leonard		Leonard
Martin							Martin		
Denise				Denise					
Kenny					Kenny				
Tyrone							Tyrone		
Jennifer							Jennifer		
Janice						Janice			
William						William			
Rebecca							Rebecca		
Tralin							Tralin		
Yolanda						Yolanda			
Louise							Louise		

Shereka		Shereka							
Cindy							Cindy		
Rachel							Rachel		Rachel
John							John		
Nina		Nina							
Brian							Brian		
Tangela							Tangela		
Deshawn	Deshawn								
Wilma	Wilma								
Joe	Joe								
							Mary		
							Gabrielle		
							Ella		
							Tom		
							Paul		
							Tara		
							Chantelle		Chantelle
							Lana		
								Derek	

NOTES

1. See *Among Friends: Classrooms Where Caring and Learning Prevail* (Dalton and Watson, 1997) for a full description of CDP.
2. Bowlby (1969) used the term *working model* to indicate that the initial beliefs a child develops act like theories seeking to sustain themselves but are nevertheless open to change.

PART ONE

BUILDING TRUST

I

BUILDING THE TEACHER-STUDENT RELATIONSHIP

I was talking to the kids early in the week about field day, telling them what we were going to do and what the events were, and Kenny said, "I've never been on a field day before."

I was surprised. "You haven't?"

He said, "I always had to sit in the room. They never let me do it."

So on Friday morning when we finished the spelling test and we were getting ready for field day, he just came out of his seat and grabbed me and announced, "I love you, and you know it." He didn't mention field day.

The weather kind of cancelled our plans for an outside picnic. It was real overcast and cold. So we ate lunch together inside the classroom. I was sitting at a table with some of the kids, and Kenny came over and said, "You're the nicest teacher I ever had."

And I said, "Well, now, what are you going to say next year when you get this teacher and she looks like me, and acts like me, and talks like me, and dresses like me?"

He said, "I don't know."

So I said, "Well, you can say, 'You're as nice as that teacher I had last year.' " And then he just started laughing because he knows that he's going to stay with me next year.

o

AS ADULTS, we believe that others like us when they joke with us, give us a soft nudge, tell us they care, do helpful things for us, ask about our lives and tell us about theirs, and make an effort to spend time with us. If it turns out that someone did any of these things in order to get us to do something for them, then we feel manipulated and mistrustful of them. The same is true for children. If we want our students to trust that we care for them, then we need to display our affection without demanding that they behave or perform in certain ways in return. It's not that we don't want and expect certain behavior; we do. But our concern or affection does not depend on it.

A solid, trusting student–teacher relationship is the foundation of a classroom community of partners. Over the course of the year, Laura was able to build a trusting relationship with Kenny, even though he was a child who was often "in trouble." She responded to his qualities of warmth and goodwill, worked with him to control his frustrations and tantrums, and conveyed her genuine affection for him, whether he was in a sulk or declaring his love.[1]

Martin Haberman (1995) calls this "conscious, premeditated caring," and he reports that it is characteristic of teachers who are successful in teaching children of poverty. "Such caring," he argues, "is not predicated on children always doing the right thing. On the contrary, it assumes they frequently will not. At that point, the professional caring springs into action and demonstrates to the child that he or she is worthy and capable—even at the lowest and worst moment of his or her offense" (pp. 57–58). Others have called such caring unconditional love or unconditional regard. And it is this kind of caring that meets our students' basic need for belonging. How do we achieve this feeling of caring for all our students? And then how do we help them see that we care?

Learning to Like All Students

Although most children are easy to like, there are always some in every class who are not. Perhaps they are defiant, disrespectful, aggressive, or disruptive. Perhaps they moan and groan and complain that everything's boring. Perhaps they tease and belittle others. Whatever the annoying behaviors are, we can soften our feelings toward these children by viewing them through the lens of attachment theory.

Children's Basic Need for Belonging

Knowing that all children want and need to belong—to be loved and protected by caring adults and to fit in with their peer group—can help us look through their troublesome behavior to see the vulnerable child behind the bothersome or menacing exterior.

It's not easy to think of children who are misbehaving, particularly children who misbehave frequently, as vulnerable and needy; they often seem so powerful and defiant. Laura's student Martin was one of the most aggressive children in the class, but he was also someone to whom she paid a lot of attention and who seemed to trust her and want her good opinion. Toward the end of the first year, when a mean quarrel with another student finally resulted in Martin slugging Laura, she struggled to understand why his behavior continued to be so erratic.

> Tuesday I had to be out of the classroom for the first hour of the day. The speech teacher watched my room, but when I walked in, Martin was on the rug instead of in his seat, and he and Denise both looked upset.
>
> When I tried to get everyone together for the morning meeting, Denise said, "He called my auntie a fat, ugly witch."
>
> Martin yelled out, "Well, you called my mom fat and ugly."
>
> Denise said, "I only did that after you said that about my auntie."
>
> At this point I said, "Well, we're not going to say things like that here. I'm ready to start the morning meeting, so let's get going."
>
> But before we could get started, Denise said, "Well, if he does it again I'm going to have to hurt him."
>
> By this time Martin came over and stood like an inch away from her and shouted, "Your aunt is a fat, ugly witch. Now hit me!"
>
> Denise looked up at me and said, "Get him off of me, Mrs. Ecken, or I am going to hit him."
>
> I said, "No, you're going to control yourself. You're not going to touch him."
>
> To Martin I said, "You need to back off and get over there and sit down. I told you we don't do this here."
>
> Instead, he got closer. He put his body on hers, like the front of his body on the side of hers, and he started pushing on her a little. And he went, "Your aunt is a fat, ugly witch! Now get up and hit me!"
>
> Denise warned, "I'm going to do it."
>
> And I said, "No, Denise, just sit there." I walked over and put my hands on the side of Martin's arms, and I said, "You need to move away, and this needs to stop."
>
> And with that, he took his elbow and slammed me right in the stomach. I mean, as hard as he could.
>
> I exploded. "You're not staying here and doing that. I don't know where you think you are, or what's going on with you. I don't know what went on this morning while I was out, but you are not staying in this room and touching me or touching anybody else. You're out."

Well, he said, tough as can be, "I'm not going anywhere, and you can't make me."

I thought to myself, "Well, that's a good point." So, I wrote a referral, and I asked Martin to take it to the office.

He reminded me, "I told you, I'm not going anywhere, and you're not making me go anywhere."

I asked one of the other kids to take the referral to the office, and I wrote on the top of it, "Martin refuses to bring this to the office."

The rest of us gathered for the morning meeting, and Martin stayed in his chair. It turned out that they were busy in the office and no one came down right away. After about fifteen minutes into the meeting, Martin started scooting his chair over by us, so I looked up and said, "Martin, just because today got off to a horrible start doesn't mean it has to stay that way. This day doesn't have to continue to be bad for you. C'mon, why don't you join us?" He sat down, and he was just ready to share when the principal showed up at the door.

He got up and went on out with her. I was glad he had calmed down. The principal didn't let him come back to class the rest of the day. She made him sit in her office. She told him that if he touched another person in the school, he would be suspended for ten days. After all the other kids had eaten, she took him down to lunch and left him to eat with Ms. Lucy, who runs the lunchroom. Ms. Lucy told me Martin was indignant, complaining that he had to punch me because I was jerking on his shirt. He told her, "I'm not having anybody do that to me!" I think he knew he was wrong, but he just has to show that he's this big tough guy.

His mother came in with Martin the following morning before the start of school, and we had a long talk. Martin had an attitude at first, but his mother told him, "You get that look off your face, and you get it off now!" He did and he was fine. After his mother left, he and I were in the classroom alone, and he just came over and he hugged me and he said, "I love you."

Sometimes he kisses me good-bye when he leaves; he'll just hug me and kiss me on the cheek and say, "I love you." And then he just leaves. I don't think he really meant to hurt me. I think it probably is a matter of self-control; he just can't control himself. On the whole he's a good person and he tries to be decent. But then he does some stuff that's so bad.

Even when Laura got upset with a child, down deep she believed that the child wanted to be loved, wanted to belong to the classroom community, and wanted to learn. She did not tolerate abusive or disruptive behaviors, but she usually attributed them to children's vulnerability, their difficulties with self-control, or their insecurity. She considered it her job to find out how to help every student develop the skills and understandings he or she needed to succeed. This belief in the deep humanity of all her students helped Laura continue to like even her troublesome students while searching for ways to help them change their problem behaviors.

In the first year, many of Laura's students were angry, aggressive, and defiant, and a few were withdrawn, easily upset, and stubborn. The sheer number of difficult students made it especially hard for Laura to maintain a caring stance. Progress was slow and Laura was frequently discouraged. In November, Leonard, one of Laura's most difficult students, left the school. Leonard had frequently refused to work, defied Laura's authority, teased and made fun of other students, and involved other students in fighting, teasing, and name calling. Although Laura had not succeeded in building a trusting relationship with Leonard, she did care about him and even shed a tear in the good-bye class meeting she arranged for him. However, once Leonard was gone Laura was surprised at the sense of relief she felt. Her class began to run more smoothly, and she begged the principal not to place Leonard in her classroom if he should return to the school.

In February, however, Leonard returned to the school and to Laura's classroom.

> Leonard's back. I thought I was going to die! I was walking through the parking lot and a voice yelled, "Miss Ecken!" I looked and there he was with his mom. And I thought, "Oh, this can't be true," but I said, "Oh, it's so good to see you all. How is school going?"
>
> Leonard's mother said, "Mrs. Ecken, we had to take him out of that school, and I had to move back out here. He had a referral every single day. Last night I had to get him out of JCYC [Jefferson County Youth Center]."

Laura was very upset to have Leonard back in her classroom. Her first response was anger with the principal for placing Leonard back in her room and resentment toward Leonard for being there, even though she knew that there was no better placement for him.

> When Leonard came back, they didn't even walk him to my room. They put the enrollment sheet in my mailbox, and he just showed up after breakfast. It's like nobody had the nerve to bring him back down here.

> He wasn't here a day before the problems started: the teasing and name calling and defiance. I know it's hard for Leonard to come back, but apparently he has come back about like he left.
>
> At the beginning of the year, a lot of times when I'd say the class was going to do this or that, he'd shout, "I'm not!" It was his way of letting me know that "I do what I want to do." Or if I challenged him, he would yell, "Suspend me. Go ahead, suspend me!"

Leonard's return upset the equilibrium and sense of community that Laura had worked hard to establish. He was a powerful personality and exercised a fair amount of negative leadership in the classroom. Dismayed by the effect Leonard was having and remembering all her earlier struggles with him, Laura was initially ready to sacrifice Leonard in order to protect her class.

> Leonard's coming back made me think about how it was at the beginning and how everybody gets along now and does what they're supposed to. There are a few rough spots—there always will be—but, basically, the children are doing excellent work. So I told him right off the bat, after the second incident, "Look, I am going to tell you how it is, Leonard. You cannot destroy this class. I am not going to allow it. I want you to be here. I will help you with anything you need to do to be successful, but disturbing people who are working and upsetting people by talking about them—that's not going to happen here. So don't bother to look at me and scream that I should suspend you, because I will. I want you to know up front, before you come back in here, that this class runs fairly smoothly and you are not going to destroy that."
>
> I am not saying that that was the best thing to do, but I just felt I needed to let him know that whatever was going on in September and October was over. I'm not going back to that.

At first, Laura saw herself entering a battle of wills with Leonard, and she began by laying down the law. Over the weekend, Laura and I discussed Leonard's return to the classroom from his point of view. Laura was able to take Leonard's perspective. She saw his vulnerability. She realized how insecure he must be feeling, having been suspended almost daily from his new classroom and then having to return after three months to the classroom he had left. She realized that he needed reassurance and support more than ultimatums, and she focused on meeting his needs. She didn't lower her standards, but she provided Leonard with the encouragement and support he needed to get his behavior within acceptable bounds. Laura's ability to empathize with and have confidence in Leonard paid off for both of them.

> Monday morning, as soon as Leonard got to school, I told him how glad I was to have him back and that I could tell that all the kids were really pleased that he was back. Then I said, "Leonard, I have been noticing that when we work in partnerships you have some problems leaving the other partnerships alone. I'd like you to think about working on that this week. When you go to work in a partnership, get your work done and don't bother anybody else." He just very seriously said, "Okay, I'll work on that, Miss Ecken."
>
> Later in the day, it was time for everyone to write down goals for the week. For Leonard, it was his first time writing goals because we didn't start writing them until after he left. Just as nice and pleasant as could be, he said, "I know what I need to work on." And he wrote, "Don't mess with other partnerships." I talked with him a couple of times during the week and asked how he thought he was doing and told him that I hadn't had any complaints. He was really, really happy about how he was doing.
>
> I've also been watching closely to see when exactly it is that he has rough spots. It's when everyone is together. It's when we are in the morning and afternoon meetings and whenever we get in a group—like to share something out. It's not so much a problem for him when we are in a lesson or they are all at their tables working. But if he's in the group and he makes that contact with others, he will turn and get into it with somebody or make fun of someone. So I'm going to tell him I have noticed what happens when he gets in the group and encourage him to work on that next.
>
> He also has trouble in the lines. He wants to cut ahead of the others. So what I have done with that, without drawing any attention to him, is I control which table group leads the line and I alternate the groups. Since we have five tables, each one is named for a day of the school week. So on Monday I say, "Now remember, I need to see all the Monday people first in line."
>
> I've also had a couple of talks with him in the cafeteria. What he does is grab his tray and then just push it down in front of people, just shove it in. A lot of them won't stop him. And it happens so fast that everybody just kind of stares at him. The first time I saw him do it, I asked him to think about whether that was fair, and I told him to go to the back of the line. The second day I said, "You know, we talked about this yesterday, didn't we?" And then he just said, "I know where

> to be," and he went to the back of the line. So I think it's going to be okay. He is already making progress.

Although Leonard still misbehaved on numerous occasions, he and Laura gradually developed a partnership focused on his continuous improvement. Once Laura changed her view of Leonard, seeing him as vulnerable and in need of her help and guidance rather than as powerful and bent on doing things his way, she was able to build a positive, nurturing relationship with him. Laura was so pleased with his progress that she decided to keep him in her class for another year. She labeled him a fourth grader, and she challenged him with fourth-grade work, but she kept him in her classroom, which was otherwise designated as a second third-grade class. Laura knew how difficult it was for Leonard to form trusting relationships, especially with adults, and she believed that he needed another year with her to reconcile his tough-guy self-concept with his concept of himself as a good and helpful person and a serious learner.

Examining Our Working Models of Children

Laura was able to develop a caring attitude toward Leonard when she changed her working model of him and his behavior. Our working models of children are works in progress; they are shaped throughout our lives, both at the conscious level by our professional training and at the unconscious level by our relationships with our caregivers, our individual childhood experiences with peers, the general cultural milieu in which we grew up, and our ongoing personal experiences. For example, if we were insecure or badly treated as children, we are apt to find it harder to trust in the goodwill of others, both children and adults. If we were bullies as children, we might be more understanding of the causes of bullying behavior in our students and, as a result, find it easier to sympathize with and care for them, even as we struggle to stop their bullying. However, if we were victims of bullies as children, we might feel irrational anger toward children who bully, undermining our ability to care for them. Reflecting on our own past as we analyze our reactions to our students can help control these unconsciously generated negative feelings.

Our working models of children are also affected by our conscious and unconscious beliefs about groups of people. None of us like to think of ourselves as biased or prejudiced, especially if we have entered a helping profession such as teaching. But we are all influenced by our environment. We may have heard our parents or grandparents characterize people from other groups as less worthy or less trustworthy. We have certainly been affected by the media, which, controlled almost by definition by people in power, generally portray people from nonpowerful groups in negative ways (Cortes, 2000). We can overcome these influences and, as caring teachers, we must.

Psychological theory and research provide strong support for the belief that at the fundamental level of human motivation, all children are alike. They share the same basic needs: to belong, to be and be seen as competent, and to be autonomous or to feel that they are the cause of their own actions.[2]

However, multicultural theory and research provide strong support for the belief that at the level of behavior, children are different. For example, they have different learning styles, politeness norms, and conversational styles.[3] If we do not understand these differences, and if we have been influenced by negative stereotypes, we are apt to hold negative or stereotypical views of groups different from our own and fail to meet the emotional and educational needs of children who differ from us by, for example, race, class, or culture.

On the basis of theory and research related to human motivation and attachment, we can anticipate that all children want to feel loved and cared for, want to acquire the skills and knowledge valued by their culture, and want reasonable autonomy. On the basis of attachment and multicultural theories and research, we can be confident that some children will fail to learn and fail to adjust well to us and our classrooms either because they have a history of insecure attachment relationships or because our curriculum, teaching, or interpersonal styles are out of synch with what they are accustomed to, or both.

Unless our beliefs about individual children are working models, subject to constant revision, and unless we consciously strive to understand the unique qualities of each student, we are likely to resent children who are troublesome. Because some children thrive in our classrooms, we are likely to conclude that those who do not thrive must have something wrong with them. We might dismiss them as learning disabled, lazy, or willfully defiant. Of course, some children are learning disabled, but often they are labeled as such because our curriculum or interaction style does not match the experience and qualities those children bring to our classroom. Some students avoid work that is either too hard or too easy, and we label them lazy rather than find work that will engage them. Some students are willfully defiant. But if we see this defiance as their desperate attempt to survive in a world they view as hostile, we will see them more as vulnerable than as defiant, much as Laura finally did with Leonard. It will be easier to genuinely care for all our students if we review our working model of each child, taking into account children's universal needs for autonomy, belonging, and competence, filtering out our unconscious biases or stereotypes, and adding all the unique information we have about the child and his or her family and culture. Courses in multicultural education and books and articles written from diverse perspectives can help us understand general characteristics of diverse groups, but they only make us aware of ways in which our students *might* be different from us and from one another. There is a great deal of diversity within every group. Our goal is to understand and value the individual students in our classrooms and their families. For this there is no substitute for getting to know them as individuals and trying to view the world from their perspective.

Getting to Know Our Students

It takes time to find out who our students are and what's going on in their lives. But it is time well invested if we are committed to learning to like every student in our classroom.

GATHERING DATA. Students' cumulative files can alert us to important information even before they enter our classroom, but some teachers do not read those records. They think by not doing so, they can give each student a "fresh start." But students cannot make a fresh start. This is one of the important implications of attachment theory. Our students bring their past experiences into our classroom. If they had conflictual relationships with their teachers in the past, they will be more ready to interpret our behaviors through mistrustful eyes. Knowing about earlier troubled relationships can alert us to the extra work we will have to do to earn a student's trust. We don't have to accept another teacher's judgment about a child, particularly if the relationship was conflictual and the judgment is negative.

Laura always reviewed her students' records and checked them against her own evaluations. When Chantelle showed up on the first day of school, her records had not preceded her, but her behavior presaged what Laura would learn later from them.

> Chantelle is a new girl. On the first day of school, before her records were sent down, I noticed right away that she walked the edge. If we lined up, or whatever we did, she would just take it to the limit. Then when we were making cut-outs of ourselves to put up around the room, I was sitting at her table, cutting out my own self-portrait, and she said, "I can't wait to see how you act at the end of the year. Last year Mrs.

> Griff was mean at the beginning of the year, and by the end of the year she was meaner. So I can't wait to see if you're going to be mean at the end of the year. 'Cause you're nice now."
>
> I had no idea, but it turns out she's been thrown out of several classes and was in a special program to keep kindergarten and first-grade kids from getting a BD [behavioral disorder] referral.

Not all of our students will convey their mistrust as clearly as Chantelle did. But if a student's records show that he or she had a difficult time in past classrooms, it's likely that such a child will enter our classroom wary and ready for trouble. Knowing this can help us be ready to work extra hard to build a caring relationship.

During the first few weeks of school, Laura, like most teachers, took great care to make her classroom a comfortable place and to connect personally with each of her students.

> When the kids come in that first morning, I really want to take some time to talk to each one, so I have this activity that keeps the whole group busy making their names real fancy on name tags while I move around the room and talk a little with each child.
>
> The first year, with Martin, I remember telling him that I knew his older sister and him telling me about his younger brother. I was also able to tell Tralin that I knew her sister. They seemed so pleased by just that little bit of personal connection.
>
> Some of the kids were new to the school or had been in different classrooms from each other the year before, so I tried to make some connections for those children. Since quite a few kids came from Ms. Blanchard's room and they already knew each other, it was nice to be able to say, "Hey, you all know each other, but here's somebody you don't know."
>
> So that was kind of a nice little time together while they were making those name tags, just to move around and talk to each of them and give them some time to talk to the others at their tables.
>
> Then right after the name tags, I like to do an activity called Question Circle that shows the kids they have a lot in common. In my classroom half the chairs are red and half are blue. So I make one big circle with the chairs, alternating the colors, and divide the kids into red and blue. I get all the kids seated and give them a question to talk about with a partner, the person next to them. I keep moving the kids; all the reds, for example, move two chairs to the right so that they keep sitting by different people. I have a whole list of things for the kids to talk about

> that I know they're probably going to have some similar thoughts on, like, "Tell about your favorite cartoon," or "Talk to your partner about what you like to do when it rains," or "Talk to your partner about the favorite thing that you like to do when you get home from school."
>
> What I hope is that they're going to find out that these kids they don't know, or who seem different, are a lot like them.
>
> When we finished our questions, I asked the kids to share something they learned about someone else. No one said a thing, which is not unusual for the first day of school. Since they apparently didn't feel comfortable sharing in the whole group, I said, "Well, I learned that a birthday celebration that someone will never forget can be a sad thing. When I was thinking of this question, to tell about a birthday you would never forget, I was thinking that a birthday would be a happy time, but my partner told me about a birthday celebration where everybody was at the grandfather's house for his birthday and the grandfather died. What was supposed to be a wonderful celebration ended up being a really sad event."
>
> I decided to share that because it kind of went along with a theme I had for this first week of school—letting them see that things aren't always what they seem. Birthday celebrations aren't always happy; people who look different from you aren't always that different—they might actually be the same in lots of ways. It fit with the message I was trying to send: "Don't have a lot of preconceptions, keep an open mind, and give yourself a chance to listen to people and get to know people."

Question Circle was just one of a number of activities that Laura did during the first weeks of school to help her connect with and learn about her students and to help her students connect with and learn about one another. Similar activities continued throughout the year. The class created charts, graphs, and Venn diagrams describing their characteristics; they drew self-portraits and made a quilt displaying important facts about everyone in their class. As time progressed and the students acquired more academic skills, getting-to-know-you activities took on a more academic flavor. For example, students shared their favorite part of a story or the most interesting fact they had learned in their research.

Getting-to-know-you activities are often thought of as purely social in nature, but getting to know how each student constructs meaning is at the heart of teaching for understanding. Getting to know our students, what they like, and how they think is not only essential in building our affection for them, it is essential in effectively teaching them.

HANGING OUT WITH OUR STUDENTS. Spending time with individuals or small groups of students—time when there is no instructional purpose—is one of the best ways to learn to like even our unlikable students. When we are not pressing our students to perform in any particular way but are simply interested in being with them and getting to know them better, even the most angry and defiant children will relax and let us see their softer side. And because we have no instructional agenda and are under little pressure ourselves, we can relax and enjoy each child's unique qualities.

Hanging out has side benefits as well. It is a powerful way to let our students know that we like and care about them, and we will also learn an enormous amount that can help us in unforeseen ways during instructional time.

One of the ways Laura chose to hang out with her students was to have lunch with a few of them every day. These times were important for her students and useful for mending and cementing Laura's relationships with them.

> On Monday I started eating with the Monday table group. On Tuesday, with Tuesday. And it's worked out great. They absolutely love it, and it's real relaxing.
>
> Well, on Thursday I had problems with Kenny. He interrupted the whole reading lesson on Thursday morning. Just tore it to shreds. Walked around the room, "Not doing this," "My partner won't talk to me," and just on and on and on.
>
> So, anyway, when we got together as a group to discuss the questions we were working on, he sat at his table and started writing what he and his partner were supposed to have been doing earlier. He yelled over at me, "Could you stop talking! I'm trying to work!" I mean, I just wanted to laugh, it was so funny.
>
> Instead, I said, "Kenny, we're going to talk about the work we've been doing and we're going to do it now. You're just going to have to work under these conditions." So he came over with the rest of us.
>
> Then it was time to line up for lunch. I was going to eat with both Thursday and Friday since there was no school on Friday. And Kenny shouted out, "I was absent on my day! And I need to eat with you like everybody else!" So I said, "Well, please get your tray and come in." All through lunch he was just so pleasant and so much fun. It was like he had no remorse at all for wrecking the morning. Just none.

During these small, intimate moments Laura and the students talked and joked and simply told one another things that were on their minds.

Laura wasn't trying to teach anything. These gatherings were simply to be with the children. They were easy times for even the most troubled of her students because nothing was demanded of them except that they treat their luncheon companions with respect. When a child had had a difficult morning, as was the case with Kenny, hanging out at lunch was an opportunity to reconnect.

In *The Challenge to Care in Schools,* Nel Noddings points out that lunch time can provide an important opportunity to build caring relationship with our students (Noddings, 1992). It definitely served this purpose in Laura's classroom. At the end of the year, eating with Laura was one of the things the class decided to write about for their book, *Remembering Our Year.*

> EATING WITH MRS. ECKEN
> Eating with Mrs. Ecken is fun because we can tell about stuff like [we do in] the morning meeting. If it's Monday, Monday gets to eat with Mrs. Ecken and it keeps on going.

Laura had a number of ways to hang out with her students. Often when she had an uneven number of students for a partner activity, she would partner with one of them. Once the class had the routines for working with partners well in hand, Laura could give the child who was her partner nearly undivided attention. In the following situation, partnering with a difficult child was made possible because a student teacher was conducting the lesson:

> I watch Louise mess with people a lot. She's a nice kid but she just messes with people, and when I talk with her about it she gets upset.
>
> The other day when Miss Rowan was going to start a partner lesson that lasted several days, I made the children's partnerships come out so that I was Louise's partner. She was thrilled to death. It's kind of letting us bond a little bit. So that's been helpful, because if she does mess with someone—like if someone comes over and wants to sit near us, maybe she'll kick their chair—I can talk to her about it as her partner, more like person to person, not so much teacher to student.

Laura also opened her classroom in the morning for kids to come in early if they wished. Some of the more needy students frequently came in to help set up the class and to talk. In *Enhancing Relationships Between Children and Teachers* (1999), Robert Pianta suggests a process called "banking time," whose objective is to spend pleasant, nonstressful time with a child.

There is no lesson, no goal beyond communicating or connecting with the child. He suggests that teachers think of themselves as prospectors hunting for the gold that is buried somewhere in any child. With preschool and primary-grade children, this interaction may need to be around an activity, such as reading and talking about a story, working with clay or blocks, or playing a game. With older students it may simply involve conversation, talking about whatever the child is interested in, honestly conveying your own thoughts on the subject, and listening with the sole intent of really understanding what the child has to say.

Nel Noddings (1994) calls such conversations "ordinary conversations" and suggests that they powerfully affect children's moral development. The goal of the conversation, however, is not to affect anything but to connect to the child and, by so doing, to build a more loving and trusting relationship. Banking time can happen during school hours if we have an aide or if our students are capable of working independently. However, because it is important for these interactions to be stress-free, it might be easiest to schedule them during noninstructional time.

Getting to Know Our Students' Families

Meeting and talking with our students' parents or caregivers early and throughout the year will help us understand our students' lives outside of school and the kind of relationship each child has with the most important adults in his or her life. A parking lot conversation with Louise's father helped Laura understand some of the reasons for Louise's low self-esteem and petulance.

> Louise's parents did not come to conference, and the first time I met the dad, I was out in the parking lot for some reason. I saw Louise in the car. Louise and the father, they look just alike. I introduced myself, "Oh, hi, I'm Louise's teacher. It's so nice to meet you. She is doing such a nice job. She's serious about school and she's getting along well with the other kids."
>
> The father referred to Louise as a fat slob, and he said, "Well, it's about time she did something she was supposed to."
>
> So I said, "Well, she does. She's one good kid."

This father's relationship with his daughter was extreme, but it was important for Laura to know about it in her dealings with Louise and in trying to establish a partnership with her father on Louise's behalf. Most parents can be relied on for support, especially if we give them specific suggestions or materials for helping their children, but some families will be unwilling or unable to provide much support at all. Whatever the case, we will need to know the parents before we know whether or how they can help us work with their children.

When Tyrone, who had made a pretty good adjustment in the class, began having problems, Laura felt sure that his mother could help. Laura had not met Tyrone's mother—she hadn't come to open house—but Laura knew that Tyrone was close to her because he often talked about her and was eager to bring papers from school to show her. As Tyrone's problems escalated, Laura decided to walk Tyrone home and have a talk with his mother.

> After a tough start and then really coming along well, now Tyrone is starting to have a whole lot of problems. He's just in constant motion and he can't focus. I was working with the whole group the other day and he started singing. So I looked over and I said, "Tyrone, I can't talk when you're singing, okay?" And he looked me straight in the face and just kept singing. So I said, "Tyrone, I really need you to stop so that we can hear what's going on." He stopped singing, but then he started doing something else he shouldn't have.
>
> I walked home with him one day this past week because I wanted to talk to his mom. It had been picture day at school, so he had on this real cute little red shirt and he had put on a gold necklace. All day long he was so proud of that necklace.
>
> When we got to his home, well, his mom wasn't there. She's been put in a treatment center, and a young aunt is taking care of him. It was heartbreaking. The aunt started screaming at the older sister, "You let him go to school dressed like that? On picture day!" His face just showed the pain. It was clear that he dressed himself and that his aunt didn't get up with him.
>
> Anyway, the aunt said that he's really upset about his mom, and nobody knows how long she is going to be in this treatment center. So, I really feel like I need to do something special, something to say, "Hey, you're not all alone in this world." But I don't know what. I don't know how to do it.

By walking Tyrone home, Laura discovered one reason why Tyrone's classroom behavior was disintegrating; she also realized that she couldn't rely on his young aunt for much support. Laura couldn't make up for Tyrone's loss, but she did have more patience with him. She provided him with more support and worked extra hard at being dependable and caring. She also helped Tyrone write letters to his mom that the social worker delivered. And she took him to visit her at the treatment center. Seeing his mom greatly relieved Tyrone's anxiety and, along with Laura's patience and extra support, helped him stay focused on learning in the classroom. As we make efforts to learn about our students, their families, and their community, we are not only building our capacity to like each of our students, we are also building our capacity to teach and we are showing our students that we care.

Helping Our Students See That We Like Them

Just as we may have difficulty liking some of our students, some of our students will have difficulty believing that we like and care about them, even when we do. Some may mistrust us because they have a history of insecure attachment relationships with their primary caregivers and their working model of relationships is built on mistrust. Others may have had a history of secure attachment relationships but have had such bad experiences at school that they have learned to mistrust teachers in general. This is sometimes the case with students who have experienced repeated failures in school—students, for example, who have had difficulty learning to read. Students who are culturally or ethnically different from us may mistrust us because we are different or because they have been taught to be mistrustful of our group. Some may have had difficult relationships with others of our group. Whatever the cause of our students' mistrust, we will need to make a conscious and sustained effort to convince them that we care in order to build the kind of nurturing relationship that will support their academic learning and their social, emotional, and ethical development.

Touching and Hugging Children

Displays of physical affection are usually pervasive in parent-child relationships, but experts disagree as to whether teachers should hug or even touch children (Johnson, 2000). For example, Martin Haberman (1995), who argues strongly for the importance of teacher caring, states that "demonstrations of affection are not a method of teaching" (p. 60). He asks us to think how we would feel if a twenty-five-year-old teacher hugged a seventeen-year-old student for giving a correct answer. Although physical demonstrations of affection are not a method of teaching academic content, they are an important way to communicate caring, especially for preschool and primary-age children.

Most preschool and primary children need and seek physical displays of our affection. They frequently want to lean against us, hug us, or hold our hand. We need to accept and return these gentle expressions of need and affection; to pull away would convey rejection. (One of the characteristics of parents whose children become avoidantly attached is their aversion to touching or being physically close to their infants.)

Although we need to be judicious in displaying physical affection and take care that our gestures of affection are designed to meet the needs of our students and not our own, there are a number of appropriate ways to physically display affection, depending on the context and the age of the students. Laura frequently touched, put her arm around, or hugged her students to support, encourage, and convey her commitment to them. Sometimes, it was the most efficient way of repairing her relationship with a student and bringing the child back into the class.

> Martin was just furious because he didn't get picked to help me, first with a math activity and then to pass out cookies. When it was time for our read-aloud, he sat back in the corner and put his coat over his head.
>
> I said, "Martin, can you sit up and take your coat off your head? We're going to listen to the story now."
>
> From under his coat he said, "I hate you!"
>
> I told him I was sorry to hear it, but we went on and started reading the story. I could see him stuck back there in his attitude and, finally, after I read for about five minutes, I said, "Martin, I need you just to come up here right now. I know what's wrong with you. You're feeling left out, so just sit up here and let me put my arm around you." That's what we did for the rest of the story and he was fine. This was on Friday. When we got ready to leave and they were lining up, he came over and gave me a big hug.

Laura often used touch to support her students in their work as well as to convey affection. She had learned that hugs were important for getting Tralin past frustrations, and eventually Tralin identified this pattern for herself and was able to ask for a hug when she needed one.

> Tralin was in a really bad mood all morning on Monday—arguing with her partner over who was doing what book page and just unhappy. At lunch time, as we were walking down to the cafeteria, she looked at me and said, "I'm in a bad mood. Give me a hug."
>
> And so I gave her a hug. And then she said, "I'll be better in the afternoon," and she was.

> That's never happened before, that she asked for a hug. In the past when she's been in a really bad mood—the work is often hard for her—and I could see that she wasn't going to come out of it, I'd just go over and hug her and say, "You know, Tralin, I've seen you do this. I know that you can do what we're doing, and if I can help you I will." I thought it was a real breakthrough that she asked for that hug.

Other ways to physically convey affection are particularly appropriate for older children. For example, standing close to a child, positioning yourself at the child's eye level, or leaning across a child's desk, if done with a friendly attitude, all convey affection. A congratulatory handshake or other gesture can communicate affection to older children. The important thing is that we convey genuine respect and caring.

Telling Our Students That We Care

All our students need our authentic interest in their efforts. Because we are successful adults, our students look to us to learn the standards for success and to know if they are meeting those standards. We therefore need to pay close attention to their successes and let them know that we admire and appreciate what they have accomplished. Students don't need what Alfie Kohn (1996) calls slobbering, manipulative praise, but they do need expressions of our genuine delight and interest in what they have done and honest feedback about their efforts.

Some students need more than just our interest; they need a direct expression of our caring. Children who have not experienced most people in their lives as caring may assume that they are not worthy of care. They need to hear us say directly that we care about them. This is apt to be particularly true for students who regularly misbehave. Because we frequently need to control these students, our relationship with them will be more conflictual than with other students, causing them to more readily assume that we don't like them. Often students will provide opportunities following some kind of trouble for us to tell them we care about them. Laura describes such a situation with Ella, who came into her class in the second year and for months had difficulty trusting Laura.

> Ella was screaming in line on the way back from the cafeteria, and when I asked her to stop she started screaming at me. I told her I wouldn't listen to that, and I asked her to sit down and write about what she could have done besides scream in the line and scream at me.

> She wrote about what she should have done, and then she wrote on the letter, "To: my teacher, Mrs. Ecken. Love you tons. Did not mean it at all. You know that. Love you Mrs. Ecken."
>
> We read the letter together, and I told her that I could see that she knows what she's supposed to do and so I hoped that she would.
>
> It wasn't a half an hour later when she started yelling at me again. And I said, "Ella, no. I'm not going to have it. Get yourself a piece of paper and write down why this is not going to go."
>
> And so she wrote, "Dear Mrs. Ecken, I should not back-talk. Do what she says. Do not say a word. Go back to my seat. Say Yes Mam, and go. I love you. By: Ella. And next time I will do what it says."
>
> She really is trying. When she handed me the note, I read it, and this time I answered her in writing: "I love you, too! I am counting on it. I know you can do it. Love you tons. Mrs. E."
>
> When she read those concrete words of affection, she just got the biggest smile.

Students with a history of insecure attachment will need to be assured over and over that they are worthy and that we care about them. Several of Laura's students needed this kind of continual reassurance, and even when Laura provided it, not all of them ever really believed her.

Sharing Ourselves

Sharing personal information is a sign of affection and of trust. Laura frequently shared information with her students about her life, her family, and even her dogs. This sharing was sometimes done informally in the context of a class meeting or while talking with students over lunch, sometimes as part of activities designed to help the class get to know one another and sometimes as a way to introduce or model academic activities. Details from this sharing were often reflected in her students' comments and in their work.

> The singers from the senior center came over and gave a performance for the school. My class took their little buddies, and then afterwards everyone got drinks and cookies and sat and talked together. The older people just loved it, talking to them and being with them. When we came back up to the room, we took a few minutes to talk about being with our buddies and the singers.
>
> They all know that at night, after I get the supper finished, I go sit in the family room with a cup of tea and my cookies and just sit and

> relax. And I've told them that the dogs always sit beside me, so I have to give all three dogs one bite of cookie.
>
> So Martin said, "You know, I was sitting down there with my buddy and those singers and I just felt like Mrs. Ecken sitting in her family room, drinking her hot tea and eating her cookies and giving them to the dogs."

A month later, when Martin was frustrated by a writing assignment and ready to quit, Laura was able to get him back on track by referring to some personal information that Martin had gathered, not from her but from her teenage son Damian. Martin drew on a past conversation with Damian to envision the steps to reaching a personal ambition. He wrote:

> I'd like to be a football player for the Greenbay Packers. I'd like to run the ball and be a quarterback. First you have to go to college. You have to have good grades and go to college. If you don't have good grades you will not be able to play for the Greenbay Packers. You will not play any sports. Like Damian he had to have good grades to play any sport.

As we openly share our lives with our students, we not only convey our affection for them but we provide them with a way to connect to our humanness and our ways of being. As we will see later, it can be particularly helpful to share some of our mistakes and foibles with our students.

Doing Nice Things for Our Students

In every classroom there are many opportunities to do something nice for our students. We can do something as simple as retrieving a pencil from the floor or commenting about a new haircut or lunch box. We can lend forgotten lunch money, make a reminder call about a field trip permission, or write a student's parents to let them know about one of their child's accomplishments. These "nice things" are not earned, and they are not offered as a way of bargaining with children. They are simply done to make a child's or the class's life more pleasant. In essence, they are an expression of the norms for life in a caring community: "When someone needs help and we can provide that help, we do. When we can do things to make the people in our community happy, we do."

One of the regular, nice things Laura did for her students was to provide them with a daily snack. The class ate lunch at 11:30, and the school day did not end until 3:20. By midafternoon Laura's students were hungry, and they loved getting a cookie, some cheese and crackers, or a piece of candy to tide them over. It was also hugely important to the class that *everyone* got a snack, even people who had not had a good day. Although many of Laura's students had received snacks in their classrooms before, usually these had been contingent on good behavior. The daily snack was another of the things the kids chose to write about in their remembrance book at the end of the year.

> SNACKS
> By Tangela
> Every day we have snacks after special area. Sometimes we eat them when Mrs. Ecken reads to us. She gives it to everybody in the class. She never leaves anybody out.

Laura also did many small things on an individual as well as a class level. For example, when Cindy was afraid that no one would pick her up from day care because her foster mother's car was broken, Laura made sure Cindy could stop worrying.

> At the close of school on Thursday, Cindy came up to me very upset. She said, "My mother's car is broken so I know she won't be able to pick me up from day care. I'm afraid I'll have to take the bus and I don't know how."
>
> She was really upset, so I told her about a time my mom's car was broken and I was afraid, but that my uncle came and picked me up. I said, "I'm sure that your mom has arranged for someone else to pick you up, but just in case you have a problem, here's my phone number. You can call me and I'll come pick you up." Well, about six o'clock that night I got a call from Cindy. She was home and she just wanted me to know that her grandfather had picked her up.

All Laura's small and large acts of kindness eventually helped her students see that she really did care for them and that they could depend on her.

We sometimes resist doing these nice things out of a fear that our students will become dependent or take advantage of us. As teachers, we have often been warned that if we are too helpful we encourage laziness or create dependency. On the other hand, the research in attachment theory has demonstrated that if we are able to meet children's needs with reasonable consistency, they will become secure in their necessarily dependent relationship with us and will gradually grow more independent and self-sufficient.

However, as most teachers have experienced, when we help some students, they seem to want more and more help, which would seem to confirm the notion that providing help encourages dependence and even laziness. Again, the research in attachment theory casts this behavior in a new light. Children with a history of anxious attachment often try to get our help, not because they need it but because they need to test our availability. If we respond by lowering our expectations and providing these students with too much help, we inadvertently convey our lack of confidence that they can succeed on their own. So there is tension here. But gradually, with insecurely attached children, as we demonstrate in a wide variety of ways that we are trustworthy, these acts of kindness will increase children's feelings of security in their relationship with us, allowing them to take more risks, develop more confidence in themselves, and grow in independence—not dependence.

Doing Fun Stuff

Although teaching is a serious business, one of the ways to convey our affection—to confirm a close and trusting relationship—is to occasionally interact with students in playful or even silly ways. Laura describes this as "acting goofy." Every teacher has different ways of having fun with a class. Laura danced with the kids at their parties, and she loved to joke and play around with them. On a whim one day, Laura pretended that she was Oprah and that the students were guests on the "Oprah Winfrey Show."

> Sometimes when we did role-plays from the partner reading books, we would set them up like a little theater and I would introduce each partnership. One day I was feeling silly and pretended that I was Oprah and that they had traveled all the way to Chicago to do a role-play for the audience. I used a fat marker for a microphone and started, "Now we have this group here from Louisville, Kentucky." And then I asked them some questions about the city: "So, tell me, what do you all do on Derby Day?" and "I heard you had this boat by the river. Can you tell me a little bit about that boat?" Kind of giving them a chance to talk about some of the things they are supposed to know about their city. Well, they just loved it and frequently they would ask to do their role-plays on the Oprah show. Sometimes I would ask them completely goofy stuff, like, "I heard you all drank so many sodas on the bus that the bathroom on the bus flooded." They would play right along, "Oh, yes, it's true. I drank five Cokes." Once I said, "Now, I hear you all have a lovely teacher. Tell me about her." Goofy stuff, but it added fun to the classroom and made us feel like a community with our own special ways of doing things.

As was the case with so many things the students liked, "doing the Oprah show" quickly became a tradition in the classroom. It was just one of the many ways Laura could increase her students' joy and convey her affection for them.

Key Points: Building the Teacher-Student Relationship

- Remember that all children, even those who appear aloof and defiant, want to be loved and protected by caring adults and want to fit in with their peer group.
- Examine and revise your working model of children by reflecting on how your personal history might influence your own attitudes and understandings.
- Remember that all children are alike in their need for autonomy, belonging, and competence and that each child is unique in skills, intelligence, temperament, culture, and life experience.
- Find natural ways to get to know each student personally.
- Find ways to get to know and work with students' families.
- Help your students see that you care about them, and share your own life to give them an opportunity to know you.

A trusting and supportive teacher-child relationship is the foundation on which a nurturing relationship is built. Achieving such a relationship with all our students requires that we see each of them in a positive light, learn enough about them and their lives to be able to understand their unique ways, and convince our students that we can be trusted to care for them no matter what—three huge tasks. Theory and research in human development, motivation, and attachment, as well as multicultural theory and research, can help us understand the unique needs and strengths that our students bring to the classroom. But as important as this knowledge is, it cannot substitute for spending time getting to know each student individually and building personal, nurturing relationships with each of them.

Doing nice things for our students is an important way to build these relationships because we are saying with our actions that we care. However, it's very important that these kind or helpful acts be done for their own sake or to convey our affection. If we do something nice but use it to bargain with or bribe children, we are being coercive, not caring (Kohn, 1993). To convey that we care and to build our children's trust in us, our kind and caring actions must be unconditional. No matter how many times students misbehave, get something wrong, reject us, or tell us they don't like us, we continue to care, continue to treat them well, continue to be there to help them, and *never* say, "I helped you when you needed help, so will you please cooperate with me now."

Doing nice things for our students simply to be nice also provides students with a model of kindness and consideration. If we encourage them to do nice and helpful things for one another, gradually norms of kindness and helpfulness will pervade the classroom. We will be helping students meet another aspect of their belonging needs, that is, feeling liked and valued by their classmates and peers. In the next chapter, we will see how Laura helps the students in her classroom learn how to be friends.

NOTES

1. Ironically, Kenny was placed in another teacher's classroom the following year. As mentioned in the preceding chapter, after school closed for the summer, the principal decided that Laura's class had too many difficult children and that it would be best to move Kenny to a different classroom. At first Laura argued against taking Kenny from her class, but she was tired and as she reflected on how demanding the year had been, she reluctantly agreed that he be moved.
2. See Ainsworth and others, 1978; Deci and Ryan, 1985; Erikson, 1963; Maslow, 1970; Ryan and Deci, 2000; Sheldon, Elliot, Kim, and Kasser, 2001; and White, 1959.
3. See Banks, 1993; Cortes, 1986; Delpit, 1995; Heath, 1983; Nieto, 1992, 1999; Schmidt, 1998; and Steinberg, Brown, and Dornbusch, 1996.

2

TEACHING CHILDREN HOW TO BE FRIENDS

We were reading the book *J. T.* as a class. Tralin and Shereka were working as partners to write a letter to the boy, J. T. Then Tralin took her pencil and started scribbling on Shereka's paper. Then Shereka pinched Tralin on the arm. Tralin came up to me and complained that Shereka pinched her.

When I asked why she would do that, Tralin said, "I don't know. I'm just sitting there writing and she pinched me on the arm."

Next I asked Shereka what happened. When I found out the whole story, I pointed out to Tralin her part in getting pinched.

Tralin scowled at me. "I'm telling my Mom on you. You're letting people pick on me in here."

I said, "No, I'm not letting people pick on you. What Shereka did was wrong." And I told Shereka she had no right to touch Tralin.

Then I asked Tralin how she would feel if Shereka drew on her paper. She said it wouldn't bother her at all. So I asked Shereka how it had felt to her, and she told Tralin it made her mad.

We talked a little more, and just as it seemed we were coming to some understandings, Shereka brought up a new piece of information. "She said she's getting me after school."

Tralin nodded, "She pinched me on the arm, and I'm going to get her for it."

I just couldn't get Tralin to see that if she hadn't scribbled on Shereka's paper, none of this would have started. She couldn't get past being pinched.

Later, Tralin was coming in from the playground and she said, "You know, I hate school. I hate it because you're not allowed to beat the people up here that bother you. I can't take care of the things I want to."

O

IT WAS OCTOBER of the first year. As confrontational as Tralin and Shereka might have appeared, they also wanted and needed to feel liked and accepted by their classmates. Like them, many of Laura's students had much to learn about getting along with others. Laura knew that creating a classroom in which her students felt safe—a classroom that satisfied their need for belonging—would mean teaching her students how to get along.

Learning to form friendships and collaborate smoothly and productively with peers is one of the key developmental tasks of early and middle childhood. As we saw in Chapter One, creating mutual trust between teacher and student is the first step. The next step is to create a classroom environment in which they feel safe with their peers and with us. To do this, we will need to teach many of our students how to be friends.

If Tralin and Shereka were preschoolers, we would consider the development of their interpersonal understanding and their social skills to be central aspects of our teaching. However, we expect our elementary and middle school students to have mastered these skills before they reach our classrooms. In fact, many of the problems we solve daily are not related to academics but to our students' undeveloped social skills. Teasing, tattling, bossing, bickering, scapegoating, and hosts of other unfriendly behaviors not only interfere with student learning and well-being but are a major source of teacher stress.

Because we often assume that school-age children have mastered the basic interpersonal skills for getting along with peers, we tend to view their failure to do so as evidence of willfulness. Accordingly, we focus narrowly on changing the motivations of our most nettlesome students. Although motivation is often part of the problem, our techniques for changing motivation are typically those inherited from learning theory (Bower and Hilgard, 1981), which are likely to make the situation worse. On the one hand, punishing children who treat their classmates badly is likely to increase their resentment toward those very classmates whom they have harmed. On the other hand, if we ignore unkind behavior we convey the message that such behavior is acceptable. And although rewarding or praising kind behavior may have some positive short-term effect, it is likely to cause the children who seldom receive this attention to resent the children who do. Even more troublesome is the fact that children who treat others well in order to be rewarded do not build an experience of themselves as people who choose to be kind.

The reasons students treat one another badly or fail to get along are complex. They involve not just a lack of will but a lack of understanding and skill. This more complete view allows us to focus on helping our students to like one another by changing their understanding of the nature of relationships and teaching them social and emotional skills.

Research in attachment theory finds that children with histories of secure attachment are generally well liked by their peers and get along with relative ease (Sroufe, 1996). Still, even these children need to learn more about forming caring relationships, particularly with their classmates who are unpopular or different in some way. Understandably, even the kindest and most congenial children may be unfriendly to those same children whom we as teachers find difficult to like. Many of these unpopular children will be aggressive or domineering, which is typical of children with insecure avoidant or disorganized attachments. Others may be withdrawn or dependent and whiny—characteristics that are typical of children with insecure, anxious attachment relationships (Pianta, 1999; Sroufe, 1996) and lead them to be victimized by their peers. Our responsibility is to find ways to like even the most unlikable and least popular children and to help our students find ways to relate well to them.

It will take time and many supportive interactions to help insecurely attached children develop the building blocks of effective peer relationships: basic trust, the ability to regulate their emotions, a strong sense of self, and the ability to guide or regulate their own behavior. Likewise, it will take skill and stamina to engage securely attached children in accepting them. Beginning on the very first day of school, we can do a lot to promote respectful and friendly relationships among our students. First, we can create a friendly atmosphere.

Structuring an Environment for Friends

Our own attitudes have a powerful effect on our students' feelings about their classmates. We need to be clear that everyone is important and to help students get to know one another well enough to experience that feeling themselves. We need to show students that we value differences in people and let them explore why that is so. And we must never convey dislike or disrespect for particular students. Their peers will quickly perceive this, and some will shun or scapegoat those students to align themselves with us. Conversely, when there is a student in the class whom most of the others do not like or respect, we can clearly convey our respect and help the other students see important strengths in the disliked child.

Helping Students Get to Know Their Classmates

In the previous chapter, several of the activities that helped Laura get to know her students better also helped her students get to know their classmates. As the students exchanged information in Question Circle, created Venn diagrams of their favorite foods, or drew pictures of their partner's favorite activities, they, along with Laura, were getting to know one another better.

Helping children get to know one another is only part of creating friendly peer interactions and a safe classroom environment, but it is an important part. Laura's student Danny, whom she was so determined to find likable, testified in his own words to the power of getting to know the other kids in his class.

> Dear Nancy and Susan,
> I used to thro rocks at you. That was befor I new you. I am sory.
> Love,
> Danny

Making Differences Okay

Every classroom is diverse. Some are diverse in more ways than others, but students in all classrooms deal with diversity. Acceptance of and respect for diversity do not come naturally. Left to their own devices, children will deal with diversity by forming little groups, connecting with some children, and excluding others. Some children will be marginalized by their peers because of their race or culture, their relative lack of academic or athletic skill, their dress, their body size, the neighborhood in which they live, or perhaps because they are frequently reprimanded or corrected by the teacher.

Laura's classroom was no exception. Some of these differences were Laura's responsibility to minimize, but others she decided to highlight as a way of helping her students be more accepting of everyone in the class.

In the beginning of the year, Laura used the activity Forced Choice to impress on her students that their differences, as well as their similarities, could be an asset to the classroom and in their lives.

> I want the kids to see that they have a lot in common—that they are alike in many ways—but I also want them to realize that it is okay to

be different. In this activity, I offer them two choices and ask them to go to different sides of the room, depending on their choice. For example, I'll ask, "Would you rather swim in the ocean or climb a mountain?" "Would you rather read a book or see a movie?" "Would you rather go to Pizza Hut or McDonald's?" I choose things that I'm pretty sure will get my kids to form lots of different groupings.

Something interesting happened this year when I asked, "Would you rather dance or sing?" Everybody rushed to the dance side; some even *danced* over there. All of a sudden they noticed that Yolanda was the only one standing on the sing side and they began to point and say, "Oooo." It was almost like they were saying there was something wrong or embarrassing to be the only one who preferred to sing.

So I said, "Well, look at that. Think how much courage it took Yolanda to stand by herself because she prefers to sing."

After I said that, a few people started to cross back over to where Yolanda was. I couldn't tell if they were coming over because they wanted to please me, or so that Yolanda didn't have to be there all by herself, or because they really did prefer to sing but just hadn't been willing to go against the rush to the dancing side. And maybe it was a combination.

In Forced Choice, it becomes really obvious that sometimes friends like different things. And sometimes that can cause a little tension or a bit of a problem in a relationship. So, when the activity was over, I brought the class together to talk about it. I said, "I noticed that during this activity some friends stayed really close together, and then all of a sudden I saw some people say, 'I've got to go over there and leave you because I like that even if you don't.'"

We talked about what might be difficult about having a friend who likes different things than you do.

Tyrone said, "If you have a friend over and you want to play and they want to eat, you should do what they want to do." When I asked him why, he said, "That's just showing respect."

John said, "You might want to ride your bike and they don't want to."

He couldn't really say what the problem was, so I said, "I think I see where you're going. If your friend doesn't want to do what you want to do, it kind of puts you in a spot, 'Do I really want to go on riding my bike and leave my friend behind?'"

When I asked what might be some advantages of having a friend who likes different things than you do, Denise related it to the Kentucky State Fair, which was going on that week.

> She said, "You might want to go to the Discovery Zone and your friend might want to go to the fair. You might be mad cause you have to go to the fair. But if you never been to the fair, you might get there and find that the fair is real good."
>
> So we talked about how having a friend who likes different things can broaden your horizons and introduce you to things that maybe you wouldn't think you would like.
>
> This is an important early conversation because as we get into the school year they will be doing a lot of work in partnerships, and there will be many situations when their partner maybe has a different idea about how to do the work than they do. My hope is that conversations like this set the stage for them to respect the differences that come up and to be more open to compromise.

Laura also used children's literature to help her students see that differences can prevent us from getting to know others and can lead us to misunderstand, avoid, or even fear them. During the first week of school, she read and discussed with them the story *Miss Maggie,* which is about a boy who overcomes his fears of a lonely old woman and becomes friends with her. Laura's students listened with interest to the story but struggled to understand its implications for them.

> When I said we were going to talk about the story, the first response was, "Is it time to go home?"
>
> I told them we still had about an hour and fifteen minutes left.
>
> Rebecca asked, "Can we take a nap?" To be fair, it was the start of the year and they weren't used to being in school or discussing stories.
>
> "Let's talk about this a little bit, "I said. "How did Nat feel about Miss Maggie at the beginning of the story?"
>
> Someone said "scared" and I asked, "Why? Why was he scared?" About all they could come up with was that she was old.
>
> So I asked them why Nat changed how he thought about Miss Maggie.
>
> Louise said, "Probably because of the bird [Miss Maggie's pet, who had died]."
>
> When I asked why they thought the bird was so important to Miss Maggie, Janice said, "Because it was her favorite bird."
>
> They were having trouble seeing the world from Miss Maggie's perspective, so I asked, "Did she have many friends?"
>
> They all answered no, and Brian said, "She lived alone; she didn't have no husband."

So I asked again, "Why was the bird, Henry, so important to her?"

This time the question made more sense to them. Janice said, "It kept her company." The next question was what I really wanted them to think about: why it's so important to get to know people who are different. I asked, "How did two people who were so different, a young little boy and an old, old woman, become such special friends?"

Brian said, "Maybe because he thought that she wasn't that old." Then he added, "Maybe he saw that she was sad."

No one else offered anything, so I expanded on Brian's last comment. I said, "Do you think that maybe when Nat went over there and found out how sad she was and got to know her a little better that he wasn't so afraid of her?"

They kind of agreed and someone said, "It's almost time to go home."

This discussion was hard work for Laura and for her students. There was so much the students needed to learn, from how to have a discussion to the importance of welcoming people who seem different from yourself. But this was a beginning. As the year progressed, Laura's students would become more articulate and able to sustain longer discussions. More important, their understanding of what it means to treat others respectfully and with an open heart would deepen.

Helping Children Find the Gold

It's difficult for children to see the positive qualities in other children whom they perceive as different from themselves. In all classrooms, but particularly in full-inclusion classrooms, it's important to help children see beyond the differences and appreciate each of their classmates' unique talents and strengths. Sometimes children will have a particular gift that we can promote as a way of helping their classmates value them. Sometimes their special qualities will be harder to discover. But in all cases, we must find ways to help other children come to respect and value the children they find hard to like.

Grouping Students for Friendship and Learning

Laura was committed to having her students get to know and to work with everyone in the class. Partner work was the primary structure Laura used to promote friendly collaboration in the class, but she used table groups (the foursomes that made up the classroom seating structure) to engineer a harmonious base from which students could move in and out of the more demanding interactions inherent in partner work.

Structuring Table Groups for a Harmonious Base

Laura assigned students to the five table groups with great care. Even though her students spent much of their day in a variety of other groupings, their home base was their table group. It was crucial for the tenor of the relationships among the four students at a table to be positive.

> When I set up table groups, I didn't place the kids randomly. They spend a lot of time in those groups, and it was time when they were encouraged to help each other. So after I got a sense of who the kids were, I made very calculated decisions about who sat where. For example, I would put a child who was struggling academically between two students who were academically strong and who would provide that child help and support.
>
> And although I tried to change children's tables and table groupings about once a month, it was very, very difficult for me to change the groups that were going smoothly. If I had a table where two calm children were managing to keep a more emotionally volatile child reasonably calm and focused, the next time I created new table groupings, those three would find themselves at a new table but with only one new tablemate.
>
> Which particular seat a child ended up in wasn't random either. Students who were easily distracted or who liked to distract others got seats that didn't face the rest of the tables. It didn't take me long to figure out that Leonard and Martin shouldn't be able to catch the eyes of the other kids or that Tyrone was better off facing a wall than whatever was going on in the middle of the classroom.
>
> Each time we formed new tables, the new groups each created a poster showing everything "This Table Likes." We left those hung up around the room until we made new table groupings.
>
> One time Louise yelled out, "Mrs. Ecken, we all like you!" I said, "Good, be sure to put that down."

Laura carefully orchestrated table groups as an important way to give children positive experiences with classmates. She also encouraged tablemates to help one another, setting the stage and providing practice for the more structured collaboration children would have to manage in their partnerships.

Pairing Everyone

Because Laura was committed to having everyone work with everyone else, whether they were easy to like or academically adept or not, partner work was a laboratory for helping students learn respect for all of their classmates. Sometimes Laura assigned partners, and sometimes she used random pairs. But she made it very clear that everyone in the class would have the opportunity to work with everyone else and would be expected to do so without complaining or hurting anyone's feelings.

At the beginning of the year, students did a lot of short partner activities. These early partnerships were formed by having students find their match: another student whose randomly dealt card had a synonym for the vocabulary word on their own card or whose card had the number that completed the equation on their card.

Students enjoyed the academic game of finding a partner, but they didn't always like the partner. Early in the first year, Laura had to deal with students' attempts to sabotage her system.

> The kids were finding their partners, and a couple of partnerships were having difficulty greeting their partners in a nice way. I was talking with them about that when all of a sudden I noticed that Martin was working with Leonard. I knew they didn't have matching cards because I had seen both of their cards.
>
> I just stopped the class right then. "I'd like your attention. We have a problem *again* with people switching cards." I said "again" real loudly because this wasn't the first time. "People don't have the numbers they drew. People have told people they don't want to work with them. So now we have to start this whole thing all over."
>
> Everyone was groaning about having to start over, and some people were really angry, so I thought I would let the people who were causing all this commotion hear from their classmates. "What do you all think of this as a class?" I asked.
>
> Somebody said, "It's painful."
>
> Tralin said, "It's mean when people say, 'I don't want to work with you.'"
>
> Leonard, who had switched cards, complained, "I've been wanting to work with Martin and now I got to and we have to do it all over again."
>
> I said, "Wait a minute, Leonard, you didn't really get to work with Martin. He didn't draw you as a partner and you didn't draw him. Yolanda drew Martin."

> Then I said to Yolanda, "Did Martin tell you he didn't want to work with you?" When she said "yes," I asked her what she did about it. I guess I wasn't really thinking very clearly, because I was expecting her to tell me that she tried to object and tell Martin that we don't treat partners that way. But Yolanda, just as innocent as can be, looked up at me and said, "Well, I told him I didn't want to work with him either."
>
> I had to say, "To be honest, if somebody looked at me and said, 'I don't want to work with you,' I'd probably say, 'I don't want to work with you, either,' just like Yolanda did."
>
> So I decided to back up to the beginning. I said, "All right, now what do we need to do when we find partners?"
>
> Somebody said, "Stay with them."
>
> And I said, "Yes, and how can we let partners know that we want to work with them?"
>
> Tralin said, "Treat them in a respectful way."
>
> Then I decided to deal with Martin directly. So I said, "Martin, look at me. You switched your cards yesterday. Now you've switched them again today, and it's a big problem because I've got all these people who are upset. They're thinking, 'We have our partners, we didn't trade cards, so why do we have to do it over?' "
>
> I went on, "I'm going to explain to all of you why we are going to have to do it again. We are going to work with anybody in this class that we draw. It's not acceptable in this class to change cards." I wanted to let them know that whenever it happened, we were going to turn around and redo it.
>
> They drew new cards and I said, "Remember to say kind words to your partner or maybe greet them and say, 'Let's go find a place to work.' But let's get it done."
>
> Of all things, this time Martin and Leonard ended up with matching cards. It was just a wicked twist of fate. They were so happy. They shouted out, "Miss Ecken, we get to work together! We're partners!" I must admit, I felt more than a little defeated by my own system.

Laura treated rebuffing a partner as an assault. Because it was her duty to protect her students from being hurt, either physically or psychologically, her response to Martin's trading of cards was clear and firm.

Although Laura's students knew that she expected them to work respectfully with all their classmates, this did not stop them from continuing to complain about some of their partners, even well into the year. But Laura did not give up. She couldn't. Getting all her students to be willing and able to work with all others was central to her goal of building her students' respect for diversity and their commitment to treating others with kindness and consideration. She also saw congenial, accepting partnerships as essential for making the classroom a place where *all* her students would feel a clear sense of belonging.

So she talked with her students about how it feels to be rejected and how important it is to make the classroom safe for everybody. She made it clear that refusing to work with a partner was unacceptable—a violation of their moral obligation to treat others kindly and respectfully. And she looked for ways to make it easier for her students to accept partners they didn't know or with whom they weren't particularly friendly.

For long partner assignments, when students would work together for several days, Laura tried to create partnerships that she believed each child would experience as positive. She also used humor to increase her students' willingness to work with their partners, whoever they turned out to be.

> With some students, if they don't get exactly who they want to work with, they'll just say, "I'm not working with them!" So what I've been doing when I introduce a partner activity is to say, "Now, we're going to work with partners in this activity, and I don't care if you get Captain Hook for a partner. If you get Captain Hook, I want you to say, 'I'm glad to be hooked up with you, let's get to work.'" And then I'll go on and say some other goofy stuff. "If you get a boa constrictor for a partner, say, 'Give me a hug, and let's go to work.'" I usually do seven or eight animals. It seems to help. It seems to get them into a more accepting mood.
>
> Well, this week we were going to get new partners for working with the book *Chicken Sunday.* Just as I got ready to name the partners, Rebecca announced, "And remember, Mrs. Ecken, if you get a tiger, say you're glad to be with that tiger and just work with him." And then three or four others piped up with different animals.

Gradually, Laura's students accepted the reasonableness of her expectations, and by spring most were able to approach collaborative work with any of their classmates with a willing heart. There were occasional objections when, for example, a child was in a particularly bad mood or when two children were partnered just after they'd had a rancorous playground disagreement. But, in general, accepting and working with partners ceased to be a problem.

Because a number of Laura's students had a fragile sense of themselves and were easily hurt, Laura didn't let her students choose their own partners for fear that some would be damaged in the process. The one time

Laura allowed students to choose their own partners, the last student chosen—Tangela—objected to being Denise's partner. She, in fact, liked Denise, but she felt humiliated being the last child chosen.

Teaching Partner Skills

Laura's students didn't acquire the good graces to work with everyone in the class without Laura's repeated intervention. Although some of her students had well-developed skills for getting along with their peers, most did not. And even the most socially adept children found it challenging to

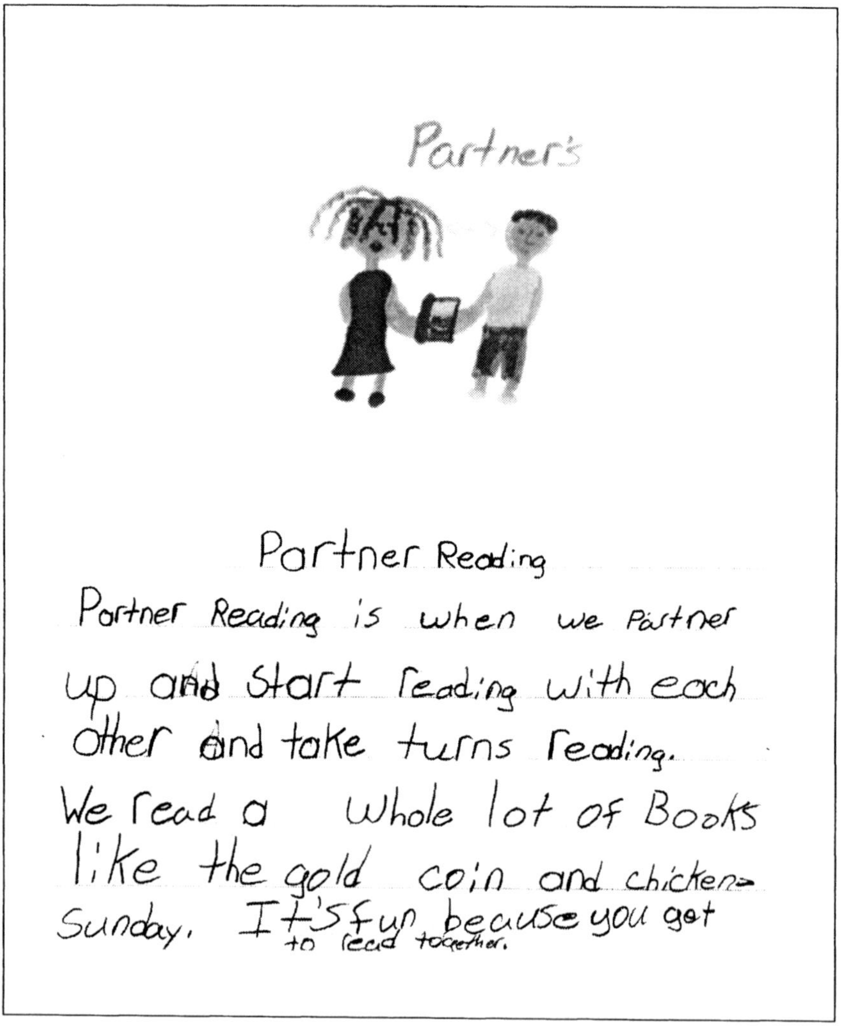

work with the children who were universally disliked and who, typically, lacked the basic skills of friendship. These skills, however, can be taught.

To teach some skills, Laura modeled or role-played approaches students could try. When she introduced partner work in the first year, for example, she found that students didn't just have trouble accepting some of their new partners; lots of them didn't even know how to say hello.

> I think it makes a big difference to provide some direct teaching in what you do when you get with a partner. It helps to teach them very basic things. I might role-play with a student how to look at your partner and smile.
>
> With Louise, for example, I think it was very important that we talked about how to let people know you want them for a partner. She didn't have a clue. She would get with a partner and then grab the pencil out of their hand or kick them under the table. After we had some conversations about how to greet our partners, she started having positive partner experiences simply because she smiled at people and they smiled back. And those smiles were a wonderful thing for that kid.
>
> The other day she and Tyrone drew each other, and it was precious because she was happy to have him and she showed it. For his part, Tyrone's been having a lot of problems in his partnerships because people see him as not serious, and he does play around some. So when he got a partner who smiled and was happy to work with him, it was just great for both of them.

Laura's understanding of Developmental Discipline led her to focus mainly on teaching social skills and ethical understanding as they became relevant—an embedded or naturalistic approach. Because Laura insisted that partners try to solve problems themselves before coming to her, when a partnership was clearly foundering, she was usually free to help.

> It was the second week of school and kids were settled in their partnerships to read *Frog and Toad Are Friends.* I noticed that Brian and Denise's partnership wasn't working out. Denise was wandering around, and Brian was reading to himself on the carpeting. I corralled Denise and we went over by Brian. I sat down next to him, but Denise wouldn't even sit down with us. I asked them what was going on.
>
> Denise said, "I've already read out of my book."
>
> I said, "Okay, a little while ago I saw you standing up back here and reading, and then I saw you over there with Yolanda and that group talking to them. Then I looked over and saw Brian reading by

himself, and I saw you walking around the room with the book open reading totally apart from him."

To Brian, I said, "Did you ask Denise to read with you?"

He said, "I asked her to come over here and read and she wouldn't."

It was dawning on me that they had never agreed on a place to work. So I asked Brian, "When did you get together and decide where you wanted to read, or did you just pick this spot, and tell her to come here?"

Brian said he picked the spot without talking it over with Denise.

Then I asked him, "What about the reading?"

He said, "Well, she said she wanted to read first but then I wanted to read first."

I asked, "How did you all work that out?"

Denise was still standing up over us and said, "He said it was all right that I could read first."

I said, "Okay, did you read?" Then it was like she couldn't attend to what we were talking about. She couldn't even answer whether she read.

So, I just stopped the whole thing and asked her to sit down with us, "Look, can you sit down so I can see you?"

So, she lay on the floor, just lay down on the carpeting and started messing with some pillows. I said, "You know, I'm trying to talk to you but you're not even looking at me; you're not even sitting. You're taking these pillows and you're like building houses with them. You're trying to build a bed to lie down on, and we talked about how we're not going to do this with the pillows." Then I was like, to myself, "Oh, my gosh, Laura, get over it, you're carrying on too much!"

I looked at Denise and I said, "You know, if you were talking to me, I would look at you and I would sit up and pay attention because I think you're an important person and what you have to say is important. I expect the same respect from you. Do you understand that?" She kind of nodded and said yes.

Now that I felt I had both of their attention, I said, "Okay, now what happened with this partnership? One person is reading by himself and one person is walking around the room. Is that a partnership?"

They both said "no," so I asked them how they could work it out.

Denise said, "Well, we can read together."

I said, "How can you work that out?" I wanted them to be clear about how they would actually do the reading as partners.

Denise said, "I can read a part, and he can read a part, and I can read a part, and he can read a part."

I said, "Do you think you can do that?" And she said "yes."

> Then to both of them I said, "In the future we're going to be doing this often, and you and your partner will need to find a quiet place to work, and you will need to sit down, and you will need to get to work together.

In this brief incident, Laura not only found a way to get Brian and Denise back on task but she reinforced the importance of working in a collaborative manner with your partner. She explained that it's important to check decisions out with your partner and to show respect by looking at the person speaking to you. And she modeled that respect in her own behavior toward them. When she came close to losing her perspective and going off on a little tirade, she caught herself and, instead of demanding that Denise show her respect, she explained how she would show respect to Denise if Denise were talking. This allowed Denise to hear Laura, and from then on the conversation turned around.

There were many things that Laura's students didn't understand about working collaboratively. Some didn't know how to say what they wanted without being bossy; some didn't seem to care about the needs of their partners, and some withdrew at the slightest disagreement or conflict. Over and over again, Laura provided brief little lessons, such as how to work fairly and considerately with a partner, how to express your needs without giving up or withdrawing, how to give reasons for your opinion, and how to look for compromise solutions. The power of these lessons came, in large part, from the fact that they occurred directly in response to specific problems her students were having.

> Ella was working with Gabrielle on a role-play. I happened to be nearby and I heard Ella say in a bossy way, "You're Sarah Ida. I'm the dad."
>
> So I asked, "Did you all talk about who you want to be?"
>
> Ella said, "No."
>
> So I said, "Well, Gabrielle, how do you feel about Ella telling you that you're Sarah Ida and she's the dad?"
>
> She looked up and in a real quiet voice she said, "I'm embarrassed."
>
> I said, "Okay, you're embarrassed by that? Ella, what can you do?"
>
> Ella snapped, "I don't know!"
>
> So I asked Gabrielle, and she said, "We could talk about it."
>
> I said, "El, what do you think about that?"
>
> And she said, "Nothing," and just sat there.
>
> So I said, "I've got a suggestion for you, Ella. If you really want to be the dad, a way you could say that to Gabrielle is, 'Maybe you could be Sarah Ida, and I could be the dad. What do you think about that?'

> Or, you could say 'I'd like to be the dad. Would you mind being Sarah Ida?' Ella, do you think that could work?"
>
> It was interesting, because she immediately agreed. "Yeah, okay, I can try that."

Laura was often surprised by how useful modeling possible dialogue was for students. Their limited experiences negotiating or problem solving meant that they had few concrete examples of their own to draw from. Laura used modeling in this way to teach them skills that they did not have.

Complex Teaching of Many Skills

Just as most students do not grasp academic concepts like place value or multiplication when they are first introduced, Laura's students did not become friendly and collaborative with their peers after one or two "lessons." They had many skills to learn, and they had to develop trust, the capacity for empathy, and an understanding of the importance of collaboration in relationships. They had to construct and, for many, reconstruct their basic understanding of social relationships, as well as acquire the skills involved in communication and negotiation. Often Laura had to work harder to help her students develop social and emotional skills and understandings than she did to teach the academic content. The vignette to follow, which took place in February of the second year, is an example of the depth and breadth of Laura's teaching in the social and emotional domains and of the patience, insight, and persistence such teaching often demands.

> Martin and Ella were research partners. They were researching eyes and ears to make a poster and give an oral presentation to the rest of the class. Ella wrote some stuff on the poster and Martin immediately wrote over it, making her words darker. Well, Ella just threw a fit. She slammed the books; she turned her chair away.
>
> So I walked over and said, "What's the problem here?"
>
> Ella said, "He's writing over my stuff."
>
> Martin's explanation was, "I'm making it better. I can't read what she writes."
>
> This is like déja vu. Last year Rachel didn't write well enough to suit Martin, and here he is pulling the same stuff with Ella.
>
> I asked him, "Why are you writing over this?"
>
> He said, "Well, look at it. You can hardly read it."
>
> I said, "No, I can read that clearly. She doesn't write like you, but it doesn't mean that it can't be read."

He went, "Well, I'm making it better."

I said, "Martin, how would you feel if you wrote something down and then Ella wrote over it because she said she was making it better?"

He actually thought about it for a minute and said he wouldn't like it. So I asked him how he thought Ella felt.

He said, "She doesn't like it."

"Yeah," I said, "that's exactly right, Martin. That's what she's telling you. So, what can we do here?"

And he said, "I don't need to be writing over her stuff."

I said, "Exactly. So do you think you two can get to work?" They said "yes" and then they were fine.

At the end-of-the-day meeting, when I asked the kids to talk about what went well during the day and what were rough spots, Martin raised his hand. "I learned that you don't write over people's work to make it better, because you wouldn't want somebody doing it to you."

I thought that was pretty good of him to verbalize that and to be able to volunteer it.

However, Laura's sense of accomplishment did not last long.

The next day during the partner research, Martin and Ella were furious and neither one of them was doing any work. I mean, they were literally in a rage. They had their arms folded and their backs to each other. And so I went over and said, "What's going on here? I know you're both serious learners, but you're not doing any learning like this."

Martin said, "She doesn't want me to be her partner."

Ella said, "Well, he just wants to write everything down and not let me do anything."

He said, "She won't do anything. She was just sitting there."

And Ella said, "That's because he was writing it all down."

So I said, "Well, how can we solve this?"

Martin started crying and said, "We can't because she doesn't want me for a partner."

Ella's also got tears coming down her face, and she said, "He doesn't want me, either."

I said, "You know, this partnership, doing both eyes and ears, you're the only people in the room who are researching two separate things. You've probably got one of the hardest reports to do. "That's one of the reasons I put you together. Martin, did you notice how Ella just gets right to work and wants to do a lot, and write a lot, and read a lot?"

He said, "Yeah."

Then I said, "Ella, did you notice that Martin doesn't play around during research? That he also wants to get right into it and learn as much as he can?"

And she said, "Yeah."

So I said, "Well, why do you think I put you two together? This is a great partnership. We've got two people who are such serious learners."

Then I said, "Ella, is it true that you don't want to work with Martin?"

She said, "No, I do want to work with him."

Then I said, "Martin?"

And he went, "Yeah, I want to work with her."

So I said, "What can we do?"

Martin said, "She can draw about the ears and I can draw about the eyes," and Ella agreed.

One week later, on the day that Martin and Ella were preparing to give their presentation, their partnership dissolved again.

They had divided the poster in half, and Ella's side about ears was all filled. Martin's side still had some room.

Well, Martin was at counseling when I read the class a book about frogs. Ella asked if she could borrow the book, and when Martin came back, she said, "Martin, I've got something else for the poster."

Martin immediately said no because he thought it was about ears and there wasn't any room on her side of the poster. Then she got mad because he wouldn't listen. She was trying to talk to him and he wouldn't listen. She put the book down and folded her arms and just sat there. This is when they're supposed to be practicing their presentation, and neither one of them is doing anything.

I said, "What's the problem?"

Martin said, "She wants to put stuff from that book on her poster and she doesn't have any room."

I said, "Elly, what's going on? What's Martin talking about?"

Ella said, "You know, you were reading to us about the frog that has two eyes up front but then he's got two eye spots in the back that help him scare away predators? I thought Martin would like that and might want to put it on his side of the poster about eyes."

Martin perked up, "Oh, I didn't know it was about eyes. I thought it was about ears and you don't have any room."

So I said, "You see what's going on here? Martin, you didn't listen and started with an attitude. And then, Elly, when he started with that attitude, what did you do?"

She said, "Wouldn't talk to him."

> I said, "Yeah, so he never even knew it was for his side. So that's a lot of time lost with that attitude. And then backing out of the situation and not communicating caused more problems."
>
> Later, when Ella and Martin made their presentation, Martin seemed pleased to point out that frog information on his side of the poster.

Ella and Martin are bright children. They were leaders in Laura's classroom, and both were clearly invested in their learning. Yet their defensiveness, lack of trust, combativeness, and utter lack of collaborative skills were practically comic.

As inept as Martin and Ella's collaboration seems, it actually represents substantial progress, at least on Martin's part. When Martin entered Laura's classroom a year and a half earlier, he quickly displayed an aptitude for mastering the academic curriculum, yet he often showed a complete lack of empathy toward his classmates. He frequently teased, bullied, and laughed at them. When Laura tried to get him to stop his hurtful behavior by asking him how he would feel if someone did to him what he was doing to others, he would loudly declare that he wouldn't mind or even that he would like it. So when Martin acknowledged that he wouldn't like it if someone wrote over his writing, it was a significant marker of progress and allowed him to empathize with Ella and willingly change his behavior.

Helping students develop the capacities for friendly collaboration is taxing, requiring not only patience and perseverance but considerable time as well. But by helping her students work successfully with one another in their academic activities, Laura was able to help them accomplish one of the central developmental tasks of childhood: developing effective peer relationships.[1]

Highlighting the Values of Friendship

Possessing the skills for effective peer collaboration is only part of what it means to be a friend. Even when Laura was focused on teaching specific skills, such as smiling at your partner or listening to your partner instead of shutting down, her teaching was embedded in a broader context—the context of a caring community. It was not enough for her students to learn to work and play collaboratively. Laura wanted them to understand both the joys and the obligations of friendship.

Friends Listen to Friends

Laura injected friendship lessons whenever she saw the need and had the time and energy to do so. Many times it would have been easy to forgo these lessons, but they contributed greatly to the students' sense of safety, as well as their understanding of how to be a kind and considerate friend. Friends' willingness to listen to one another's problems was one aspect of friendship that was valued in Laura's classroom.

> During the morning meeting, Louise said that her mom and dad got in a really big fight and her dad left and he didn't come back for two days. Later, Louise was Tyrone's partner and when they started to work, Louise said that she wanted to tell Tyrone what her parents were fighting about. Tyrone told her to quit talking and get to work, and that hurt her feelings. Because Louise was mad at Tyrone, she refused to do any work and Tyrone wouldn't work because Louise wasn't helping him.
>
> So, I went over and I said, "What's going on here? Nobody's writing. Nobody's talking. This doesn't look like partner work to me. This doesn't look like any work."
>
> Tyrone said, "She didn't want to do the work. And I told her to quit talking and let's get the work done."
>
> Louise got mad. She said, "Ms. Ecken, I was trying to tell him about my mom and my dad and what happened over the weekend, and he just told me to be quiet and get to work."
>
> Tyrone, who often has trouble getting to work, looked at me, "That's right, isn't it, Ms. Ecken? Because we're supposed to be getting this letter written."
>
> I said, "Tyrone, you're right. You've got a job to do. But when I hear what Louise is saying, I'm thinking that there may have been a better way to handle it. When bad things happen to people, when people are really upset, sometimes they need to talk. So is there something you could have done differently?"
>
> Tyrone said no, so I said, "Well, Tyrone, could you have said, 'Louise, I know you need to talk about this, but right now we've got the work to do. Can we sit together at lunch?'"
>
> He agreed that would work, but then he said, "This is a home thing. She shouldn't be bringing this to school."
>
> I told him, "Tyrone, that's never been the case here. We can talk about things that bother us, and we try to help each other."
>
> Then I said, "Louise, say something about your mom and dad to Tyrone, and let's let Tyrone practice what he could say to not hurt your feelings."
>
> She said, "Tyrone, my mom and dad got in a big fight this weekend."
>
> Tyrone said, "Well, we've got to do our work right now, but can we maybe talk about it at lunch?"
>
> Louise said, "Okay."

I asked them both if they were all right with that. They said they were, and then they got started working.

This was really a lesson about the values inherent in friendship. Laura was helping Tyrone understand that it's as important to listen to a friend in need as it is to get your work done. She provided him with a way to accomplish both, but the more important lesson was the lesson in caring.[2]

Friends Don't Embarrass Friends

Although children get lots of practice embarrassing one another on purpose, they don't always recognize how some of the things they do or say may embarrass someone else. When Leonard blew the whistle on a new child in the classroom, Laura had to give Leonard an impromptu friendship lesson.

> Leonard was drawing an African American sports figure. The new boy, Derek, was trying to get in with Leonard, so he sort of walked over by Leonard to make conversation. What he said was, "Why don't you draw a white person?"
>
> Leonard just screamed out, "Ms. Ecken, Derek is back here talking about people's color. I'm trying to draw and he's telling me to draw a white person."
>
> So I said, "Derek, come on back to your own place." Then I went over to Derek and explained that we don't get into white person–black person in here.
>
> I asked Leonard to come up to my desk so we could talk privately. I said, "You know, Derek is new in our class and I can see from the past couple of days that he really wants to be your friend. How do you think he feels about you yelling that across the room?"
>
> And Leonard said, "Mad."
>
> I said, "Yeah, it might have hurt his feelings a little bit, especially since he's trying to be your friend, and you go embarrassing him in front of the whole classroom. What could you have done when Derek said that?"
>
> Leonard said, "I could've told him that we don't talk about people's color in here."
>
> I agreed, "Yeah, you could've said that and taken care of it yourself instead of embarrassing somebody who's brand-new and trying to make his way into the classroom. Can you take care of it?"
>
> And so he walked over to Derek and said, "Derek, I'm sorry I did that. Next time I'll just talk to you."

Laura took this opportunity to teach Leonard a lesson in friendship, not to correct his shorthand. She said, "We don't talk about people's color." In fact, Laura and her students did talk about people's color. They addressed racial insults whenever they came up, and they often read about and discussed the experiences and struggles of people from different races and cultures. But Laura's primary aim was to help her students understand the common humanity shared by all groups and that they shared with each other. By the time Derek entered the classroom, Laura's students had internalized the value of accepting others for who they were and not judging people by their color. Leonard had experienced the sting of racial name calling earlier in the year and was quick to take Derek's comment as a kind of racial insult. Laura chose instead to focus on how to avoid embarrassing an uninitiated classmate.

Friends Forgive

Kids are always hurting one another. Sometimes these hurts are accidental; sometimes they are the result of poor self-control, and sometimes they are clearly intentional. And even when children clearly intend to cause harm, the actual harm can end up being greater than the children anticipated. Laura had many opportunities to teach her students how to forgive; often these lessons were indirect. For example, every time Laura wiped the slate clean after a transgression, her students experienced the value of forgiveness. Beyond her own modeling of forgiveness, she also directly taught her students to forgive.

> I was walking the class back to the room. I met Mary-Sue [the principal] in the hallway, and I stopped to say hello and to tell her about some things that were happening in the room while the kids went on. When I got to the classroom door, Martin and Leonard were in this big fight, screaming and yelling at each other. Leonard was visibly shaken. He was in such a rage that the color was out of his face. He said, "I'm gonna get him!"
>
> I said, "What happened?"
>
> Leonard said, "He locked me in the classroom."
>
> Martin said, "I did not. Tralin was holding the door, too."
>
> I said, "Martin, Tralin, what happened?"
>
> Tralin said, "He went in the classroom and we held the door and wouldn't let him out."
>
> Martin said, "Tralin was doing it!"

But Leonard said, "You did it," and with that he took a swing at Martin.

Martin took a swing back, only Martin didn't hit Leonard. He hit me.

I said, "Now look what you've done. You've hit the teacher. You two guys. This cannot happen here. You have got to get yourselves under control. Leonard, you walk in the room and sit down and take it easy."

Then I turned to the whole class and said, "Guys, just go in, get your book boxes out and read. I want to talk to Martin and Tralin in the hall."

To make a long story short, the class knows not to go in the room unless I walk in with them. Well, Leonard forgot, but he realized once he got in the room that he wasn't supposed to be in there. He tried to get back out, but Martin and Tralin wouldn't let him.

I asked them why they did it and why they didn't let him out when they saw how upset he was, but they just thought it was funny. So I said, "Martin, look at what's happened. That's your dearest friend. He's really, really mad at you. He's taken a punch at you. You tried to hit him back and hit me. Think about what's going on because of the decision you made. Is it really worth all this?"

He said, "No."

I said, "What should you do if somebody goes in the room when they're not supposed to?"

He said, "Don't lock them in there. Let them out."

I said the same things to Tralin. "Leonard is so upset. He doesn't even want to look at you or talk to you. Is this worth it?"

And she said, "No."

I said, "You two need to think about what you can do." They both said they were going to tell Leonard that they were sorry.

Tralin went in first and she told Leonard that she was sorry. He wouldn't speak to her. He wouldn't even look at her. And so she sat down at her desk.

When Martin walked in the room and told Leonard that he was sorry, Leonard ignored him.

Next thing I knew, Tralin put her head down and started crying as hard as she could. She was really sobbing. Leonard was standing by me right then, so I said, "Leonard, Tralin really feels bad about what she did. And when she told you she was sorry, you wouldn't even look at her. Is there anything you can do? She is really upset."

He said, "I'll tell her it's okay."

I said, "Well, is it?"

And he said, "Yeah."

So he walked over, and then he stopped, as if thinking, "Oh, gosh, I really don't want to do this."

Then he looked over at me, and I said, "It'll be okay." And so then he tapped her on the shoulder and he said, "Tralin, it's okay."

Laura's students had much to learn about friendship. The deepest challenges were those of accepting and valuing their classmates and sometimes themselves. Laura's model of accepting and valuing each of them was probably the most important source of this learning. They also needed to experience the joys of peer friendship and learn its obligations. And they needed to learn the many skills involved in friendly, collaborative interaction—such skills as perspective taking, communication, and negotiation.

And so Laura taught them. Such teaching takes time, but because it happens most effectively in the natural course of events, Laura structured much of her students' academic learning into partner collaborations so

Key Points: Teaching Children How to Be Friends

- Help students get to know their classmates as individuals and see that differences are okay.
- Help students discover their classmates' hidden talents.
- Group students for friendship and learning.
- Engage students in supportive partner activities and enforce a class policy that all students will work with one another eventually.
- Address the importance of greeting and treating all partners with respect.
- Teach partner skills through role-playing and as the need arises, and allow time for empathy and understanding to develop.
- Help students understand (through stories, conversation, and discussion) that friends listen to friends, friends don't embarrass friends, and friends forgive.

that she could work with them on social and emotional skills at the same time that she engaged them in the academic work of the classroom.

Helping her students acquire the skills, attitudes, and understandings required to be a friend was essential to Laura's goal of creating a caring classroom. A more abstract goal was to develop her students' awareness that they were part of a community—a community from which they drew benefits and to which they had responsibilities. Laura knew that she was primarily responsible for the nature of the classroom community, but in the next chapter we will see how she helped her students build a commitment to it and accept responsibility for shaping and maintaining their own community.

NOTES

1. For more information on the nuts and bolts of Laura's approach to partner work, see *Blueprints for a Collaborative Classroom*, published by the Developmental Studies Center.
2. This vignette brings up the role of families in children's lives and the degree to which children's family lives should be kept private and outside the classroom. Because most of Laura's students lived in the same housing project, they knew a great deal about one another's parents, and in the beginning of the year many of their taunts and insults were about their parents. Laura found it impossible and unwise to prevent her students from talking about family situations that were important to them. Often, knowing what was going on in her students' lives was important in helping Laura understand their behavior. Laura took the position that children could talk about whatever they wanted to in morning meetings, but she tried always to take a very respectful stance toward her students' families. Sometimes she needed to make it clear that the values of the classroom were different from a value expressed by a student's parents—for example, when Louise's parent told her she could not play with "black boys" or when Kenny's mother insisted he fight a child who had harmed his younger brother, or when Tyrone justified his stealing by saying that's the way his family gets things. And occasionally she had to call protective services if a child reported the bloody beating of a sibling or to arrange for foster care when a child told about living alone.

3

BUILDING THE COMMUNITY

I will not say that I don't want her for my partner and I will not have to write no more and I will not make her feel sad.

I will try to make her happy. I will not make her cry and I will not say that I am going to beat her up. I will try to say some nice thing to make her happy.

I say some nice thing like if she fall out of her chair I might help her up and I might say "Are you OK?" and if she needs some help I will help her and if somebody say that I am stupid for helping her I am going to say that I am not stupid.

I can help whoever I want.—Yolanda

WHEN LAURA asked Yolanda to write about her problems working with a partner, Yolanda conveyed not only her own struggles trying to be kind but her sense of isolation. She mistrusted her classmates and worried that they would make fun of her *for being nice*. Laura knew that to meet her students' need for belonging, she would have to help them see that they were not a group of isolated individuals but part of a caring community from which they derived benefits and to which they had obligations. It took more than a year to accomplish this goal.

A number of educators have stressed the importance of school and classroom community for building students' sense of belonging, their commitment to democratic values, and their learning.[1] Noddings (1997) also points out that communities can be oppressive to the individuals in them unless they support diversity as well as shared values. Laura instinctively recognized the parameters of a successful community and appreciated and supported each member's uniqueness while building a core of shared goals and values.

Being part of such a community means seeing oneself as a member of a definable group with whom one has a shared history and shared goals and values—a group that provides comfort and collegiality and to which one feels loyalty and responsibility. Seeing oneself as part of a community requires trust—something in short supply for those of Laura's students with histories of insecure attachment relationships.

Building a Sense of Group Membership

Laura had two basic strategies for helping students build a sense of group membership. She used class meetings to let students experience being members of a group, and she reinforced students' identification with the group by referring to the class as a community with certain characteristics.

Holding Class Meetings

Class meetings were a time in Laura's room for students to gather—psychologically and physically—and experience themselves as a group. Sometimes they met on the carpet in the book corner; sometimes they pulled their chairs into a circle, and sometimes they stayed in their table group seats. The purpose was to share, whether personal news, class accomplishments, class plans, or ways to solve problems.

Laura began every day with a class meeting. She used these informal morning meetings to touch base with all her students, to give her students a chance to touch base with one another, to introduce the day's work, and to set the tone for the day. In the first year, students used the time to share personal news. In the second year, they were still free to introduce their own topics, but the meetings focused on books children were reading at home.

Laura also frequently ended each day with a class meeting. End-of-the-day meetings were often short (there was hardly ever enough time to get everything that was planned into the day) and generally provided opportunities for the students to reflect on the day's or week's accomplishments and rough spots.

Although Laura did not require her students to speak in the class meetings, she knew that each student would have to participate at least occasionally to experience membership in the group and to be seen by classmates as part of the classroom community. When Laura noticed that a student was not talking in the meetings, she tried to find a way to make it more comfortable for the student to contribute.

In the first year, Laura would often draw a quiet student out in private conversation and then point out topics from their talk that would be interesting to share with the class. For example, at the beginning of the first year William was often silent in class meetings. It started to bother the other kids, and they sometimes made comments like, "He always passes." Laura thought that William might be passing because he couldn't think of something to say fast enough, so she decided to help him plan in advance what he might share with the class.

> I ate with William on Monday. He's very comfortable and talkative during lunch. When he told me something that I thought the class would be interested in hearing, I said, "Oh, William, that's so interesting. Can you tell the class that tomorrow morning?"
>
> Then he told me something else and I said, "Do you mind sharing that with the class on Wednesday?"
>
> He kept telling me things, and we went through Thursday and Friday. Then he told about a dream he had, and he said, "Can I tell that next Monday?"
>
> I said, "Now look, you're set for this whole week and next Monday. So can you share every morning?"
>
> And he did.

This small amount of support was all William needed. He not only shared regularly in class meetings but he contributed more in class discussions as well. Laura used a similar approach when new students entered the class during the year.

Not being patient listeners was a problem for more students than not being able to share. Laura's students did listen to one another, but too often they listened only long enough to be reminded of a similar experience of their own that they wanted to describe. The meetings would soon get out of control, with several people talking at once. At first Laura tried to stop these eruptions. She gave the students little lectures on the importance of listening, and she even had the class write about why it's important to listen to their classmates. Eventually, she found that when lots of people wanted to comment on a particular topic, she could keep control of the meeting and not cut students off by briefly stopping the meeting and inviting children to talk with a partner.

Using Inclusive Language

Laura made an effort to use inclusive language, constantly referring to the students as a class: "We're the kind of class that likes to learn" or "Look at all the things this class has learned this week." Before starting a unit of study, she would engage the students in making a list of the things they, as a class, wanted to learn. And at the end of the unit she would help them reflect as a class on their learning.

> I tried to make the class something that people were happy that they belonged to. And so I would always say things like, "We're the kind of class that knows how to help a new person" or "This class is serious about learning." So they could just feel that connection and know that this was something they belonged to.

Building a Shared History

Although it was important for Laura to point out to the class ways they could be characterized as a group, it was more important for them to have the kinds of experiences together that would let them make these observations for themselves. Laura helped students build a shared history by involving them in creating classroom procedures, by structuring regular ways for the group to share learning experiences, and by supporting them in establishing class customs.

Creating Shared Classroom Procedures

For students, every new classroom brings with it a new set of procedures. Involving the students in the discussion and sometimes the creation of classroom procedures is an important way to establish that they are part of a community.

On the very first day of school, Laura held a class meeting to introduce the procedure for using the restroom. It was customary in her school for teachers to escort their students to the restroom and to wait with the line while students went in one by one. Laura did not want to waste academic time for this exercise, and she saw restroom use as one of the areas in which her students could learn to take on more personal responsibility.

> I started the meeting by explaining that I wanted to do the restroom a different way than maybe they were used to. I said they would each just go to the restroom when they needed to, and I gave them three basic reasons:
>
> 1. I didn't want to interrupt the class.
> 2. Everyone doesn't really need to go at the same time.
> 3. We were going to be doing a lot of work, a lot of lessons, and we really couldn't learn in the way that we needed to if we had to keep taking breaks and hauling the whole class out to the restroom.

I told them my plan: "When you have to use the restroom, please go stand up by my desk and I'll nod for you to go out. The one thing that I do ask is that we only have one girl or one boy out at a time."

Then I told them that it would take a lot of responsibility to use the restroom in this way, and I asked, "What can you all do if you take on this responsibility? What would it look like if you did this in a responsible way?"

I planned to make a list of the behaviors they mentioned and out of that to create a set of rules for using the restroom.

Someone immediately said, "We need to walk down the hall," and I wrote "Walk" on the chart.

Tyrone said, "We don't want to be doing flips and cartwheels down the hall."

I asked, "Well, why not?"

Denise said, "The principal might be out there, and if you don't see her and she sees you, you're going to get in trouble."

I didn't want them to think that responsibility was about getting in trouble or not. I wanted them to think about being responsible because that will make our school a better place. I said, "What I'm thinking is you're going to go out and use the restroom in a responsible way and the only person that's going to see you is you."

But they weren't there yet. John added that you wouldn't want to do flips, even if people couldn't see you, because they might *hear* you! Then Martin said, "You might hurt yourself."

That was closer to the right track, but before I could follow up, John said, "If you're going to go, make sure you use it when you're there."

And so I said, "Well, yes, but you know we're talking about being responsible people, and a responsible person is not going to go up and stand by the desk and say they have to use the restroom just so they can go walk out in the hall and see what's going on out there."

That idea about checking out the hall must have inspired Martin because he immediately said, "I've got to use the restroom."

I thought, "Well, at least we can practice this a little bit."

To the class I said, "Okay, what should he do?"

They said, "Go up and stand by the desk." So, it was really kind of fun because while he's going up and standing by the desk, I started the meeting again to show them we're going to keep on with our learning, even when somebody has to go to the restroom. I nodded to Martin that he could leave, and we continued to list what it would look like to walk down and use the restroom responsibly. They came up with a good set of guidelines that kids put on a poster later.

RESTROOM GUIDELINES
Don't play in water.
Don't waste the soap.
Walk in the hall.
Be quiet in the hall.
Go to the restroom and come back quickly.
Be quiet in the bathroom. Wash your hands, dry with 2 towels.
Turn the water off, dry them and leave the water alone. If you drop paper towels, pick them up. Flush the toilet once.
Don't waste toilet paper.

Laura decided on the restroom procedure without student input, but she had a class meeting to help her students understand the procedure and the reasons for it. She engaged them in a discussion of the specific behaviors that would be expected of them, not by telling them how to behave but by asking them how they would behave if they were behaving responsibly and why it was important to behave in those ways. Although her students knew the things they needed to do to "use the restroom responsibly," they didn't quite understand what "responsibility" meant.

Laura used the restroom discussion to introduce responsibility as an important theme for the classroom. She knew her students would need to understand what it means to be responsible and to take more responsibility for themselves. Laura also wanted them to realize that being responsible is an intrinsic good that makes the community—in this case the classroom and the school—a better place. The concept was a difficult one for her students.

After we had generated a pretty good list of guidelines for using the restroom, I tried to get the class to understand *why* they should follow the guidelines they were coming up with.

I went back to Tyrone's example of not doing flips in the hallway and why you wouldn't do that.

Brian said, "Somebody might see you and do it too!"

Then Denise said, "A little person might see us and get hurt. You could get someone else hurt because of the stuff that you would be doing."

I wanted them to recognize how Denise's idea fit with being responsible because it's the right thing to do, so I asked how they might *feel* if they went down to the restroom and used it in a responsible way.

Leonard said, "Happy?" But he couldn't really say why.

Janice said, "You'll feel good that you didn't get in trouble."

> Denise took it a step further. She said, "You'd feel good because your teacher taught you what to do and you did it and she might be looking at you and give you something."
>
> I asked, "Is there another reason why you might walk down the hall quietly and use the restroom in a responsible way?"
>
> Nina said, "You have to do it in a responsible way because the principal might catch you."
>
> I said, "Now, do we really want to walk down that hall quietly just because the teacher or the principal might be watching?"
>
> Denise gave a tentative "Yes," and everyone else just looked at me.
>
> So I said, "I'd like this class to be the kind of class that could go down to use the restroom and come back, not because the teacher is looking but because our school and class will run a lot better. I'd like to think of you as being responsible because you want to learn, and because you want other people to learn, and because you don't want to get hurt. Does that make sense to you all?"
>
> Every single one of them said, "No."
>
> I thought, "Okay, Laura, this is enough for today."
>
> I said, "Well, that's just something we'll have to work on."

It was clear to Laura that she had much work to do before her students would understand and embrace responsibility to the community as an intrinsic good. In their minds it was important to do the right thing because someone might see you, whether to punish or reward you. Not surprisingly, the responses of Laura's students clearly illustrate that they are at the very beginning stage of moral development—a stage variously described by psychologists as heteronymous or oriented to adult authority (Piaget, 1932), oriented to obedience and punishment (Kohlberg, 1969), and oriented to individual survival (Gilligan, 1982). Still, notions of personal responsibility were beginning to surface, as in Denise's comment that little children might copy you and get hurt.

This was just the start of an ongoing conversation. Laura knew that her students would need to learn to accept personal responsibility, as well as to trust her and their classmates, in order for her classroom to become a caring community. There would be many more opportunities to explore the meaning of responsibility and its importance, and class meetings would be an ongoing way for the class to develop shared classroom procedures and understandings.

Creating Shared Learning Experiences

Although her students had different learning needs, interests, and abilities, which Laura addressed throughout the day in individual and partner experiences, she also worked to create shared learning experiences and common learning interests for her class as a whole.

Laura's students spent a lot of time building their individual reading skills, but reading was also something that the class was able to share. Reading aloud to the whole class every day was a core piece of Laura's academic program, as well as an important way to help her students share meaningful experiences and feel connected as a class.

> I read aloud every day. It's just a great pleasure to sit down with the whole class and relax and enjoy a book.
>
> I usually choose books that would be too difficult for most of the students to read on their own but that they will find really interesting. It's good to have a book that the whole class can rally around.
>
> When we talk together about a really good read-aloud, it gives the children a chance to share in how their classmates are thinking. Lots of times, these discussions are a way for us to talk about some pretty big ideas. And since I'm doing the reading, it kind of evens out the playing field for a lot of the children who are poor readers. They get a chance to be good thinkers and to offer something to the group that they might not be able to otherwise.
>
> Laura read aloud poetry, biographies, and expository text, as well as picture books and novels. She loved having everybody involved in the same book; it was an important unifying force in her classroom.

Because Laura's students spent the bulk of their academic time working and learning with a partner, she also tried to find ways to connect students across the individual partnerships. Typical partnership activities were to write role-plays based on a book the whole class was reading or to conduct research on unique aspects of a general topic the class was learning about. Laura frequently gathered the class together and invited the partnerships to share their work with everyone else. Students were able to experience not just themselves or their partners as learners but the classroom as a whole community of serious learners.

Creating Class Customs

Sometimes it is the small, seemingly unimportant things a class does together that help students the most to identify themselves as a group or community. Laura introduced a few customs to the class, but, even more, she supported the class in inventing their own special ways of building their feelings of community.

SINGING. Like most elementary school children, Laura's students loved to sing. She made time in the morning meetings for group singing and the camaraderie it can inspire. She also taught students several songs that reflected the values she wanted her classroom to embody, including "We All Sing with the Same Voice," "Up, Up with People," and "Best Friends Should Be Together."

As she did with most of the activities in her class, Laura used singing both to build community and to build her students' academic skills and motivation.

> Singing together is fun. It feels good and it's a bonding thing—learning songs together and memorizing them. The songs were pretty long, and the kids got a real sense of accomplishment when they were able to sing them without having to look at the words. But mostly it was a bonding thing; we have our class songs and we sing them together.

The role of singing in building a sense of community may be obvious, but the importance of singing and music in the classroom is often overlooked in favor of more testable academic subjects. The songs became very important to Laura's students. They sometimes asked to perform them for visitors, and at the end of the school year one of the things they wanted to do was sing all the songs they knew as a class.

WISH FOR THE DAY. Midway through the first year, Laura began ending the morning meeting with a wish for the class. Students liked this new custom so much that they had to create another custom—a class job—actually, for dealing with it.

> I started ending our morning meetings with a wish for the day. They weren't always the same, but they focused on something positive about our class like, "I wish that everyone has a good day and is able to get all their work done." Soon one or two students wanted to add to my wish. Pretty soon almost everyone wanted to make a wish, and it was taking too much time. So we made it one of the class jobs, and different people became responsible each day for making the class wish.
>
> A little later on, after some of the boys became involved in football, they introduced a kind of huddle to follow the class wish. We'd all put our hands in the middle and shout, "Just do it!"

LUNCHTIME WITH MS. ECKEN. One of her students' favorite customs was lunchtime with Laura—taking turns by table group eating in the classroom with their teacher. When a suggestion came up to jigger this core custom, Laura needed to be open to hearing the students and to shaping their suggestion to be consistent with the overall good of the class.

> One Monday, everybody from Monday's table was absent except for Leonard. So I said, "Leonard, you can eat with me by yourself today if you'd like. But if you'd like to eat with more of your classmates, you

> can wait till tomorrow. On Tuesday there will be a whole table of kids. It's your call."
>
> Leonard said, "Why can't we all eat lunch with you?"
>
> Well, I didn't want to give up the intimate time I had when we ate lunch in a group of four and I told him that.
>
> Then Martin said, "Can't we all just eat with you one day a month, like the whole class?"
>
> So that's what we did on Monday. The whole class was so happy to eat together that day, and a couple of people told Martin what a great idea he had. Martin just beamed.
>
> So now we all eat together on the first Friday of each month. We extend the lunch period from the usual twenty minutes to maybe thirty or forty minutes, and I bake cookies or brownies for a little treat.

Martin and Leonard's suggestion that the whole class eat together and everyone's enthusiasm for the idea were clear evidence that the students were seeing themselves as part of a community; the monthly lunch became a means of deepening that community spirit.

TAKING A BOW. In the second year, the students suggested a way to honor the individual accomplishments of other community members. Children took one of Laura's light touches and turned it into an expression of pride in their classmates.

> In the first year, when students were learning how to perform role-plays for the class, I very theatrically showed them how to bow at the end. The children loved it, and so after their performances they would always take a bow and the class would clap for them.
>
> One day during a morning meeting, I was congratulating someone for good decision making and Martin yelled, "Let him take a bow!" So the student did, and the class spontaneously clapped.
>
> After that, when I would compliment someone for making a good decision or accomplishing something that had taken extra effort, students liked to say, "Let her take a bow" or "Let him take a bow," and everyone would clap.

Highlighting Shared Goals and Values

Healthy communities are defined in important ways by their shared goals and values. A clear goal of school is to promote students' academic learning and to value learning. Another clear goal is that students understand

and practice the values of a democratic society. Laura had these goals and values in mind whenever she structured experiences for her students.

What We Hope to Learn

Laura believed that her students wanted to learn, even though she fully expected that they would not always want to learn what she was responsible for teaching. To emphasize the goal of learning and help her students realize that they all shared that goal, every year Laura held a class meeting during the first week of school to discuss what the students hoped to learn during the coming year.

> In our meeting, I had three things I wanted them to talk about: "What do you want to do in school this year," "What do you all want to learn about," and "What kind of activities do you want to do?" I really wanted to hear what are they interested in, what they think school is all about, what they think kids do in school.
>
> Tralin started it off with she wants to play kick ball; Leonard said he wants to go on a lot of field trips; Brian wants to paint. And John and Martin both said they want to learn how to read.
>
> Then Brian said he wanted to learn about the Earth, and Tyrone was real interested in math, especially, he said, "take-aways." Little Jennifer, who had been pretty quiet, said that she wanted to learn about plants and how to keep them healthy. Denise wanted to learn about snakes.
>
> We had a pretty good list going, so I just asked them, "What is this telling us about ourselves as a class?"
>
> People were quiet, so I said, "Well, here's what it tells me. This is a class that likes to have fun, likes to do things. This is an active class. And this is a class that wants to learn!"
>
> I wanted to set that up right away, that sense of, "Hey, guys, you all have high expectations for yourselves and I do, too. I recognize all these things about you. You have all this you want to do, and I'm right here to help you do it."

Of course the students at six, seven, and eight couldn't possibly know what they needed to learn or even have a clear idea about the kinds of things they would enjoy learning. Nevertheless, the class meeting established that they wanted to learn, that their teacher wanted to help them learn, and that learning was a shared goal and value of their classroom community.

Laura emphasized this goal with end-of-the-day class meetings that she introduced the first week of school.

> We're going to have class meetings at the end of the day for students to see what they've learned. I decided to keep a learning journal and record what they tell me for each day.
>
> On Friday I said, "Let's talk about what we've learned and what we've done this whole week."
>
> Martin, who had a goal of learning to read, just right away said, "Hey, we learned how to read books."
>
> Leonard said, "Well, we've done charts and we learned about the charts."
>
> Tralin said, "We had meetings to talk about how to do things." I was really pleased with her saying that because I wanted them to know that this was going to be a place where we were going to sit down and talk about things and have input.
>
> Louise talked about learning to find her partner by finding the person with a matching card.
>
> Jodie talked about making the chart where we set the goals for what we wanted to learn.
>
> Then Tralin said, "We learned how to greet new partners, and we have to remember to say people's names because sometimes we forget their names."
>
> Tralin's comment made me think that the meetings and lessons in how to greet partners had maybe given her some security, some sense that she knows how things are going to go in this classroom.
>
> When they didn't have anything more to add, I said, "I've thought of some things that we learned this week that haven't been mentioned yet. We learned about Nat and Miss Maggie and that people who are different can be friends. We also learned that it is easier for us to work together when we learn something about each other.
>
> "And," I said, "I think something that we learned this week that was really, really important is that in this class we are going to work with everyone."
>
> I felt pretty good about the week and ended with the idea that this is going to be a class where everybody works with everybody. I hoped that they would be excited about that, even though it would be a tall task.

This meeting helped the students recognize all that they were learning, underscored their shared goal of learning, and enabled Laura to assess what and how students were learning. She heard from them some of the things they remembered from their week together, what they themselves saw as learning, and the meanings they constructed from the experiences of the week. The meeting also enabled Laura to interject a value for the classroom that was non-negotiable: the value of interpersonal respect, which was embodied in her statement, "In this class we are going to work with everyone."

How We Want Our Class to Be

Laura knew from experience that it would be difficult for her students to consistently treat one another fairly, kindly, and with respect, yet these values were non-negotiable. They needed to be the values of the classroom community. She also knew that unless she insisted on these values, provided a strong model, and actively helped students live by them, the children would fail to coalesce as a caring community. She knew that, in his or her own way, each child wanted to be treated fairly, kindly, and with respect. Her goal was to help her students eventually come to understand that what they wanted for themselves they should provide for others. She also wanted them to understand that the classroom rules and her actions to maintain the community were not arbitrary but necessary to ensure that everyone would be treated fairly, kindly, and respectfully. So during the second week of school, Laura held a series of partner activities and class meetings designed to raise her students' awareness of how they wanted to be treated and how they wanted their class to be. She started by asking for concrete examples of things that made them feel good and not-so-good about being in school.

> After they talked with a partner, we got together to share as a class.
>
> Denise said it didn't make her feel good when someone told a lie on her at school.
>
> I asked, "Has anyone else ever had that happen at school?"
>
> A whole bunch of people raised their hands, so I asked them why they didn't like it.
>
> I figured that if having lies told on you is happening all this much, then probably these kids have done some of it themselves. So I said, "Has anybody ever maybe done that to someone?"
>
> Then there was dead silence and nobody responded. So I said, "Well, you know, I've done it before. I was out in the hall with a bunch of kids and my friend and I were making noise. The teacher came out and asked who was doing that and I didn't want to get in trouble. So I pointed at someone next to me and said, 'She did it.' Does that sound like something anyone else has ever done?"
>
> Tralin told about a time she and her sister snuck outside when they weren't supposed to be out. "My mama came out the door and said,

> 'What are y'all doing?' I said, 'Playing hopscotch.' She said, 'Who told you you could come out here?' I pointed to my sister."
>
> I asked Tralin, "How did that make you feel when you told that lie?"
>
> She said, "Well, my sister was sad and I was sad."
>
> I said, "This is important for us to think about. The person who gets the lie told on them feels bad, but so does the person telling the lie."
>
> Yolanda gave us another example of something that feels bad at school. She said, "I fell down in my chair and everybody was laughing." It seemed like a lot of other people had had that happen to them, had been laughed at.
>
> Then I asked them to share some of the ways their friends had treated them that made them feel good or glad to be in school. Silence. I couldn't help thinking that they were a lot more familiar with making people feel bad than with making people feel good. I tried again, and this time I included the teacher in the question, "Can you think of some ways that you've been treated by a classmate or a teacher that felt good to you?"
>
> Martin said, "Yeah, when the teachers help us learn how to read."
>
> About half the class agreed with Martin that they feel good about learning. But that was it for what makes them feel good at school.

This meeting was just the first step in getting Laura's students to think about how they wanted their class to be (and not be). At this point, they were aware of things they did to harm one another, but they didn't have any examples of ways their friends had been kind or helpful. However, even though Laura's students appeared to be at the lowest stage of moral reasoning, they possessed innate characteristics that would help them develop morally and on which Laura could build. Martin Hoffman (1978) has shown that even children as young as eighteen months are capable of feeling empathy and a pull to help another in distress. Larry Nucci and Elliot Turiel (1978) have shown that preschool and kindergarten children are aware that a morally wrong action such as hurting someone for no reason is wrong, even if adults say it is right. Laura's class meetings, conversations, and appeals to her students' feelings were designed to build on these developing moral capacities of her students.

The next day, their discussion focused on what they could do to have a classroom they wanted to be part of.

> I explained that I would write all their ideas about how they want their class to be.
>
> Someone said, "We want to respect each other," so I wrote that on a chart.
>
> Someone else said, "We want to be quiet."

I said, "Do we want to say 'be quiet' or do we want to talk about *when* to be quiet?"

Louise said, "We want to be quiet in the circle when we're talking."

Janice interrupted her and said, "No, when Miss Ecken is talking."

I said, "Now, wait a minute. Isn't it important that we're quiet when you are talking also?" I'm trying to get them used to the idea that this is our classroom and we're all important—that we need to listen and show respect for everybody, not just the teacher.

Some more things they said:

"Don't tell lies that can hurt people's feelings."

"Help clean up."

"Don't fight!"

"Listen when someone is talking."

"Share your book if you are finished reading it."

Martin said, "We would like to be respected." I asked him what that meant, but he wasn't able to say.

We went on and made a pretty long list.

Because Laura's ultimate goal was to have her students think in terms of general prosocial values, she needed a way to help the students turn their laundry list into a set of class norms—agreements that would help her students to think in terms of broad prosocial values such as fairness, responsibility, and kindness. The next day, the class tried to put all the things they had listed under one of these three values. Laura expected that their specific examples, such as "Help clean up," could help them understand the values she was after—in this case the value of fairness. Not surprisingly, the children had trouble thinking in terms of values rather than specific instances of a value.

I tried to get the class to categorize the various behaviors on their list under one of the values. But, really, they couldn't see the point.

When we took "fairness," for example, I said, "Can you give me an example of how someone could act in a fair way?"

Rebecca said, "Like share your pencil. If they don't have one you can let them use one."

I said, "Well, what I'm hearing is that when you're in a situation where you have something and it belongs to you, when you are with someone else who needs something you could give it to them. That sounds like sharing and being kind more than being fair.

"When I think of the word *fair,* I might think about taking turns on the bean bag chairs and how if you've been on one before, it's fair to let someone else have a turn."

> This meeting didn't work very well. The kids didn't really have a very good understanding of the values. They thought some things were good and some things were bad. But at least this initiated the conversation. We'll keep coming back to it.

This was not a neat and tidy process. Laura's students struggled with the meanings of such terms as *responsibility* and *fairness,* and their suggestions of ways they wanted their class to be contained a mixture of general statements such as "Be nice" and highly specific statements such as "Share the markers." Some of their suggestions were likely the result of their own thought, whereas many were simply restatements of things they had been told by adults. Nevertheless, these class meetings began the process of establishing shared norms and values. They also began what was to become an ongoing process of discussing what it means to be kind or fair or responsible in a variety of situations.

Eventually, as the students became more accustomed to class meetings and one another, they also set norms and guidelines for specific activities, such as the following norms for working with partners.

> RULES FOR PARTNER WORK
> Find a quiet place to work.
> Work without disturbing others.
> Be serious about your work.
> Be fair and take turns.

Building Interdependence and Responsibility

Because members of a community are interdependent, they benefit from the positive efforts of other community members. To help her students experience the positive aspects of interdependence, Laura frequently had them work together to create various products for the class—a quilt composed of drawings of each of them, group poems that included lines written by each of them, and lists of ways they had improved as a class or things they had learned as a class. Different groups of students made signs for the class to help remind them of "Ways We Want Our Class to Be," "Rules for Partner Work," and "Restroom Guidelines." Eventually, the students took responsibility for various routine classroom chores.

Taking Responsibility for Class Jobs

Laura was in the habit of asking students to do little jobs as the need came up, such as answering the phone or taking the attendance to the office.

She did not think it was worth the trouble to come up with a whole system for assigning class jobs. That changed one day in March of the first year, after Yolanda asked if she and Leonard could pass out the afternoon snack. Because no students had ever had this job before, when Laura said, "Sure," fairness became an issue.

> Thursday when I was passing out snacks, Yolanda asked me if she and Leonard could do it the next day. I agreed, so when it was snack time on Friday, she and Leonard washed their hands and started passing out the cookies. Well, that just ticked Martin off big time.
>
> I'm forty-four years old. My thoughts are, "Who cares who gives out the cookies as long as everybody gets one?" But I knew that I was going to have to deal with it, like get a big list of who's going to pass out the cookies. In fact, I probably need to work out some kind of fair system for rotating class jobs. I need to look into that, I guess. It's just a lot of trouble.

As reluctant as she was to get involved in a system for assigning class jobs, Laura opened it up for discussion in a class meeting the following week.

> I began by saying, "I can see that you all want to take over more and more of the jobs in the classroom, that you feel more a part of everything."
>
> So we made a list of all the things that we do. They came up with go check the mail, do the attendance, make the wish for the day, wash the tables in the cafeteria, run the tape recorder, erase the board, and get out the snacks. We agreed to put everyone's name in a pocket chart next to every job and draw names for each job each day until everyone had done everything.
>
> The one place we got hung up was when they suggested answering the telephone as a job. I said, "That's something that helps in the class, but there are only four people in the room who are tall enough to answer the phone, so let's not include it for this."
>
> They all said, "That's not fair! Then nobody should be able to do it!"
>
> I said, "Let's look at it this way. A lot of times I am teaching or I am meeting with a student or we're right in the middle of something, and it's a big help to me if I can have someone answer the phone." Everybody except Martin and Kenny said they could understand that.
>
> Martin and Kenny just went on and on about it not being fair, and so finally I said, "Look, guys, this is my call. I'm the teacher in the class. I'm not going to interrupt lessons to answer the phone, and I've

got to have somebody answer it who's tall enough. If you have another suggestion, I'll listen to it, so let me know."

Martin said, "You are lazy. You don't even do your own job. If you do your own job and answer the phone yourself we wouldn't have this problem. You're nothing but lazy."

I ignored being called lazy. I said, "Martin, please walk over there and see if you can answer the phone."

He went over and tried to answer the phone and said, "Nope, can't do it and nobody else in here should be able to do it."

Then Kenny joined in, "Uh-huh, she's lazy. She won't even do her own job, she just wants the kids to do her job and answer the phone. She won't even do her own job, she's lazy."

That was it. After trying so long to be patient, I just snapped. I said, "I'm not going to be called names by you two. If you can't sit in here without doing that, then you're out."

To the rest of the class I said, "Let me tell everybody in here. You are not going to call me names. That's not the kind of class we said we wanted, and it's not the kind of class I want to be in."

Anyway, we finally went on, and—it was the strangest thing—immediately they were making their nametags for the pocket chart and having the best time. They were proud of the ways they can contribute.

I told them, "You know, you're trying to take over a lot of what goes on in this class. It shows what serious learners you are and how serious you are about the class going well." Really, it was a wonderful meeting other than that telephone.

That afternoon, something else came out of that meeting. Janice is usually so nervous about being in the group that she always wants to be sitting about three feet away. But at the end-of-the-day meeting, she happened to be sitting right up beside me. Everyone was telling me what to write about our day, and it got so that I couldn't keep up with writing and calling on people. Janice saw my problem and she said, "I'll call on the kids for you if you just want to write." So, she did. I felt that it directly came out of that jobs meeting—seeing something that you can do and offering to be part of the class and help things run more smoothly.

About a month later, Laura returned to the issue of the telephone. As outrageous as Martin and Kenny's response had been, Laura wasn't really satisfied herself with the way things had been left.

I came in on Tuesday and I said, "I thought over spring break about how upset you all were about answering the phone and how you thought it wasn't fair since some of you aren't tall enough to reach it. So what if we have a person that reaches the phone and then an answerer, so everybody will have an opportunity to talk on the phone?"

They were like, "That's great! Oh, thank you for thinking of that!"

Now it's a highlight of the day to see who gets to answer the phone—who gets to reach it and who gets to answer it.

It's working beautifully. When the phone rings, the reachers say, "Hurry up, come on here and answer this!" Every now and then it's one of the answerers yelling, "Hurry up, get me that phone!" It's working fine and they're all happy about it.

Building a classroom community was not a smooth and easy process. And Laura's patience was often sorely tried. It was not always clear how to strike the right balance between taking the time to work things out and getting on with the work at hand, between doing things herself and giving her students the latitude to increase their responsibility.

Reminding

In the beginning of the first year, after the students and Laura worked out how they wanted their class to be, Laura invited her students to share in the responsibility of maintaining a caring classroom by reminding their classmates whenever they were not following the guidelines set out by the class. Laura believed that once her students knew how they were affecting the class and how their actions led their classmates to see them as "not nice," they would try harder. Rather quickly Laura came to see a much wider set of causes of her students' misbehavior: their untrusting view of the world, their lack of social and emotional skills, their need to protect their personal sense of competence, and their misunderstanding of the nature of relationships. Still, she wanted to share as much responsibility with her students as she could.

This decision to let students "remind" one another caused a lot of problems for Laura, and many times during the year she doubted its wisdom. Whereas some students could handle this level of responsibility, several could not. They needed considerably more guidance and control than Laura initially provided. There were times when students were shouting "reminders" across the room at their classmates, frequently for things Laura herself would have chosen to ignore.

Although most of Laura's students were gradually able to handle reminders, a few seemed to use reminders as if they were weapons, continually disrupting the class with their admonishments. It was as if these students feared that there was not enough of Laura's love and attention to go around, so they kept trying to edge their fellow classmates out of their teacher's good graces. At the start of the second year, Laura considered putting a stop to reminders altogether.

> Last year Martin and Yolanda, especially, spent the whole time policing the room. They'd yell reminders out, even across the room. They were continually interrupting lessons and messing with people.
>
> Tangela, for example, has a very hard time sitting still. She's always fixing her hair or moving in her seat. I'd be reading a book to the class and be right in the middle of a very interesting part of the story, and Tangela would put her hands up to fix her hair. Really not a problem until one of them would interrupt the whole class by shouting out, "Get your hands out of your hair, Tangela!"
>
> That needs to stop.

However, the students were proud of being trusted to remind their classmates, and many had learned to use reminders in helpful ways, not only with their classmates but with Laura as well.

> One day Janice wore a rawhide jacket with all this long leather fringe on it. She started tearing off the strings and giving them to people. I'm in the middle of this lesson and everybody is busy tying themselves up with these things. So, I said, "Give me those strips right now, every one of you all."
>
> I held out my hand and, apparently, Tyrone had been chewing on his. When he put it in my hand I said, "Gross, Tyrone, you had it in your mouth."
>
> Immediately, Tyrone just turned around and threw himself down on the floor. I said, "What's wrong with you? Sit up, we're in the middle of a lesson."
>
> Just that quick, Kenny said, "I can tell you what's wrong with him. You embarrassed him in front of all of us."
>
> I said, "I did?"
>
> He said, "Yeah, you let every one of us know he had spit on that. You should have said that quietly."
>
> That was on Monday. On Thursday we were doing a math lesson with these little cubes. Well, Kenny had one in his mouth. I said, "Get that out of your mouth, you're going to choke."
>
> He looked at me and rolled his eyes and kind of gave me this "Shush!"
>
> So I whispered, "Get it out of your mouth."

On reflection, Laura realized that involving the class in giving reminders was generally working as a positive force in creating a classroom community. Instead of asking her students to give up the practice of reminding others, she decided to provide the class with additional guidelines and stop any child who used a reminder in a hurtful or inappropriate way.

At the start of the second year, she explained to the students that when she was teaching a lesson or working with a group of students, that was a time when she was running the class and she would do any reminding that needed to be done. However, when they were working in their partnerships, or were in the cafeteria, or whenever she wasn't nearby, they should remind their classmates if they started to behave inappropriately.

This worked pretty well. Not, as we will see next, because the students followed Laura's directions exactly but because they were growing in trust and were less worried about their classmates as their competitors. They gradually got a better sense of when they could helpfully remind one another, even when Laura was in charge.

Experiencing the Benefits of Community Membership

In the second year, with twelve returning and eight new students, Laura's class began to jell rather quickly into a community. Laura's returning students—Brian, Louise, Leonard, Martin, Jennifer, Cindy, Tyrone, John, Rachel, Rebecca, Tangela, and Tralin—were active partners with Laura in building a community spirit in the classroom. A month into the second school year, Laura realized that her class was running far more smoothly than it had been at this time the year before. All her hard work was bearing fruit. Both she and her students were enjoying the class more.

> Last week we did a role-play based on an incident from the book, *Shoeshine Girl.* The role-play was a phone conversation that might have occurred between the shoeshine girl's Aunt Claudia and her mother or father.
>
> When we were getting ready to go out into our partnerships, we talked about some ways to decide who's going to be which character in the role-play.
>
> Leonard said, "Remember, it's not like you're going to turn into Aunt Claudia. It's just a role-play."
>
> We all had to laugh. That came from last year. There were times we had people just say absolutely, "No, I will not be that person," and then they'd just shut down.

> So, that was good. It was something Leonard learned from last year. And I think his saying that helped, especially the people who weren't in the class last year.
>
> As I was moving around the room, I could hear that they were able to negotiate who was going to be which character and that they were really working together.

Laura's new students entered a classroom that was well on its way to being a caring community. Her returning students set a supportive tone right from the start, encouraging their classmates' good behavior even when Laura was in charge.

Taking Leadership for Helping

Laura had always encouraged her students to help one another, saying things like, "Now, remember, we're all working together. If you can help your tablemates, please do so." In the second year, she was able to create an even more helpful atmosphere by actively encouraging her students from the previous year to help the new students and to take a leadership role in the classroom.

> One of the new students, Gabrielle, is very young. She's a beginning second grader, and she has a lot of trouble concentrating and getting her work finished. But she's an excellent reader—she reads on a fourth-grade level. I put her in a partnership with Rebecca for our work with the book, *Go Fish*. Then I had a little talk with Becky.
>
> I said, "You're a big girl, and little Gabrielle is having some rough spots. She's having trouble staying with the group, staying focused, and getting the work done." I asked Becky to help her, and I talked about a few things that Becky could do that would be helpful to Gabrielle.
>
> And it was the sweetest thing. The next day Becky's mother came to the classroom in the morning, and she said, "I just wanted you to know that Becky is so pleased that she's a helper this year. She told me all about working with this little girl Gabrielle."

By late October, a general spirit of helpfulness and responsibility had begun to pervade the classroom. Laura was thrilled by the way her students seemed to be taking responsibility for their community. They began helping one another without any prompting from Laura.

> This year I do the math early in the morning. It's on their tables when they come in. As soon as they finish their math, they get out their jour-

> nals and they can write about anything they want. I take the math as people finish and correct it right that minute so that I can talk to each person about any problems they are having. I'll always circle what's wrong and ask them to go ahead and fix it.
>
> Tyrone, when he gets finished with his own math, he just goes over and starts helping people. He doesn't even ask me. One day Chantelle had missed five problems. I said, "Chantelle you got fifteen of these right. This is really good, but see if you can get these other five." And Tyrone just went over and said, "Would you like me to help you with that?"

Soon the new students, as well as the returning students, were extending themselves in helpful and kind ways. Even Chantelle, who came in with an aggressive stance toward her classmates, gradually began to take on some of the more caring norms that children were establishing.

> Little Mary [a new second grade student] wants to read chapter books so badly because everyone else is. So she's reading the Babysitters' Club books at home with her parents' help. She might read one or two chapters at night and then tell about it in the morning meeting. Everybody claps when she does that. But sometimes she gets mixed up when she tries to describe what happened in the chapter. So Chantelle, who's read every Babysitters' Club book and is kind of a class expert, jumps right in and helps Mary out. It's really nice and Chantelle is so happy she can be helpful in that way.

Her students' generosity and spontaneous helpfulness to one another were part of mounting evidence to Laura that her classroom was becoming a caring community—one that her students were both benefiting from and taking responsibility for. As a group, they were losing the fierce competitiveness that isolated them from one another and that perpetuated a lack of safety in the classroom. Laura let her students know that she saw and appreciated their helpfulness and growing responsibility, and she increased the opportunities for them to share in responsibility for nurturing the classroom community.

Seeing Classmates as Colleagues

By December of the second year, although Laura's students still got into the normal arguments and tussles with one another, they began to take on important aspects of Laura's supportive role in the classroom. For example, they no longer needed Laura to point out their classmates' accomplishments.

They noticed and honored their classmates' accomplishments on their own initiative.

> Martin got upset about something, but then he pulled himself together and let it go.
>
> Well, somebody in the class noticed it; I forgot who it was, and said, "Can Martin just stand up and take a bow?"
>
> He stood up and took a bow, and everybody clapped for him. He was so happy that somebody noticed that he shook something off and had put himself back together.

Classmates were also beginning to defend and protect one another, sometimes even calling on the entire class to temper its behavior.

> We were going to do a math activity of making a ratio of how many candy corns taste good with how many peanuts if you eat them at the exact same time. In science right then we were talking about solids, liquids, and gases, and how you describe things with mass. One thing you do is tell about the characteristics. So I said, "Let's combine our math and science and start off by describing the characteristics of the candy corn and the peanuts to your partner." The peanuts were Spanish peanuts with the skins on them.
>
> After they examined and tasted the candy corn and the peanuts and talked with their partners, we met as a group. When Mary started to describe the peanut, she said, "Well, the peanut has no taste."
>
> And people were like, "What?"
>
> Tyrone, who was her partner, said, "Let her finish."
>
> So she said, "That little brown thing that was around the peanut—it doesn't have any taste." Then everybody was okay with that; they understood what she meant.
>
> Tyrone said, "See? Sometimes people start off confusing, but then you understand." He was letting everybody know to give her some time to tell what she needed to.

In both of these examples Laura was present, but the students assumed the responsibility for their community. What they seemed to understand far better than Laura's verbal directions were her behaviors. Once they learned to trust her and to trust that she could keep them safe, they took on many of her behaviors and even her words. Laura was really delighted as her class grew in community spirit, and she was not alone.

At the end of Friday I said, "Let's talk about the things that went well this week and things that we just want to celebrate." We usually talk about rough spots too, but we had too many successes to do that.

Jennifer said, "P.E. went okay this week. It usually doesn't."

Becky said, "We are all reading better."

Chantelle, who is new to the class this year and has been having a lot of trouble treating her classmates respectfully, said, "Not many people are getting smart and sassy."

And then Martin said, "Well then, Chantelle, you should get up and take a bow." So Chantelle had to get up and take a bow, and everybody clapped.

Louise said, "When we went to art, all of us listened."

Brian and Leonard, who were sitting together, both said the same thing happened in science, that when they went to science, everyone listened and got right to work.

And then Chantelle raised her hand again, and she said, "I had two good days without so many reminders."

So Brian said, "Well, let her take a bow again."

When she stood up to take this bow, she bent way over and her rear end stuck out.

Becky said, "Chantelle, there's a way to bow without your butt sticking out."

I said, "That's not school talk."

Then Becky got up and showed her how to bow, like a ballerina.

Paul said, "Now, there you go."

Then John said, "When we were making words, people listened."

Becky said, "And no one was talking during it."

While Becky was saying that, Tangela said something smart to Martin and he was about ready to say something back.

So right while Becky was talking, she turned around and—the way teachers do, they'll be teaching and they'll say something to somebody and then continue the sentence—Becky stopped in the middle of her sentence, and she said, "You can ignore that, Martin." And then she turned around and kept telling about how no one was talking during our making words lesson, and that we could all hear.

Louise said, "Our morning meetings went well. People listened."

Brian said, "When we got out the book boxes, we read and we kept reading."

Chantelle said, "People weren't disrespecting Mrs. Ecken and the class."

> John said, "When we did the lesson on the couch and read those words to Mrs. Ecken, people didn't interrupt."
>
> Chantelle (and I think this is because we had a little talk about her kind of slipping in her reading) said, "People are learning lots of new words, and we have to keep reading."
>
> And then Ella said, "Becky got to the third-grade reading level." Becky had announced her progress in an earlier meeting, and everybody had clapped, so Ella was reminding us about that.
>
> Mary said, "Everybody's getting done in math."
>
> Martin said, "When we went to read to the little buddies today, no one was running around."
>
> Lana said, "It was fun finding a book to read to your buddy."
>
> Nikki said, "When we were doing math and learning base 5, nobody tore the base 5 pieces."
>
> Paul said, "When we went to P.E. nobody ran. We just jogged."
>
> Chantelle said, "Tralin and Martin put themselves back together when they were ticked."
>
> By this point in the meeting, Martin had left for home already so he could avoid an older boy who has been threatening to beat him up. So Ella said, "Well, we should have said that when Martin was here."
>
> Brian said, "The games went perfect this week."
>
> And then we had to leave.

It's clear from the students' words that they saw their classroom as a community and that they took considerable pride in their classroom. It's also clear from their words that this classroom doesn't run in a perfectly smooth way. The fact that no one tore the base 5 pieces or ran around when they were with their little buddies would hardly be something to celebrate in a perfect class. There were countless ups and downs. But as imperfect as the classroom was, it's also clear that a real community was being built and that the students saw themselves as responsible members of that community.

Laura worked hard to help her students see themselves as part of a caring community from which they drew benefits and to which they had responsibilities. She saw this not only as important for achieving harmony in her classroom but as preparation for citizenship in a democratic society. She considered this attention to community part of her social studies curriculum, as well as part of her approach to classroom management.

Laura used a variety of activities to help her students see themselves as part of a community. She engaged them in setting goals and norms for the community. She provided lots of opportunities for shared experiences, helping them build a shared history. She used class meetings to help them feel part of the whole class and, together with her students, created special customs that helped define them as a group. Perhaps most important, she encouraged her students to share in the responsibility for creating and maintaining their community, and she helped them do so.

This was not an easy process. Laura was frequently discouraged, especially during the first year. But gradually, because of her perseverance and goodwill, because she made the classroom safe and helped children learn

Key Points: Building the Community

- Build a sense of group membership by using class meetings to share personal news and class accomplishments and to involve the students in planning and problem solving.
- Use inclusive language. Frequently refer to the class as a whole, for example: "This class sure likes to learn!"
- Build a shared history by creating shared learning experiences and involving students in developing class procedures, customs, and rituals.
- Highlight shared goals by generating with students lists of things they hope to learn and trying to weave these into the curriculum.
- Highlight shared values by engaging the whole class in thinking about how they want to be treated and how they want their class to be.
- Build interdependence and responsibility by asking and helping the students take responsibility for the classroom.
- Encourage students to help one another, the class as a whole, and the teacher by organizing the environment to support student interaction and being open to students' suggestions.

how to be friends, and because down deep even her most angry and withdrawn students wanted to be part of a caring community, Laura was successful in meeting her students' basic need for belonging.

Sometimes, however, Laura worried that her focus on belonging was diverting her from students' other basic needs—for competence and autonomy. In the next chapter, we will see how she eventually achieved a balance.

NOTE

1. See Bryk and Driscoll, 1988; Dewey, 1958; Goodenow and Grady, 1993; Maehr and Midgley, 1996; Noddings, 1992; Solomon, Battistich, Kim, and Watson, 1997; and Wentzel and Caldwell, 1997. For an in-depth discussion of the research on the role of community in student development, see the article, "Students' Need for Belonging in the School Community" by Karen Osterman (2000).

PART TWO

MANAGING THE CLASSROOM

4

MEETING STUDENTS' NEEDS FOR COMPETENCE AND AUTONOMY

Dear Mrs. Ecken,
Why can't you be nice to me?
Chantelle

LAURA KNEW that it was not enough to create a classroom in which her students felt liked and accepted if they weren't also meeting high standards in their learning and behavior. Satisfying her students' need for belonging was necessary but not sufficient. When Chantelle interfered with other students for the second morning in a row, Laura's response was not "nice," in Chantelle's estimation. Instead of checking in with Chantelle or negotiating with her, Laura focused on Chantelle's and the other students' need to develop competence.

> Chantelle came in a little rough on Monday morning. She was bugging the people around her and laughing, and she kept getting up and bothering other people who were trying to work. I had to remind her several times to sit down and leave people alone.
>
> On Tuesday morning when she started the same stuff again, I said, "Chantelle, we're not talking right now. You're to sit down and you're to do your work. Now."
>
> A while later she was wandering around, so I said, "Are you finished with the assignment?"
>
> She said, "No, Ms. Ecken."

So I said, "Then you need to be seated, and I don't mean maybe or perhaps. This is work time and I will not tolerate anything else."

Next thing I knew, she had gotten into a fight with Tom and she was getting ugly with him. I went over to her and said, "Look, it's this simple. You keep your mouth closed, and when you do talk to people, you do it in a respectful way. I'm not spending every morning carrying on with you."

She settled down some. A little later I noticed she was fooling with this piece of paper, all folded up. I didn't know what it was, but I took it and said, "You need to be doing what we're all doing."

When we began the next lesson, she got into it and started having a good day.

It was probably 1:30 or 2:00 when I felt the piece of folded-up paper in my pocket. I opened it and read, "Dear Mrs. Ecken, Why can't you be nice to me?"

So I went over to her. "Chantelle," I said, "I just read this. What's it all about?"

She said, "In the morning, you were just not nice to me."

I said, "Chantelle, I want to explain one thing. We have really high standards in here. I am not *not* being nice—I am holding you to the same standards as everyone else. I am trying to help you get your work done, to help you do what everyone in the class does."

She kind of got it; she said, "Oooh, okay."

I didn't have any trouble with her the next morning or the rest of the week. In fact, she's really had lovely days. She's been bubbling over with happiness, so I asked her, "How does it feel to leave people alone, to be friendly, and to be able to work with them?"

She said, "It really feels good."

I said, "Sure, it does. Look at yourself, look at yourself!"

It was Laura's responsibility to be sure that her students were becoming competent. Sometimes she was quite tough and firm in order to keep them on a path that would lead to their competence. At the same time, she wanted to be understanding and make allowances for the difficulties that many of them faced in their lives outside of school.

I'm trying to send a very strong message: "We are learners," and there are certain things that have to take place for learning to occur—there are certain things that I'm not going to put up with. Because of the pressures from outside, from what's going on in their lives, I am walking a very

> thin line. But I don't know what else to do except maintain the integrity of how the class needs to be for everyone to learn.

In order to achieve the delicate balance between holding her students to high standards and making allowances for their personal struggles, it was important for Laura to realize that her students' psychological need to be competent was at least as great as her desire to help them be competent. All children, as part of their evolutionary heritage, have three core psychological needs. They need to experience competence and autonomy, as well as belonging.[1]

The need for belonging emerges in the first year of life; the need for autonomy arises somewhere around eighteen months, and the need for competence is present early in the second year (Erikson, 1950; Sroufe, 1996). From then on all three needs are present. To build a truly nurturing relationship with each of her students, Laura struggled to find ways to simultaneously meet all three of these sometimes-conflicting needs.

Building Competence in Reluctant Learners

Although some of Laura's students entered her classroom confident in their basic competence, a number had serious learning problems that had deprived them of a sense of competence, at least as related to academic learning. Because they felt incompetent, these students did all they could to avoid engaging in whatever learning activities Laura devised. Not realizing the extent of their learning problems, Laura saw them, at first, as defiant and lazy.

> I've got a problem with Yolanda and Tralin. No matter what I say we're going to do, no matter what, they whine and moan and groan.
>
> Tralin will say, "It's boring. I don't want to do this. I wish I was at another school."
>
> I've talked to them about it. I've tried to let them see from my perspective that it's not easy to teach. When I plan lessons and look at the books we're going to read and plan the activities we're going to do, I always try to think about what they want to learn. I look at the list of what they say they're interested in. I look at what they need. I've let them know that it's very hurtful for me to sit and hear them whine and cry and carry on about it.
>
> If I stop and say, "What's the problem," which I try to do, it takes time. And it doesn't change anything. I finally end up just saying, "Look,

> I'm the teacher and it's my job to plan these lessons so that you can learn and grow. This is what we're doing." It takes time away from the learning.
>
> With Tralin, I've started doing a lot of one-on-one meetings, because if you give her a sheet with two or three things to do on it, she's out of whack. She'll start crying. So I outline for her how she can get through it: "Let's do this first, and once you've got this done, move to this." And I try to be encouraging. "You can do it. I've seen you do it. You might have some problems with it. People have problems with things, but you can do it."

Even with Laura's extra help, the following week Tralin's lack of confidence spilled over into a general refusal to cooperate.

> It started when I did one of those games to pull the class back together—snap your fingers if you're ready—and Tralin just said, "No."
>
> I asked her when would she be ready and she said, "Never!" She just got really, really upset.
>
> So I called her grandmother and set up a conference for the three of us.

At this point in her relationship with Tralin, Laura was frustrated. She couldn't have known that over their next two years together, Tralin was going to provide her with a classic lesson in how important competence is to children.

> It turns out Tralin is really upset about not knowing how to read well and not knowing what to do. So we made an agreement that when the class goes into partner work, I will visit her partnership first—to make sure that they're clear on what the directions are and to give them some help if they need it to get started. Tralin agreed to quit moaning and groaning, even when the work looks too hard.
>
> That's worked out a lot better. A couple of times she's started whining and I just very quietly say, "Remember, we have an agreement. Anything you need help with, I'll help you."

The other strategy that emerged from the conference was for Tralin to practice with her grandmother the book that she would be reading the next day with her reading partner. Tralin and her grandmother left the conference with a copy of *Daniel's Duck* for Tralin to read at home.

When I met with Tralin's partnership the next day, she said, "I can read this. I've been practicing it." She just had the biggest smile. So I sat with her and her partner a little while and listened to her. It wasn't fluent, but you could tell that she had studied every word. She took her time and she could do it."

Once Laura realized that Tralin's resistance to learning activities was not defiance or laziness but her lack of competence and her fear that she could not succeed, her attitude toward Tralin changed. And as Laura provided Tralin with the support she needed, Tralin gained confidence in her ability to succeed and became a more willing student.

Laura soon discovered that a number of her students were struggling in both reading and math. She set about on a conscious effort to get her students to be and to see themselves as competent people and serious learners.

Year 1: Becoming a Community of Readers

Laura's first priority in building her students' competence was to develop their reading abilities. Improving her students' competence in reading would have a pervasive effect on their sense of themselves as learners and their approach to the wider curriculum.

Administering the Slosson Oral Reading Test confirmed Laura's fear that some of her students were reading at the primer and even pre-primer level. The test also revealed that a number of students who were successfully reading at or near grade level were not reading phonetically. In previous years, Laura's students had been older, more accomplished readers. She had always focused on reading comprehension and had not needed to worry much about phonics. With her new class, however, it became clear to Laura that she needed to revamp her reading program. In December of the first year, she added to her existing reading comprehension program a more carefully structured approach to daily individualized reading, as well as daily direct instruction in phonics.

The kids love using the dry-erase boards, and every morning we get them out for what we call *word study.* I give them a letter, a blend, or a syllable, and I say, "On one side of your board write real words, and on the other side you can put nonsense words. Make as many words as you can with this sound." Then they read their words and nonsense words to each other.

If I say the *en* sound, for example, the kids who are advanced write words like *Kentucky* and *open.* And the kids who really struggle come

> up with *pen* and *Ben.* But they can all do it. Kids like Tralin and Rebecca and Cody are so happy that they've got something to do that they *can* do, and that they are learning to read.
>
> For the daily individualized reading, I needed to give them more guidance about what to read. Instead of just letting them read a book of their choice for those fifteen or twenty minutes, I made everybody a bag with books that I felt they could read. For the kids that are having a lot of trouble, I used some of the Dr. Seuss books that I've heard them read before and a bunch of easy readers. I chose some little chapter books for Martin and Cindy and a few of them who are reading at a more advanced level.

Laura made the phonics lessons inviting by capitalizing on her students' intrinsic interest in writing on the dry-erase boards, creating tasks in which all her students could find both challenge and success, and keeping the lessons short and game-like. Laura's more structured approach to daily individualized reading was, on the surface at least, more restrictive of her students' autonomy. The students could only choose from a set of books that were at their easy reading level; they had to actually read the entire time—not write, draw, or look at pictures—and they had to read aloud in a quiet voice, allowing Laura to walk around the room and monitor their reading.

Although there were some complaints at first, within a few weeks Laura's students no longer experienced the reading program as overly restrictive. Laura helped her students want to do what she was requiring them to do. She helped them see how important the practice reading was to developing their competence as readers, made a serious effort to help them find books they would like, and offered them a choice of books within a limited range. But perhaps the most important thing she did to help her students become willing readers was to give them hope that by reading every day they would eventually become competent readers—a hope that her struggling readers had previously begun to doubt.

> We talked about Michael Jordan. I told them that he didn't make his basketball team when he was a sophomore in high school—he got cut. But he practiced and he believed in himself and he became a very good basketball player. I told them that my goal is for them to be able to read as well as he plays basketball. It takes a lot of practice and that's what we are going to do.
>
> So, we talk about that a lot when they're reading. If somebody is not into it, I say, "Remember, we're practicing. This is the way you

> learn to read and become a good reader. It doesn't just happen; you have to keep practicing."
>
> And people have what they can read at their level. It's not like I'm asking anybody to practice something they can't do.

By the end of the first year, nearly all of Laura's students had improved their Slosson reading scores by more than a grade level, which was noteworthy in a school where one year's growth relative to one year's attendance could not be taken for granted. As their competence grew, so did their willingness to read and engage in learning activities that involved reading. By increasing their competence as readers, Laura also increased their sense of autonomy because they wanted to do what they were required to do—learn to read. They willingly read every day. By the end of the year, these individualized reading periods often lasted for thirty or forty minutes. And the students understood and enjoyed what they read. Laura was pleased by the progress of all her students, but she was particularly pleased by the progress of reluctant readers like Tralin.

> Tralin's still not a great reader, don't get me wrong, but she can get through things. She has added a little chapter book to her book box [after a few weeks, Laura replaced the book bags with book boxes] and it's been very motivating. She'll be asking, "When are we getting our book boxes out? I've got to see what's happening." Or she won't want to stop when it's time to put the book boxes away. Every now and then she'll come up and give me a report of what's happening in the story.
>
> Tralin's and the class's progress in reading was encouraging. At the close of the school year, each of Laura's students went home with a reading log to record their summer reading, a public library card they each got during a field trip to the library, and a few books that they had been given as part of the schoolwide Reading Is Fundamental book giveaway program. Laura hoped that during the summer they would continue to read and build their reading skills.

Year 2: Increasing the Supports and Challenges

Even though her students had made definite progress in reading during the first year, many were still reading below grade level. Over the summer, Laura decided that she would increase her focus on reading and more thoroughly integrate it into the study of various curriculum topics that she was obligated to cover. Buoyed by her students' progress during the first year and their increased willingness to read, and convinced by research that kids get to be better readers by reading—the more the better—Laura decided to add home reading to her program.

She also thought that if the students read in the evening, the morning class meetings might focus on what they had read the night before and thus contribute more to their overall academic development. In the first year, a lot of class time was devoted to class meetings. Even though Laura believed that class meetings were crucial for building class community and contributed substantially to her students' oral language development, she began to worry that class meetings were taking too much time away from the academic curriculum. However, Laura and the students loved these meetings, and Laura didn't want to give them up or even shorten them. Having her students read for homework and share something about their reading in the morning meetings seemed to be a perfect plan. It would allow her to retain the community-building benefits of daily class meetings and increase the time students spent reading and discussing books.

This plan was harder to put in place than Laura expected. When her students returned in August, both Laura and the children were surprised and discouraged to find that the students were less able to read than when they had left in May.

The first indication came when Laura reinstituted the individualized daily reading program. She decided to allow the students to choose books on their own for their book boxes, so long as they stuck with the difficulty level they had been working in at the end of the previous year. Tralin was only one of many students who struggled to read the books they had chosen. Laura needed to help them select less challenging books while reassuring them that they would get better with practice.

> It was the beginning of the second week of school, and Tralin called me over to ask me a word in the *Arthur* book that she was reading. Then she immediately asked me two more. So I decided to stay with her and listen to her read.
>
> I said, "Remember, if you have five words on a page that you can't read, the book might be too difficult, and you might want to choose another book."
>
> As she read on, I kept helping her. The book was too difficult and she was really struggling.
>
> I said, "Tralin, what does it feel like to read this book?"
>
> She said, "It's hard."
>
> I said, "Yes, it is hard. For book box time, I'd like you to just enjoy a book. This is not a time to do hard work. This is a time during the

day when we're going to read and relax. I'd like to see you have a book in your hands that you can just read and have a lot of fun reading."

I asked her if she had a book she could read more easily. She pulled out *Put Me in the Zoo* and read the first few pages comfortably. So I said, "Well, how does it feel to read this?"

And she said, "Fine."

I said, "Well, when we're reading in the book boxes, that's what we want to do; we want to feel fine. It's not a time to be struggling. This doesn't mean that you don't go back to the *Arthur* book in a few weeks when you get back into your routine."

Seeing how much of their reading skills her students had lost over the summer made Laura more determined than ever to help them develop not only strong reading skills but also a love of reading. On Monday of the second week of school, Laura held a class meeting to introduce her home reading plan. After a summer of not reading, several students were less than enthusiastic. They didn't want reading to interfere with out-of-school life, and they let Laura know it.

I had a class meeting to talk to the kids about the way we were going to do homework this year. I had decided that the kids could pick out a book, take it home, read it, and then just keep a record of what they were reading and maybe make a couple of little comments.

I started the meeting by asking, "Why do you think having reading for homework is important?"

Lana said, "Well, we'll learn how to read."

Rachel said, "If you read a book about Martin Luther King, you can learn about him."

Brian said, "Yeah, then you can remember what you read."

I could see that Tralin was upset so I said, "Tralin, tell me what you think and be honest. You can say what you think."

She said, "I don't like doing it. I want to do something else."

I asked, "Well, what don't you like about it?"

She said, "You've got to write all the answers."

I said, "Tralin, it's not writing answers. It's writing the title of the book and the date, who wrote the book, how many pages you read, and a few thoughts."

She said, "Well, I don't like writing."

John tried to be encouraging. He said, "Well, you know, it's just going to take a little bit of time—first you read it, then you just write a little bit about what you read."

> But Tralin was pretty upset and she looked at him and said, "I just want to go outside and play!"
>
> John kind of looked at Tralin and then looked at me and said, "Well, me too!"
>
> It was funny because at first he had been saying that the homework wasn't going to be so bad, and then he realized that, of course, he would rather be out playing, too.
>
> At this point I felt a little defensive and worried. As I was trying to explain the logs, Tralin just yelled out, "I'm not doing my homework!"
>
> And Martin, who I thought would enjoy taking a book home, just very belligerently said, "I don't want no books!"
>
> So I said, "Okay! Now listen, guys, I've made a decision as the teacher of this classroom that reading is important. Learning to read takes practice. When we do book boxes at school and read during the day we are practicing, but I think we need to practice at night as well. I have also made this decision so you can learn things. There are so many places you can go in a book."
>
> Tralin screwed up her face and said, "How you going to go in a book?" She didn't have a clue what I was talking about.
>
> Rachel said, "It's like you're in the book when you get interested in reading it and you're staring at it—it's like you're in the book."
>
> That didn't help Tralin any. In a very unhappy voice she said, "I don't understand any of this stuff!"
>
> I just said, "You know, it might be because reading is hard for you right now, but once you get good at it you're going to see that reading is just so much fun."
>
> Then I ended the meeting. I knew that some people weren't ready yet to understand that this was going to be a good experience. I had to get people where they were reading comfortably before they would understand that.

Laura needed to balance her students' felt need for autonomy with their real need for competence. She stood firm. She tried to soften her students' resistance by explaining her reasons and assuring them that they would soon come to enjoy reading. But she was not negotiating; she was requiring her students to read. She believed that they would not see the value of reading until they became better readers, and they would not become better readers unless they read. So, like many a good parent, she relied on the strength of her relationship to get her students to do what they would not willingly do on their own.

The next morning, even though many students did not want to talk about their reading homework, Laura was already able to see its potential.

> It was real interesting. I went around the circle by table groups [to start the second year, Laura assigned seats for the morning meeting]. No one in the first group wanted to share. I thought, "Oh, great! They're just going to refuse to talk."
>
> I went on to the next group. Martin's in that group and he had his hand up.
>
> He said, "Well, last night it was just me and my sister and we kept reading the book and she loved it. First, I read it and then she read it, and Max the cat was sitting on the bed."
>
> I had to stop and say, "Now that's just a sweet picture, you and your sister on the bed, with Max the cat just lying there listening. What book did you read?"
>
> When he said, "*The Two Crazy Pigs,*" everyone laughed at that because bunches of people know that book.
>
> Then Brian said that he wanted to share. He read a book about Michael Jordan and he found out something that he didn't know—that Michael Jordan used to play football.
>
> Then John said that he and his mom also read *The Two Crazy Pigs* and that they were laughing so hard about that book that they couldn't get anything on paper.
>
> I knew that was his way of letting me know that he did not write in the reading log. I didn't say a thing about it. The fact that he was talking about enjoying the book with his mom was enough. I just thought to myself, "It is the beginning of the year; my primary goal right now is to have the kids read."
>
> After John, the next entire group passed. Still, I thought, "Well, this is okay; they don't have to share. We'll just keep going and hopefully people are going to hear about other people reading and it's going to be okay."
>
> I got to Tralin's group and Tralin wanted to share. I was surprised after all her complaining the day before.
>
> She said, "I was at my granny's house and I was doing my homework. And I was reading to my baby cousin. And when he saw a picture of a baby, he said, 'Baby.' "
>
> I said, "So you were reading the book to him. How'd that feel?"
>
> She said, "Fine." Then she went on, "My auntie came in and he said it again."

> She had this big smile on her face, so I could tell she was feeling proud. I said, "You know what? You're helping that baby become a reader because that's how it starts. When little bitty ones are born and you start reading to them, they get interested in books and they find out that reading is fun. So you're helping someone become a reader."

Laura did not offer her students any prizes or points for reading, nor did she threaten to punish them if they did not read. The one coercive step she took, which was asking them to write down what they read, fell by the wayside. Most of her students had come to trust her and actually wanted to do as she asked—unless they could talk her out of it. When she insisted that they read for homework, they read. Across the year, sometimes it was clear that a student hadn't done the home reading. This happened only occasionally and Laura didn't make anything of it. She knew that many of her students lived in circumstances that would sometimes make it difficult for them to read or do any homework. She just kept up her expectation and provided the opportunity for the students to talk about and share their reading during morning meetings.

By December, students spontaneously began bringing their books to meetings, to show them and sometimes read excerpts to their classmates. As this process evolved, it further increased students' motivation to read.

> It started with Lana and Chantelle sharing a Shel Silverstein poem, "I Got Stung by a Bumblebee," that they found in a reader. Then other people started looking in the readers for poems. They also started sharing other stuff they saw in the readers. Martin found something about Jane Goodall, and they all wanted to read that because we had already read a book about Jane Goodall in class. Some of the guys were sharing the sports books, reading aloud something they didn't know about a famous sports star. And John takes home science books almost every single night, so he's been sharing from the science books.
>
> It's like they're doing little book talks. And so it gets people interested, and they end up taking all kinds of things home.

As the students began reading more, they began, as Martin had with Jane Goodall, to make connections between their home reading and their in-school curriculum. Laura supported and encouraged these connections. For example, in January, when the class began writing personal narratives, Tralin took home an English textbook she found in the class library. The next morning, she tried out something she had come across in her reading.

> When it was Tralin's turn to share in the morning meeting, she said, "I found this section in the English book about personal narratives, like we're trying to write. And I'd just like to ask the whole class a question."
>
> I said, "Okay, go on."
>
> So she asked everyone, "What is your favorite part of your favorite meal?" She read that right out of the book.
>
> Right away I said, "Partner up. Find somebody to partner with." And so they all turned to a partner and talked about their favorite part of their favorite meal.
>
> After they talked with their partners, we talked as a group about the favorite part of our favorite meal.
>
> And then we had to thank Tralin for helping us think about our personal narratives. I said, "You know, that's what serious learners do. If they're working on something or are interested in something, sometimes they do a little research. That's what Tralin did last night. She looked at what we were working on and researched it herself in the English book." So then, of course, everybody had to give her a big hand.

In addition to building her students' motivation to read, Laura carefully monitored their reading progress. When they were engaged in their individualized reading, she would move from student to student listening to them read and providing help as needed. She also periodically tested their decoding skills. They showed steady improvement, which Laura shared with them. However, even though her students were reading more and better, they were still making reading mistakes that indicated that their knowledge of phonics was too limited. For example, when they came to unfamiliar words, Laura noticed that a number of students guessed at the words based on context and an initial letter or two. Although this process worked reasonably well for books classified as easy readers, Laura feared that it would leave her students at a serious disadvantage once they tried to read more challenging text.

Believing that some of her students needed more work with phonics and would probably benefit from more systematic instruction, Laura began a program developed by John Shefelbine (Shefelbine and Newman, 2000) that involved daily, fifteen-minute instruction in reading polysyllabic words. To Laura's surprise, her students loved these lessons.

> Because some students were still shaky on the different vowel sounds, I began with flash cards of short- and long-vowel syllables, like *mim* or *mi*. We focused on whether the vowel is at the end of a syllable or

not at the end. I also had a set of flash cards of common syllables and word parts, like *ment*, or *est*, or *per*, and each day I introduced five new ones to practice along with some we had already done. Last, we would read together several polysyllabic words, syllable by syllable, and then fluently. Most of the polysyllabic words came from books we were reading in class—the biographies or science books, or the partner reading books. The kids loved that—coming across words from our phonics lesson in their regular reading.

Depending on how quickly we were going through things, the phonics lesson would only last ten or fifteen minutes. And that's another thing the kids really loved about it. It was fast and, as they say, you got a lot of bang for your buck.

When I was monitoring their reading during book box time, I had a way to show them how to attack difficult words. I'd just do the same process on an individual level. I'd isolate each syllable and ask, "Where's the vowel?" "Is it short or long?" and guide them through the whole word.

These lessons helped all the kids. It was wonderful to see the struggling readers like Rebecca and Tralin really get a handle on the decoding process and to see the better readers like John, who were on the brink of real fluency, have a way to figure everything out and just go.

At the end of the year when the kids put together their class book remembering the year, Jennifer, one of the most accomplished readers in the class, chose to write about the phonics lessons.

The Dividends of Competence

Laura's strong focus on reading paid huge dividends. As her students realized their growing competence, they became happier and engaged the curriculum more willingly. Their increasing competence also made it possible for Laura to afford them more autonomy in class assignments. The research projects she devised in Year 2 are the best example of this. Laura gathered many easy-to-read books on a range of social studies and science topics—for example, biographies of historic figures or books about many different animals—and assigned partnerships but not specific topics. The partners worked together to learn about the topic they chose and to report back to their classmates. The students loved these projects, as Laura found when she introduced the second one of the year.

I explained to the class that we were going to work with partners and do more research, and people started cheering, like they were just thrilled silly.

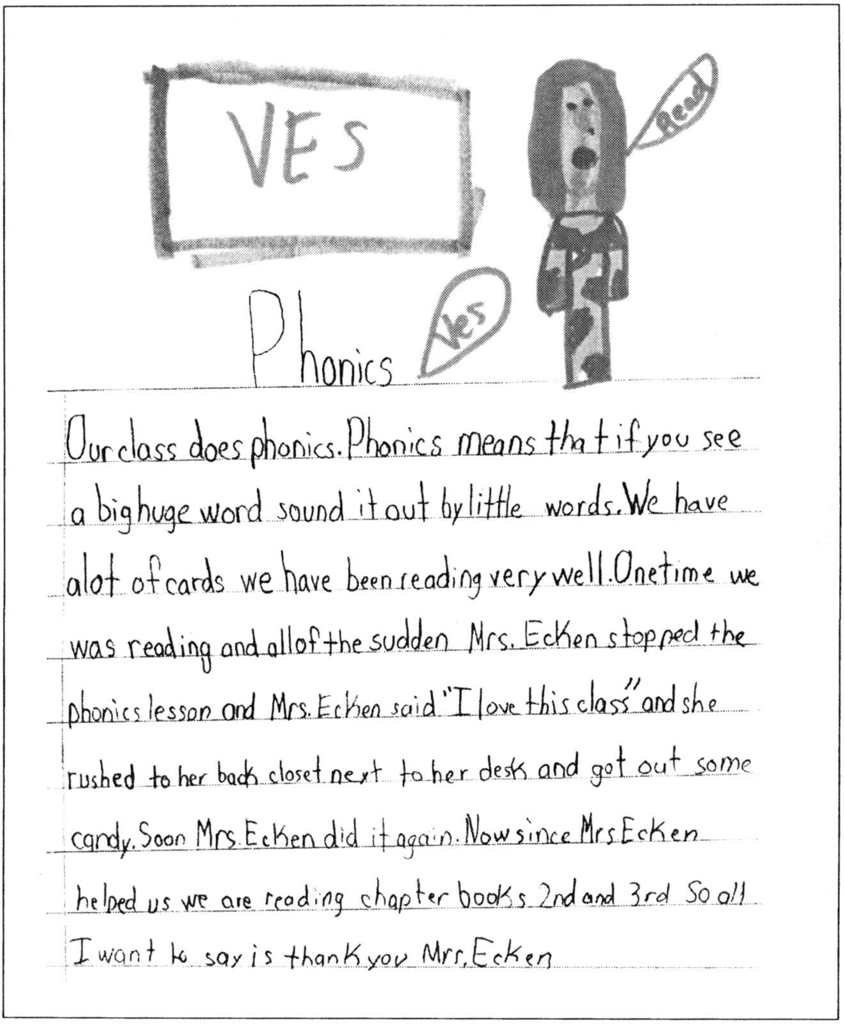

I said, "We're going to do some research on water and weather, because they kind of go together, and you'll see this as we go on with the research."

I had them make a list with their partners of the things that they would like to study or know about related to water or the weather. I explained before they made their lists that there were some topics that I wanted to be sure we covered in our research, like clouds and storm formation—and I named a few other things—and I explained that if it turned out no partnerships chose some of those topics, I might ask people to do them.

After each partnership made a list of things that both of them wanted to study and do research on, most people had five or six things on their

> lists. It worked out fine because what was on everyone's list was pretty much what I wanted to do. They even added a few things that I hadn't thought of.

Laura's approach to class research projects brings to mind the child-centered approach to teaching advocated by Carl Rogers in *Freedom to Learn* (1969) and exemplifies the balance that she eventually achieved between meeting her students' need for competence and granting them the autonomy they wanted and needed. Although her students had no choice about the general topics of study—for the most part they were mandated by the Kentucky state curriculum—Laura maximized their freedom within those topics. For example, the state curriculum dictated that her students would study the water cycle. However, in introducing this topic Laura gave each research partnership the opportunity to list the things they were particularly interested in learning about and then assigned each research partnership the open-ended task of reading about and reporting to their classmates what they learned. Laura was able to support her students' needs to be competent in the mandated curriculum, as well as to help them develop into autonomous academic learners—students who wanted to learn school topics because they saw the learning as interesting and relevant to them and who had some choices in how to do it.

Balancing Autonomy with Authority

Over the two years, finding ways to meet the students' felt autonomy needs while also meeting their needs for belonging and competence was a slow and difficult process. How much autonomy students can handle in the classroom will depend on their level of understanding about the purpose and role of school in their lives and their level of self-control. Many of Laura's students had little of either. It will also depend on their level of trust and their understanding of the nature of relationships. Several of Laura's students were deeply mistrustful, seeming to believe that controlling others, whether through dependency or aggression, was a matter of survival. For the class as a whole, students' low levels of self-control and trust amplified the normal developmental tensions of balancing autonomy with authority.

Being Clear About What Is Not Negotiable

At first, and throughout most of the first year, Laura tried to meet her students' autonomy needs by giving them lots of freedom, allowing them to take much responsibility, and offering explanations for why they needed to behave in fair, kind, and responsible ways. At the same time, she tried to provide enough structure to keep the class running smoothly. And because her long-term goal was for her students to become personally responsible for their learning and behavior, she was somewhat reluctant to impose structures or to use her authority to require the behaviors she hoped they would learn to do on their own.[2]

By the end of the year, she felt that she had provided too little structure, engaged in too much negotiation, given her students too much autonomy, and exercised too little authority. To begin the second year, Laura felt compelled to make some changes.

> Because I'm so used to starting each year with many of the same students I had the year before, this past year I hadn't thought through all the procedures I would need for a class of almost all new students to run smoothly. So this year I've put some new structures in place, like seating assignments for the class meetings and initials on the pencils, so that they're not fighting about dumb stuff. But mostly I've been concerned about having better ways to let students know what's expected.
>
> Last year there was too much ugliness and making fun of people. I feel I spent too much time trying to negotiate with certain students and trying to get them to see why they needed to be kind. I spent a lot of time talking, but too much teasing and unkind behavior went on.
>
> It was important at the beginning of this year to let them know that this was going to change. For one thing, I was not going to talk and negotiate when someone was being unkind. Last year we didn't have the concept of our classroom being a "safe" place. So I introduced the vocabulary "safe" and kept talking about "safety." I made it very clear to all of them how important this was. Whenever I needed to, I would say something like, "You're not going to mess with people and stay here because this is a place where people are going to be safe."
>
> One day Leonard said, "I like people to mess with me."
>
> I told him, "Well, then do it out there. You're not doing it here. This is a safe place."
>
> When Tangela said, "I like to mess with people," it was the same thing.
>
> I said, "Well, you're not doing that here. This is a safe place."
>
> I think last year my tendency was to be too tentative. I didn't know the children very well. You've got to take some time to build a relationship with them. It was difficult for me to come down too hard on that kind of stuff because I worried about rupturing my relationship with them. And I think that was hurtful because I let some things go

> on that shouldn't have. I should have sent a very clear message at the beginning that people were going to be safe psychologically as well as physically. And this year that very clear message has been sent.

Laura decided to be more forceful in her demands that the students treat one another and her with respect and kindness, and to use the term *safety* to help them understand why. Safety and kindness were not negotiable. Nor was Laura's expectation that students would be serious learners. However, because reasoning and negotiating with students are essential for meeting their need for autonomy and for developing their ability to monitor and guide their own behavior, Laura continued to look for other opportunities to increase their sense of autonomy.

Recognizing When Students Know Best

Developmentally, Laura's students couldn't help but strive for autonomy, and they frequently challenged her authority. Yet they also understood how important it was for Laura to exercise her authority in the classroom. In mid-October of the second year, when the home reading program was well under way, Laura called a class meeting to ask students' help solving the problem of books disappearing from the classroom library. To her surprise and frustration, they insisted that she accept the responsibility of protecting their supply of books.

> Last Friday Martin asked me if he could take a book home. At first I said no because we had a rule that no books go home on Friday. I was afraid the books might get lost over the weekend. But he really wanted to take that book home.
>
> He said, "It's really a good book. I've already finished chapter two, and I really want to finish it over the weekend."
>
> So I let him take it.
>
> Then a week later, Louise's little brother brought in a book for his class that he told Ms. Lawrence was his sister's, but it had my name on it. Louise said she didn't know how her brother got it, but I do.
>
> The kids have those zipping plastic bags for protecting the book they're taking home, and a lot of times lately the book they're supposed to be returning isn't in the bag. The bag is empty, but they say, "Oh, I already put it back.".
>
> Or Chantelle's mother told me Chantelle comes home with three or four books at a time. It just makes me wonder how many books they're stealing.

I don't want to have to be like a policeman checking those book bags and counting books every day. And I don't want to discourage them from reading. They love the books and choosing which one to take home and trading with their friends. But they've got a responsibility in making it work.

So we had a meeting about the books. I started by saying, "I want to talk about our classroom and the concerns I have that books are disappearing. If the books disappear, where do they disappear from? From our classroom. Who makes up this classroom? We do."

So then I said, "These books belong to everybody. If you take books home and don't return them, pretty soon there aren't going to be any books. You're really just stealing from yourself."

We talked for a while about how we know our classroom is a community, and then I asked them to talk with someone sitting next to them about a plan for how to make sure we're taking one book home at a time and bringing it back. Almost every pair came up with a plan that had to do with me writing down the names of the books and who's taking them, or me sending a note home, or me checking the book bags, or me checking their lockers.

So then I said, "Can you think of a plan that I don't even have to be involved in? I'm not saying I won't be involved, but let's try to think if there's another way."

Martin said, "I don't think nobody should take more than their fair share."

I agreed, "Yes, that's exactly what we're talking about. Take your one book home at night and bring it back. If you already have one at home, don't take another."

At this point, Lana said, "Well, I was wondering if we could take two books instead of one, because maybe we don't have anything else to do at night and we already read our one."

Everybody jumped on that idea. They all started saying, "Can we take two? We need to take two!"

I'm sitting there thinking we were having this meeting about too many books disappearing at home, and now they want to double the number going home!

But that was the general consensus, to take two books home. So, we went back to deciding a plan, only now the question was, "What can we do to make sure that the *two* books come back?"

We couldn't get away from something that involved me, so at the end of the day I'm writing down the number of books someone takes, and in the morning I check it off if they bring them back. It seems to

> be working out, and several students have even brought back more books than they took.

As with the classroom library policies, Laura was open to negotiating with her students on many issues. And although it was essential for her to hold firm to core decisions affecting her students' safety and learning, she needed to be open to working with her students to devise alternative plans when her decisions were limiting to their development.

It contributed greatly to her students' sense of autonomy that Laura asked for their help in solving the problem of the disappearing books and that they could convince Laura to change the policy about how many books they could take home. However, it was also essential for Laura to be willing to exercise her authority for the overall good of her students. Her students knew, better than Laura, how tempting it was to keep the books at home. They knew that they needed her to monitor the returning of the books to ensure that they all had fair access to the classroom library.

Responding to Students' Differing Autonomy Needs

As teachers, we can do too much negotiation or too little. We can exercise too much control or too little. With each group of children and each individual child, we need to adjust the balance differently. One of the things that makes teaching especially difficult is that the need for autonomy and the ability to handle autonomy responsibly is different for different classes, for the same class across the year, and for different students within a class.

For some of Laura's students, autonomy was a major concern. They had not reconciled their need for autonomy with their need for adult guidance and help. Toddlers struggle with this, but it is usually accomplished by three or four years of age in children with histories of secure attachment relationships. A few hated to be given a reminder or told what to do. Like eighteen-month-olds, they found it difficult to accept adult authority, experiencing any attempt to control their behavior as a threat to their zealously guarded autonomy. Laura discovered that these students would much more willingly comply with a request or a command if she simply made the request clearly and then left the student to comply in his or her own good time. She gave her students the time to think over whether the request was reasonable, affording them the space to decide to comply without further pressure while subtly conveying her trust in their goodwill.

This was not Laura's initial or intuitive response. Like most teachers, she believed she needed to stand over noncompliant students to see that they did comply. At first she saw these students as oppositional or defiant, and her relationship with them was conflictual. For instance, it took Laura a while to realize Leonard's high need for autonomy, and her relationship with him had a stormy beginning. Once she realized how important it was to let him come around on his own, and he realized that she really cared about him, they developed a solid partnership. Laura didn't lower her expectations of Leonard; she simply learned to make her requests in a way that left Leonard some time to decide for himself that he would comply.

> After the class finished performing their role-plays based on *The Gold Coin,* we talked about ways to improve their scripts by tying them more realistically to the story.
>
> Leonard refused. He said, "I'm not doing that. Mine's good enough." And Louise, his partner, agreed.
>
> I said, "You know, Leonard, this is an opportunity to make it better. It is pretty good. But pretty good's not good enough when you've got an opportunity to make it great. And that's what you're getting right now."
>
> He said, "Well, I'm not doing it."
>
> And so I said, "You know what? That's your decision."
>
> I left it alone and the next thing I knew, he and Louise were working and getting their role-play all fixed up.

Being aware of Leonard's autonomy pattern helped Laura recognize a similar pattern in a new student, Derek, soon after he entered the classroom.

> I've noticed that Derek is a lot like Leonard. You've got to walk away and give him time. Leonard and Derek both, when I talk to them, we can talk through it, but they have their arms folded and they're not real open.
>
> Sometimes they may sit for five minutes before they'll ease up. And they're never going to do that with me sitting there. Once I realized that with Leonard, things went a lot better. And it took me a couple days to notice it with Derek, because at first I would sit there and try and get him to make a commitment. Then I just started walking away from it, and most of the time he pulled himself together and did the right thing.

Laura learned to adjust her responses to the unique needs of each of her students while continuing to provide adequate guidance and support. And sometimes, of course, Laura gave the same directive to different students and got compliance, but with entirely opposite attitudes.

> When they're reading in their book boxes, sometimes some of them won't settle down to read, and they'll be talking to people at their table and fooling around. So I'll say, "Why don't you have a seat at the back table and sit down and read?"
>
> I've done that with Rachel a couple different times. She was talking so much with her group that I had to ask her to go to the back table where she wouldn't be distracted. The second time I asked her, she actually thanked me. She's reading about the environmentalist Rachel Carson, and she said, "Ms. Ecken, thanks for asking me to sit back there where I could read. My book is really interesting."
>
> When I had to ask Tyrone to go in the back to read, he slammed the book box down, kicked every chair he could reach, and started mumbling, "Oh, I hate this." He slammed himself in the chair at the back table, turned the chair away from the room, and just sat there with his arms folded. I didn't say anything to him because I was reading with somebody, but the next thing I knew he had started to read.

Fortunately, Laura was involved with another student and chose to ignore Tyrone's display of anger. Given some space and freedom from distraction, Tyrone eventually did what he needed to do during book box time. He read.

Many students with a history of insecure attachment relationships find it difficult to trust enough to accept the reasonable exercise of adult authority. But when the authority is reasonable and they are in a caring environment, these students will often comply if they are not pressed too tightly. Laura's main goal with these students was to gain compliance with her reasonable requests without having to be coercive. An important bonus for her students of being given time to comply on their own was their experience of being able to balance their need for autonomy with her need for authority and their need for support. By providing these students with ongoing practice in reconciling their autonomy needs with the needs of legitimate authority, Laura increased their level of trust in her. Eventually, she worked with these students on their displays of anger or "attitude"; with increased trust the anger and displays diminished.

The Freedom to Grow

Like most teachers, Laura wanted her students to take increasing responsibility for themselves. She wanted them to manage their own behavior based on principles of fairness, kindness, and personal responsibility. But her students had much to learn before this would be possible. They needed to learn to control their emotions and their behavior, to accept legitimate authority, and to view their classmates as friends rather than competitors. They needed to grow in trust, empathy, and the ability to forgive. They needed to understand the reciprocal nature of relationships and their role as members of a community. Like all children, Laura's students needed a delicate and ever-changing balance of external control, guidance, support, and autonomy in order to develop their capacities to be responsible for themselves—to become autonomous learners and moral agents.

Over the course of the two years, Laura changed the balance of control and autonomy in order both to meet her students' immediate needs and to foster their further development. She continuously looked for ways to provide her students the freedom to act on their own initiative, even as she sought to control and guide their behavior. As her students' needs and abilities changed, Laura adjusted her policies and her teaching to support their further development. For example, while Laura created procedures to limit her students' opportunities to engage in contentious behavior, such as issuing pencils with students' initials on them, she relaxed these procedures as her students' ability to handle autonomy increased. Even though such procedures did nothing to alleviate the deep-rooted causes of students' contentious behavior, they made it easier for Laura to manage her classroom, helping her to gain the time and the patience to deal with the deeper causes.

Gradually, as her classroom became a safer, more caring place and the students came to trust Laura and each other, Laura relaxed her control. She provided more opportunities for her students to take initiative and assume responsibility for their own behavior. She worked hard to be open to following her students' lead while continuing to provide support, guidance, or control when necessary. Her students understood that their suggestions and initiative were welcomed, and they frequently took responsibility for their own behavior and for their community.

Laura consciously planned for ways to give her students more responsibility, but many occasions for student initiative were unplanned. They happened because the general atmosphere of the classroom invited initiative. For example, one day in November of the second year, Martin wanted to take a book home even though he had lost his plastic book bag. The series of events that followed illustrate the delicate balance of autonomy and control that Laura hoped would foster her students' ability to take responsibility for themselves and their community.

> Martin had lost his plastic book bag and he wanted to take home this really nice book. I said, "Martin, I really wish you had your bag for this, because it'll keep it clean. You can take it, but you've got to be careful."

> Well, Chantelle tracks everything I say or do. Whether it pertains to her or not, she's right with me. So she came over and said, "Mrs. Ecken, I can bring Martin a bag tomorrow for his books."
>
> The next morning she walked in with this bag for Martin. It was one of those zipping plastic bags, just like the other kids have, and she's got it decorated with his name on it. He was so thankful for that.
>
> It wasn't more than a few minutes later when she announced, "I don't have a pencil. I can't find my pencil."
>
> Well, Martin had brought in three new pencils so he got up and gave her one. He said, "You can use my brand-new pencil today."
>
> By the end of the day the pencil had disappeared. Martin was really, really mad at Chantelle. I said, "You know, Chantelle, if somebody lets you use something, it's your responsibility to keep track of it."
>
> Well, she didn't know where it was, or what happened to it, and neither did any of us. So he left kind of ticked with her.
>
> The next morning, Tangela showed up with the exact same pencil, with the exact same eraser on it. But now it had a pencil holder on it. She swore her sister Jataria gave her the pencil. Martin was out of whack because he knew that was his pencil.
>
> I said, "Now Martin, Jataria could have given Tangela this pencil. Obviously there are pencils with erasers like this in the world because you bought one. So we just have to believe Tangela."
>
> Toward the end of the day, I talked privately with Tangela. I said, "Tangela, you know if that's your pencil or not, and you know if Jataria gave it to you. But if it's not yours, try to think in your mind, what would be the right thing to do?"
>
> About fifteen minutes later, she walked up to me, took the pencil holder off the pencil, and said, "Well, he's not getting my pencil holder!"
>
> Then, without my saying a thing to her, she walked over and said, "Here, Martin. Here's your pencil back."
>
> He looked at her and said, "Thanks for giving it to me, Tangela."
>
> It was just so sweet—it's like they just figured out that they were going to do what was right about the pencil.

Early in this saga of book bags and pencils, it would have been easy for Laura to keep to established rules and not allow Martin to take home the book without the book bag. Laura's empathy for Martin and her growing trust that he would treat the book with extra care led her to a less controlling response. It would also have been easier and safer for Laura to bring a plastic bag from home or insist that Martin do so instead of letting Chantelle make a bag for Martin. After all, this incident was between

Laura and Martin, and Chantelle might fail to bring a bag, prolonging the problem unnecessarily. When Chantelle had no pencil, it would have been easier and consistent with classroom procedures to insist that she use one of the pencils from the class supply of short pencils, thus impressing upon Chantelle the importance of being responsible for her pencil. And it would have been faster and less risky for Laura to use her authority to make Tangela, who had a history of taking things that didn't belong to her, return Martin's pencil.

The actions Laura took instead reflected her goals related to autonomy: to provide her students with as much autonomy as they could responsibly handle and to build their skills and understanding so they could handle increasingly more autonomy. Thus Martin had the opportunity to be especially careful with a relatively new class book. Chantelle had the opportunity to autonomously help Martin and Martin to autonomously behave generously toward Chantelle. With Laura's support, Tangela had the opportunity to see, based on her own thought rather than Laura's authority, that returning the pencil to Martin was the right thing to do. And Martin had the opportunity to forgive Tangela and accept the pencil graciously. Had her students responded differently at any point, Laura would have responded differently. She might have had to use more control, provide more explanation, or do more teaching. However, Laura needed to risk allowing her students to take the initiative to behave well, both to provide them with the freedom to grow and to gauge for herself the level of support and guidance they needed.

During the first year, Laura focused her energies on building her relationship with her students, their relationships with one another, and their sense of community. As she prepared for the second year, Laura came to believe that in her effort to meet her students' needs for belonging and autonomy, she had given insufficient attention to their need for competence. Laura also realized that she had allowed her students more autonomy than at least some of them could responsibly handle. At the start of the second year, drawing on the strength of her relationships with her returning students, Laura decided to exercise more authority and to increase the academic focus of her classroom.

For example, she added to her reading program the requirement that students read at home each night. When her students balked at having to read for homework and Laura could not get them to see the value of home reading, she used her relationships and her authority to insist that they do so. Laura also structured her classroom more tightly in order to eliminate some of the sources of ongoing conflict and wrangling, and she responded more firmly to her students' misbehavior, especially to acts of unkindness or disrespect. However, even as Laura was adding more structure and being firmer about her demands, she was constantly on the alert for ways to involve her students in decision making, to provide opportunities for them to exercise meaningful autonomy, and to develop their ability to responsibly handle increased levels of autonomy.

By two months into the second year, in part because of the changes she made and in part because Laura could build on the strength of her relationships with her students from the previous year, Laura's class was running more smoothly. Her students' interconnected needs for autonomy, belonging, and competence were being better met. Because the majority of her students trusted that Laura really cared about them, she was able to use her authority to get them to more fully engage in learning activities. As her students found themselves learning and enjoying their learning, their trust in Laura increased. As their trust increased, they were more willing to comply with her requests. Gradually, Laura was able to establish a productive partnership with her students based on mutual trust.

An important ingredient in this partnership was Laura's trust in her students' sometimes deeply hidden desire to learn, to be competent. Often when students misbehave in our classrooms or resist doing their assigned work, the issue behind their behavior is related to their lack of competence or confidence. This was true for several of Laura's students but none more so than Tralin. At first, Tralin's resistance caused Laura to resent her. This could have led to deterioration in their relationship and a cycle of increased demands by Laura and increased resistance by Tralin. Or it would have been equally unfortunate if the result had been decreased demands by Laura and limited learning by Tralin. Instead, Laura persevered to uncover the cause of Tralin's resistance and, believing that Tralin was clearly capable of learning, embarked on a plan to increase her support for Tralin. This was not a quick process; Laura tried many things to support Tralin. It was not until Tralin mastered reading that she came to see herself as a capable learner and became a willing learner.

An equally important ingredient in forming a collaborative partnership with her students was Laura's ability to help them acquire the understandings and skills they needed to be able to responsibly exercise increasing levels of autonomy. Forming a nurturing relationship with students involves using authority and our knowledge of them to help them responsibly meet their growing need for autonomy. Children frequently make mistakes and frequently misbehave as they struggle to understand and adapt to their

Key Points: Meeting Students' Needs for Competence and Autonomy

- Adjust learning activities to match student skills, and provide additional scaffolding for students who are struggling.
- Help students see that learning is interesting, relevant, and important by, for example, connecting learning activities to students' lives and interests and providing opportunities to share their learning with others.
- Build hopefulness in struggling learners by helping them see how they are making progress.
- Stand firm on the importance of learning, but make allowances for special stresses in their lives.
- Provide students with as much autonomy in their learning as they can handle.
- Balance autonomy with authority. Clearly communicate what is negotiable and what is not.
- Look for and be open to opportunities to engage students in negotiation and problem solving.
- Make allowances for students with strong autonomy needs. Give them time to comply on their own, ignore "attitude" until you have established mutual trust, and problem solve with them to come up with a way to help them comply.
- Allow students freedom to grow. Be prepared to adjust rules in response to student growth, encourage student initiative, and allow students sufficient freedom, for example, to spontaneously help others.

world. Finding the right balance—exercising the right amount of authority and guidance and allowing the right amount of freedom—is no easy task. In this chapter, we have seen some of the ways Laura achieved this balance. In the next, we will see in greater detail the many ways that Laura struggled to manage her students' mistakes and misbehaviors.

NOTES

1. See DeCharms, 1968; Deci and Ryan, 1985; Erikson, 1950; Maslow, 1970; and White, 1959.
2. Actually, Laura limited her use of authority during the first year because she believed that was what I wanted her to do. She was trying to make sure she was using every aspect of CDP as much as possible. She knew that negotiating with children and helping them engage in perspective taking were important parts of Developmental Discipline, so she was reluctant to abandon or temper her use of them, even with the students for whom they were not working. At the close of school, when Laura had time to step back and reflect on her year, it became clear to her that she couldn't go on negotiating endlessly with the students who continued to tease or make the classroom unsafe for others. This was not only taking too much time, it was making the classroom unsafe for those students who were the victims of teasing. Laura decided that in general she needed to use more authority and structure the second year, and I agreed with her.

5

MANAGING MISTAKES AND MISBEHAVIOR

TAKING A TEACHING STANCE

Tuesday I had a substitute while I went to an in-service. The kids looted the room. We've been together almost eight months, and it was like, for what? They went through everything and just took what they wanted. They ripped boxes open in the cupboard. They took yellow stickies, toothpicks, paper towels, anything. Tangela went through my desk drawer and took my markers and pen.

When Mack [the special education teacher who worked with some of Laura's students] got back at quarter to three, Denise was taking stuff that he keeps on a ledge by his back table—stickies, paper clips, just a few supplies he needs.

He said, "Denise, what are you doing?"

And she said, "Everyone else is taking her stuff. I am getting me some, too."

Then Tyrone, he's got his pockets full of things, he said, "I took stuff. I wanted it and I took it." He's lived his whole life being raised on stealing. Everything he's had, that's how his mother got it. It's why she's in prison.

The stealing reminded me of when we read the book *J.T.* When J. T. reaches through the car window and takes the little radio that's on the front seat, my students didn't see what was wrong with that.

I said, "You know, one of my car doors is broken and I can't lock it. I've got some stuff sitting in that car. What do you think about somebody just walking by and taking it?"

Denise said, "If you don't have your doors locked, it shouldn't be in there."

So, I think whoever started taking stuff in the room, everybody saw it and just thought, "I'm going to get me some," like Denise said to Mack.

But here is what just ticks me off the most. When they went through my boxes, they didn't even open them. They ripped them. They just ripped them open. I know it's crazy to get mad over something like that when there were other things to be madder about, but they just ripped that stuff with such disrespect.

When I first asked them about what went on, everybody denied doing anything, but everybody was telling on everybody else, what they had taken.

So I said, "Bring my stuff back tomorrow. Just bring it back. And I want to tell you all something. We have a relationship. We are this close"—I put my two fingers together. "That's how much we care about each other. So you don't do that. You don't do that, period. Much less to somebody you care so much about."

And I said, "I care so much about you."

At the same time, I was in such a rage that probably nobody was even listening to me. Oh, I was really ticked.

Nobody brought anything back. I guess they didn't want to admit they took it, and I didn't give them a way to bring it back so that they wouldn't be losing face.

LAURA AND I discussed this over the weekend, and we both agreed that more needed to be done. It wasn't good for Laura or for the children to simply let this incident pass. Laura decided to bring the incident up again with her students and give them a chance to repair the damage they had done.

We had a morning meeting and after everybody shared, I said, "I want to talk about the room and what happened with the sub."

I said, "The room's a wreck. You all ripped the boxes open, you got into things and messed them up, and stuff is missing." I asked them for their help in getting things returned and getting the room back to the way it was.

They got real excited. They said they could clean the room and fix it up, and they said they would bring stuff back and put it where it belonged.

I said, "You know, that would be a good way to end this. I'd like for it to be over. If we could fix things and get the room put back together, then that would end it. It's a way to make up for what you've done."

At that point, people who had said they had never done anything admitted they took stuff. William, for example, said he took paper towels.

Only Yolanda and Tralin weren't happy. They said they didn't do anything, so they weren't going to clean anything up.

What happened then is the class said, "Yes, you did! You took her sticky notes, Yolanda!"

Yolanda said, "I did not. Tangela gave them to me."

I said, "Yolanda, whose sticky notes were they?"

She said, "Yours."

I said, "Well, if you took them from Tangela when you knew they were mine, that's like taking them. You took something that wasn't Tangela's to give to you."

She kind of agreed and offered to clean the board.

I said, "The board does need cleaning; that would be something really good for you to do."

Tralin sat there in a huff because the kids told her she took sticky notes too. I came over and sat down with her and I said, "Tralin, what's the problem?"

She said, "I didn't take anything of yours and I'm not cleaning anything up."

I said, "Tralin, did you write on those sticky notes?"

When she said yes, I said, "Well, they were mine."

And then she just looked at me and said, "Okay."

So I said, "Would you like to help get those books back together on that bookshelf?"

She was all right then and went over and got started.

After a few minutes, Leonard came up and said, "Ms. Ecken, this feels great to make this up to you."

Then Kenny came up and said, "You know, Ms. Ecken, this is just like at home. When I jump on my bed and tear it up, my mother makes me put it back together."

I said, "Yeah, it is kind of like that, isn't it? We got things in a mess so we're putting it back like it needs to be."

Martin—how he came up with this I don't know—told me, "You know, this really made me think about what it would be like in prison

> if you steal stuff and do stuff. Just makes me think I don't want to go to prison."
>
> It took about an hour, and they got everything straightened up.
>
> When it was over, I said, "What did that feel like to be able to do that?"
>
> There weren't a lot of different thoughts. It was mainly what Leonard had said: it felt good to be able to make up for what happened.
>
> William said, "I'm going to bring the towels back and I'll put them by the sink."
>
> So on Friday I said something to him like, "Did you remember the towels?"
>
> He said, "I already put them back."

This incident happened in March of the first year, and it was initially devastating to Laura. By this time in the year, she had established a good relationship with her students. She could hardly believe that the students she cared so much about and who she knew cared about her could do such a thing to her. She took the trashing of her room personally, and she felt betrayed. At first, her confidence was shaken; she began to doubt the value of her work and the progress her students had made in developing self-control and respect for her and the rights of others.

But, in fact, as their eventual behavior showed, her students had made considerable progress. It's just that their grip on self-control was very tenuous and for most still dependent on Laura's guiding and reassuring presence. They were successful in partnership with her, but they had not yet achieved the ability to be successful on their own. When they had a particularly inept substitute teacher, they fell apart. And for some of them, perhaps, when they started to fall apart, they blamed Laura for not being with them and struck out at her.

Whatever the causes, this situation allowed Laura, once she got control of her own emotional response, to provide her students with a very deep kind of reassurance—the reassurance that she still cared about them and was not going to punish or desert them, even though they had done something very bad. Laura's trust that deep down her students really were sorry and did want to repair the harm they had done enabled her to refrain from punishment or from trying to force them to make amends. By asking for her students' help, she allowed their best motives to surface, and she provided the space and support for them to reflect and to autonomously engage in the moral act of restitution.

This incident, while particularly challenging, illustrates Laura's general approach to managing misbehavior: convey unconditional caring and

trust; provide scaffolding or support for appropriate behavior; explicitly teach needed concepts or skills; and provide opportunities for reflection and, where possible, restitution.

The parallels between Laura's approach to classroom management and discipline and her approach to academic instruction are striking. In both domains, she tried to provide a challenging but manageable environment, instruction, support for her students' efforts, and opportunities for reflection, self-discovery, and correction or reparation. The discussion about creating guidelines for using the restroom, which you will remember from Chapter Three, is one example.

Because Laura's students, like students in every classroom, brought widely different social, emotional, moral, and academic skills and understandings to the classroom, this general approach often looked very different depending on the situation and the student involved. Laura's approaches ranged from the expedient of structuring the environment to the teaching and trust-building partnerships she established with misbehaving students.

Creating a Manageable Environment

Like all teachers, Laura designed a set of procedures for handling common classroom occurrences. For example, she had signals to get her students momentarily quiet and attentive, routines to begin and end the day, ways to transition between activities, and agreements about how to move around the school. Because each group of students is unique, teachers create different and more or fewer procedures and structures, depending on what they see as the needs of each group. Although the goal is to provide students with as much autonomy and responsibility as they can handle, in making the environment manageable it is often necessary to create structures that limit student autonomy by limiting their opportunity to misbehave.

Laura's judgments about where to structure her classroom to prevent the opportunity for misbehavior and where to allow more autonomy were guided by a cost-benefit analysis. If Laura believed that providing autonomy would result in unproductive wrangling, she limited autonomy or provided a structure to prevent anticipated problems. One such problem was the management of the classroom pencil supply. At the start of the second year, Laura decided to try to eliminate what had been a persistent problem during the first year: students taking and fighting over pencils.

> I came up with a plan to handle pencils this year. First of all, it's too expensive. Last year I would put new pencils out and they'd be gone. The kids would take them all home. Or the powerful people in the class would take the real long ones and just dare somebody to touch them.
>
> I'd get ready to do a lesson, and I'd have three or four of them fighting over pencils. And you can't ignore it; you can't say, "Figure it out." You have to stop and deal with it, because they're ready to hit each other over a stupid pencil that doesn't even belong to them. This went on all the time.
>
> So I gave them each a new pencil with their initials on it the first day of school. Now at least we know whose pencil is whose, and there's a collection of short pencils for anyone who loses their special pencil.

Of course, the problem that needed to be handled was not a problem about taking pencils. It had to do with the competitive, even combative, stance of several of Laura's students, the students' general lack of social and emotional skills, and their failure to see themselves as part of a community. The pencils were one manifestation of these wider problems, but by addressing the pencil problem with the simple structure of issuing pencils with students' initials on them, Laura saved herself some time and energy for issues she considered more important or that were not so easily controlled.

Lining up was another source of irritation that Laura tried to control with a structure—rotating the order in which the table groups lined up by days of the week. The Monday group would be first on Monday, the Tuesday group on Tuesday, and so on. However, this structure still left room for wrangling about the order of the individual students in a group. In this case, Laura could have also assigned an order within the groups, but instead she chose to have the students apply their own structures.

> The kids just couldn't stop rushing and trying to cut each other off to lead the line. I knew we had to have a class meeting about fairness.
>
> When we were talking, I said, "You know, if you're in the Monday group and you lead the line to lunch, don't you think it's fair for somebody else to lead it when it's time to go to the library? And then, if we go outside, maybe somebody else will step forward? And then somebody else when we go home in the afternoon?"
>
> Everybody agreed that was fair. The idea didn't come from me; it came from Louise. Earlier in the day she'd said to me, "You know, Ms. Ecken, this person's already led the line today, so don't you think maybe I could lead it?"

However, as late as March in the first year, some of Laura's students were still arguing over who would be first in line.

> Denise and Tyrone are both in the same group, and they've been into it big time about who's going to lead the line.
>
> When I would ask, "Who led it to the library?" "Who led it to lunch?" Tyrone would just lie, claiming that he didn't lead the last time.
>
> Everybody else would be saying, "Yes, you did!" Then he'd say he forgot.
>
> Finally, I just asked myself why I was still dealing with lines, and that's what I told Denise and Tyrone. I said, "Every day I hold this line up talking about who led here and who led there, when you all already know. So we're going on, and if you two have to be last in line every day because you can't figure out how to stand in it, that's your business. I'm

> not taking any more time talking to you about who's been first, because you all know what's fair and that's what I expect."

Laura believed that Tyrone and Denise really did know how to come up with a fair way to share the privilege of leading the line, and she was angry with them for failing to do so. Over the weekend, Laura and I talked about the fact that in times of strong desire it is sometimes difficult to guide one's behavior with reason or moral principle. In light of this conversation and with some distance from the situation, Laura thought that perhaps Tyrone and Denise couldn't think about fairness in the very moment when each desperately wanted to be first in line. She decided to make it easier for them by asking them at the beginning of the day on Monday to come up with a fair plan, before leading the line was an immediate issue.

Monday morning, just as the kids were entering the classroom, Laura took Tyrone and Denise aside.

> I said, "Before you come in the room, you two need to come up with a plan for the line, because I don't have the time or the energy to deal with it any more."
>
> Denise was real huffy and started to walk into the room.
>
> I said, "Oh no, Denise, right now. You need to stay out here with Tyrone and get yourselves a plan."
>
> A little bit later, they were so happy. They had this plan that Tyrone was going to line up first for lunch and Denise was going to get in front of him for special area. They were just thrilled.
>
> Then, on Tuesday when I noticed them lining up, I said, "You know, guys, there are two other people in this group."
>
> Before I could say another thing, Denise said, "Yeah, we got to get a plan with them," and she turned around and started talking with them.

Handing the problem over to Tyrone and Denise at a point when they would have a reasonable chance of solving it got Laura out of the enforcer role and conveyed her confidence that they could come up with a fair solution. Having them share their plan with her served as a kind of oral commitment or contract and also meant she could help them adjust their plan, if necessary.

Scaffolding

Scaffolding, in the sense in which it was first introduced by Wood, Bruner, and Ross (1976), involves providing students with the right level of support so that they can succeed at academic learning tasks that might otherwise be beyond them. The assumption is that the students want to succeed but need a little help or support to do so. Laura applied this concept not just to academic learning but to helping her students behave appropriately. Laura used scaffolding to help students solve particular problems on the spot, as well as to help them climb out of patterns of behavior that were causing them trouble.

Scaffolding Solutions to Impasses

Sometimes Laura's supportive responses to misbehaving students made her classroom discipline invisible. Early in the first year, before students were comfortable working in partnerships and before they knew one another well, Tralin and Janice were paired to work on a new book together. They refused even to do the first activity. Laura provided the scaffolding that both girls needed to solve their problem.

> Tuesday we started the *Outside Dog*. I put the students in partnerships and asked them to get to know their partner by talking about the kind of pet each of them would like. They had three questions to get them started.
>
> After their interviews, partners were supposed to come up and tell me about each other's pet and then go make a picture about the pets.
>
> Janice and Tralin absolutely refused to work with each other. Janice went over and sat on the couch and Tralin stayed put in her chair.
>
> At first I didn't do anything; I just said to the class, "In fifteen minutes, we are going to get together and you can introduce your partner and tell about their pet."
>
> I thought I would let Janice and Tralin figure out on their own that they had put themselves in a position that they really didn't want to be in. So I acted like I didn't even notice that they were not working together.
>
> I walked around commenting on people's work, and when I got close to where Janice was sitting, she said, "I don't want to sit where she's sitting."
>
> I said, "Oh, well, that's your decision, that's your choice," and I just went on.
>
> Then I went over in Tralin's direction and she said, "I don't want a pet. I don't ever want a pet."
>
> I said, "Tralin, don't you ever think that you would like to have a dog or a cat, or maybe a goldfish or—"
>
> "Hate them!"
>
> I said, "Why aren't you working with Janice?"
>
> She said, "Because I don't want a pet. I don't want to do this."

> "Well, you know," I said, "Janice probably wants to tell you about her pet, and we're going to meet in about ten minutes to hear about everyone's pet."
>
> So Tralin got up and walked over and she started talking to Janice. I heard her say, "Do you want a pet?"
>
> Janice told her all about her pet, and then Tralin decided she did want a pet. They went on with the activity like nothing had ever happened, but they weren't near finished drawing their picture when it was about time for the class to introduce their partners.
>
> I met with them and said, "I know you're not finished; you got started late and you will have some time later, but that does not mean you can't come up here and introduce your partner. You don't have to have a picture to do it."
>
> So they did it. They introduced each other and their pets. Since then we have done several more partner activities for *Outside Dog*, and those two have done fine.

There was no formula here, no threat, and no coercion. Laura simply tried to figure out what she could do to help the girls comply with her reasonable request—the class assignment. She allowed the girls some time to sit in their respective places, and she moved near to them to allow them to initiate a conversation with her. When she didn't find an opening with Janice, she moved near Tralin. When Tralin seemed unresponsive, she didn't issue an ultimatum but suggested a solution—that Tralin could ask Janice about a pet she wanted even if Tralin herself didn't want one. She also reminded Tralin that the class would be getting together in a few minutes to share their work. Laura believed that Tralin wanted to do the work and wanted to have something to share with her classmates, and so she tried to provide the support Tralin needed to override her emotional response and manage her own behavior in a positive way.

A final important feature of Laura's response was that she did not make the girls suffer the "natural consequences" of their stubbornness. Instead she did everything she could to help them be successful, even though they got a late start. She wanted them to experience success, even if it required her help.

Private Signals for Problem Behavior Patterns

When a misbehavior was recurrent, or part of a pattern, Laura usually took the time (not necessarily at the moment) to talk through the problem with the student and engage the student in devising a plan to prevent future occurrences. Again, her goal was to be in a partnership with the student, but in these cases it was important to be explicit about what problem they were trying to solve so that the student could recognize it and be accepting of direct help. We saw an example of this in the last chapter when Laura and Tralin agreed that Tralin would stop groaning when a new activity was introduced and Laura would immediately check in with her to see if she needed help. Laura engaged in this kind of explicit scaffolding with a number of her students.

For example, throughout the first year Rebecca would angrily withdraw from classroom activities and often refused to engage in learning activities. Because Rebecca did not complain about the learning activities themselves, at first Laura thought that Rebecca's problem was just stubbornness or a need to be defiant. However, as Laura reflected over the summer, she detected a pattern in Rebecca's behavior suggesting that Rebecca refused to do certain assignments because she was afraid that she couldn't do them. Laura talked this over with Rebecca, and they agreed that Laura would be better at providing Rebecca with the help she needed, and Rebecca would be better at signaling her need for help without withdrawing.

> One of the times Rebecca called me in the summer we talked about her throwing fits in the class and being asked to leave. I said, "Rebecca, you know what I think is happening when you throw those fits? I think you think the work's going to be too hard and you can't do it. So instead of trying to do it or asking for help, you throw a fit.
>
> "How about if you need help, you ask for it? And if I see you getting out of whack like that, I'm just going to say, 'You're doing that thing again.' Then you will know that I see that you're going off the deep end about something."
>
> So we agreed to try that.
>
> One of our first activities this year was to make a bunch of charts to get to know about our class: How Old Are We? Brothers and Sisters Venn Diagram, When Are Our Birthdays?
>
> All together we reviewed the first two charts. I asked, "What does this chart tell us?" and wrote on the board what people answered.
>
> When we came to the birthday chart I said, "Okay, I'm going to give everyone a piece of paper, and this time instead of doing it as a class, look at the chart by yourself and write down what it tells you."
>
> Rebecca started folding her arms and scooting back in the chair. I went over and whispered, "You're doing that thing again. Do you need some help with this?"
>
> And so we looked at it together. I told her a couple of things that she might want to write down, and then she saw how to do it, and she was fine.

> So at least we can have a conversation when she gets out of whack. It doesn't mean she's always going to unfold those arms, but at least now we have a starting point.

Laura's faith that Rebecca did indeed want to do the work and her willingness to help Rebecca get over her initial fear helped to keep Rebecca engaged and trying. In her conversations with students over ways she might support them in controlling their behavior, Laura provided them with the words to describe their feelings and actions—a first step in gaining cognitive control over emotions and behaviors.

Laura's observation to Rebecca, "You're doing that thing again," was a kind of private signal to scaffold Rebecca's ability to recognize a behavior that didn't work for her and make a better response. Laura found private signals, whether verbal or nonverbal, very effective in reminding misbehaving students of their partnership with her and her trust in their good intentions.

With Martin, however, Laura encountered a pattern of behavior that was too complex to be handled simply with a private signal. But that is how Laura started working with him on his pattern of embarrassing or hurting the feelings of other students. Because Martin could be so helpful and endearing at times, Laura believed that he didn't mean his nasty remarks and that they were a kind of habit.

> This morning Leonard brought up the homework, and before I could even comment, Martin said, "He never does his homework!"
>
> Last week, Candace said she wanted to sing a song, and before she could finish the sentence, Martin said, "You don't know any song! You're not singing anything!"
>
> In the morning meeting on Wednesday, John showed his brand new shoes and told about getting them from J.C. Penney.
>
> Martin didn't hear the part about J.C. Penney and asked John where he got his shoes.
>
> Before John could answer, Kenny yelled out, "Don't make fun of those shoes!"
>
> Other people said, "He's not making fun of them; he's just asking where he got them!"
>
> Kenny said, "Well, he keeps making fun of mine. He keeps asking me where I got those $10.99 boots, so I thought he'd make fun of John's."
>
> Then Candace started to talk, and Martin began making fun and rolling his eyes and laughing, and he got everybody else laughing.
>
> She asked him to stop and I said, "You know, it doesn't make me feel very good that we're sitting in a classroom and laughing when a member of this class wants to talk."

People kind of straightened up and Candace was telling her story, so then Martin looked over at Louise and said, "You stink," like he's whispering.

Louise got this look on her face and started pulling on her shirt and said, "Martin, I can't help it if I stink." He just kind of dropped it.

At the end of the meeting, somebody's wish for the day was, "I wish we could obey the teacher today. I hope we have a good day and work in our partnerships, and I hope we can obey the teacher."

Martin said, "Yeah, right, like we're going to obey the teacher."

At that moment all I said to him was to try, but a little after lunch, when people were working on something, I asked him to come and talk with me.

I asked him what he meant by saying, "Yeah, right, like we're going to obey the teacher."

He said, "Well, Ms. Ecken, we're going to do what we want."

"Martin," I said, "when I look at you during the day, most of the time you're right on target with us and doing what we all do—doing as I have asked. That's a way of obeying the teacher."

He just said, "Okay," like he understood that he was obeying but without admitting it.

But, of course, where he doesn't obey is when I ask him not to say mean things to people.

I said, "I've noticed that when people want to share, you immediately want to jump in and comment on it and mess with them or say something ugly about it. I'd really like to see you work on that."

Later, when we were in the middle of a lesson, somebody said something and Martin said something back to them, so I asked him if he remembered what we talked about.

He said, "Could you just give me the thumbs-up signal to remind me?"

I had to laugh thinking about it. What's that going to look like when anybody comes in and Martin's insulting people and I'm giving him the thumbs-up?

As Laura came to understand, Martin's insulting behavior was part of an entrenched way of dealing with the world—a stance that directly followed from his mistrust of Laura and his classmates. He desperately wanted Laura's care and good will, but he could not trust her enough to let her also give her care to others or to depend on her to give it to him willingly. Instead, he constantly demanded her care and tried to keep others from getting it. Martin's teasing and hurtful remarks did eventually decrease, dramatically, but it took more than private signals to help him stop.

Explicit Teaching to Foster Social and Emotional Skills and Understanding

Because a number of Laura's students were deeply mistrustful and had poorly developed social and emotional skills, they were often quick to take offense, responding with anger to unintentional or relatively harmless actions. Some were easily hurt and tended to withdraw, seemingly unable to defend themselves. Some dissolved at the slightest frustration. Some would strike out when things did not go their way. And they frequently denied any responsibility for their own behaviors. When these children entered Laura's classroom, physically and cognitively they were six-, seven-, and eight-year-olds, but socially and emotionally they were like toddlers, struggling for levels of autonomy they could not handle and unable to regulate their emotions or monitor their own behavior.

Although the long-term process of building trusting relationships was essential to eliminating the main cause of these behaviors, Laura also needed to find ways to teach her students the social and emotional skills they were lacking. For example, particularly during the first year, a number of Laura's students withdrew or became angry and disorganized at the tiniest disappointment or slightest suggestion that they needed to do something differently. They would respond this way whether the suggestions were about their academic work or their classroom behavior. In order to keep her class running smoothly and help her students grow in social, emotional, and moral understanding, Laura often responded to student misbehavior with explicit instruction in social and emotional skills, along with more subtle support or scaffolding.

> When the kids came back from computer class, they were really, really angry. The computer teacher came down and told me that a lot of people didn't finish the cards they were working on but that she had told them not to worry. She told them she would check with me whether they could come up on Thursday morning to finish. I told everyone that was okay with me, but when I tried to start the reading lesson, they started slamming stuff and laying their heads down.
>
> Finally, after trying to start the lesson for two or three minutes, I said, "Okay, guys, I can't teach with this going on. I know you didn't get your cards finished, but this is part of growing up. Mrs. Clarkson said you can come Thursday morning. Shake it off."
>
> That didn't work. So I said, "Put your heads down—for five minutes—and think about what we need to do and how we're going to get it done, because I cannot go on with this lesson like this."

After about four or five minutes, I got the book and I went back on the carpeting. I said, "All right. Anybody who is ready to do the lesson, meet me on the carpet."

Well, only a very few of them came—maybe four or five—but I kind of had a feeling that the others wanted to. So I said, "I'm going to start this lesson on the count of three. Anybody who's not back here cannot come in, cannot interrupt us in the middle of it."

So I counted, "One, two," and then everybody was back there except for Nina. At that time I didn't realize she hadn't come. I thought they all were back there—it looked like the whole entire group.

So we did the lesson; we read the story and talked about it a little bit. Then they set out to write role-plays.

Faced with a group of extremely agitated students, Laura at first tried to help them see that they should not be so upset—that their emotional response was out of proportion to what had happened. Her request that they "shake it off" was a lesson in emotion regulation. However, it didn't work. Her second lesson in emotion regulation—asking them to put their heads down and think about how to get engaged in the lesson—didn't work either. But still, time had passed and it's likely that her students' emotions had subsided somewhat. Hoping this was the case, Laura asked them to come to the carpet where she was waiting to start the lesson. When only a few came, Laura still gave the others a little more time by counting to three before going on with the lesson. She did threaten them, but the threat was that they would not be able to join the lesson once she had begun. As it turned out, all the students engaged in the learning activity with enthusiasm, even the one child, Nina, who had refused to come to the carpet.

Nina was Kenny's partner. When we left the carpeting and the kids spread out in the room to do their role-plays, I noticed that Nina had her chair turned to the back of the room. And Kenny was doing all the writing.

So I walked over there and said, "Nina, are you and Kenny talking this over?"

She said, "No."

Kenny immediately said, "She never came to the carpeting. She doesn't want to do this. So I'm just doing it myself."

I said, "Nina, what's the problem?"

She said, "I didn't get to do my card. I didn't get it finished."

I said, "You know, practically the whole class didn't get it finished, but you can go up Thursday and get it finished. What's the problem?"

She said, "I'm really mad about it."

> So I said, "Well, you know, you've got this to do now, and if you don't come on, you're not going to get finished and Kenny's not going to have a partner. Do you think it's fair that Kenny has to write the whole thing? Your part and his part too?"
>
> She said, "No. But I'm really mad."
>
> I said, "Well, I tell you what, I need a message delivered to Ms. Davis. Will you run this note down to her and stop and get a drink, and then see if you don't maybe feel like getting with this?"
>
> When she came back in, she sat down with Kenny and read over what he had written. She said, "Can we change this one little part? It would sound better if I said this." He agreed and they just went on with the role-play. They got it done.

It was more important to Laura that Nina get involved in the lesson than suffer the consequences of her "poor choice" not to join the class for the lesson. Nina was caught up in her anger, which probably escalated as she sat by herself while the rest of the class listened to and discussed the story. By asking Nina to run an errand for her and suggesting that she get a drink on the way back, Laura subtly conveyed that she cared about her and gave her some time to pull herself together and make her own decision to join in the activity.

Nina and Kenny were not the only partnership to have trouble with this lesson.

> Tralin was working with Rachel. While I was with Nina and Kenny, I heard her say, "It's what I put and I'm not changing it!"
>
> Rachel said, "It doesn't sound right."
>
> The reason it didn't sound right was that Tralin was doing something they still do sometimes—she was writing a story instead of a role-play. Apparently she had gotten almost half a page written before Rachel said, "It doesn't sound right."
>
> So I went to them and said, "Tralin, I know you've done a lot of work on this; I can see that. But if it doesn't sound right, you might want to think about it. And you might also want to think about how we are when we work with partners. It doesn't always have to be your way. Just because you put it, doesn't mean that you have to stick with it.
>
> Tralin said, "We've already done it!"
>
> I said, "I know, but you know what? Serious learners, sometimes if things aren't going well, they'll just start over and think of something else and get on the right track. You've got time; you could just turn the paper over." Then I left them and went on.

About fifteen minutes later, we all got together so partners could present their role-plays. They were right on target. People were really getting into the book and making the role-plays real.

Afterwards we talked about the successes they had, and a couple of them said, "We got right to work."

I said, "And did you get finished?"

They said, "Yeah, we got finished and we practiced it."

I said, "And how does it feel?"

One of them said, "It feels great!"

So we talked a little bit about that. I was hoping maybe this would give them the message that not only do you get your work done and you learn something but there's an added benefit that you feel this sense of accomplishment. You feel really good about yourself and about what you've done.

When they talked about the rough spots, Nina said, "I didn't want to do it. I was really, really mad. But then Mrs. Ecken talked to me and I knew I wasn't going to get anything done with how I was acting, so I took a walk and I came back and got finished."

Then we had a little talk about that—that sometimes you need to just get away from your anger, to take a break from it so that you can come back and do what you need to do.

I told them, "You can use that in your life. If you're in a situation where you just can't seem to get over it, walk away from it for a little while. Take a little walk around and come back."

I think that was helpful to them. A lot of times, they don't know how to handle getting mad, how to save face, how to quit being mad.

Then Tralin said, "I had a rough spot. I'd written a whole lot and it didn't sound right, but I'd already done it. And then you know what? I just turned the page over and we started again."

It sounded so simple when she said it: "I just turned the page over."

I said to the class, "You know, serious learners do that. Sometimes you get stuck and you're heading down the wrong path. You've just got to stop yourself and look at what you're doing and think maybe I need to start this over and do it in a different way."

So, I keep trying to send these messages to them.

Laura's approach with her class and with Nina and Tralin in this activity was to use minimal coercion, to try to work in a partnership with her students but not to hesitate to use her authority when she needed to. For example, she could have told her angry and complaining students to sit down and engage the lesson, sending the first few who caused trouble from the group, but she would have had a group of reluctant learners and several who were not engaged at all. She could have ordered Nina to work with Kenny or made her stay out of the lesson, leaving Kenny to work on his own. Either way it would have resulted in an angry Nina and less learning for both children. She could have demanded that Tralin start over or hovered over her to see that she did, but by making a suggestion and leaving Tralin to decide whether to comply or not, she gave Tralin an opportunity to practice the important emotional skill of self-regulation. And Nina and Tralin's pride in their accomplishments gave Laura an opening to provide the whole class with brief but highly contextualized lessons in the emotional skills of "getting away from your anger" and "starting over if you find yourself going down the wrong path."

When such scaffolding works, it provides the student with an opportunity to practice self-regulation, and it further builds the teacher-child relationship because teacher and child both experience the success of their partnership.

Such scaffolding doesn't always work, of course, and in these cases the student may not be able to escape the unproductive behavior. When this happened with Laura's misbehaving students, she usually tried to reflect with them in a way that would help build their understanding and skills, for the next time they felt stuck.

> On Tuesday we were out walking laps of the yard for exercise. Tyrone and John were on either side of me, and they wanted to know about the Vietnam War. So I was trying to explain it to them when Martin came up and got in between Tyrone and me. Tyrone told him to move and when he didn't move right that minute, Tyrone threw himself on the ground and started screaming and yelling.
>
> I said, "Tyrone, come on. Get up and let's go."
>
> He wouldn't. We just kept on walking.
>
> When we came around again, I said, "Tyrone, you're just hurting yourself. Come on. Get up here. If you want to talk about something or tell me what's wrong, fine. I'll be glad to listen. But you need to get up off the ground."
>
> He wouldn't.
>
> We walked one more time around and lined up to go in.
>
> Then Tyrone came up to me and said, "We were talking about Vietnam. I wanted to know what happened over there and you were telling John and me, and Martin just came and butted in."
>
> I said, "Well, Tyrone, you threw yourself on the ground instead of standing up and telling me what was going on and what you were upset about. So how can I deal with that?"

> He said, "I don't know."
>
> I said, "You've got to tell people what you're thinking and what's going on so that they can help you.
>
> "When you threw yourself down on the ground, what did you do? You pulled yourself out of the walk and you pulled yourself away from the explanation—because I kept explaining what went on. And you sat there and didn't even get your exercise. What could you have done instead?"
>
> He said, "I could've just told you."
>
> I asked him why he didn't, and he said, "Because Martin wouldn't move and it made me mad."
>
> I said, "Well, you could've told me that, too, couldn't you?" And he agreed.
>
> At the end of the day when the class talked about what went well and what didn't, Tyrone spoke up. He said, "I had a rough spot and I didn't take care of it. I just sat on the ground, but that doesn't help if you don't tell people."
>
> And so I said, "Okay, let's talk about this a little bit."
>
> And Tyrone kind of talked that through. He's beginning to see that throwing fits is no way to get your point across. And that's an important thing for all of them to learn.

Laura tried to take the long view with her students. She needed to figure out how to be supportive without supporting their immaturity—without supporting behavior that would be ruinous to their futures. This was not always easy for Laura, and she sometimes felt that she was being too tough. It was difficult, for example, for her to leave Tyrone sitting on the ground, but she believed that he desperately needed to stop his tantrums and that he was capable of doing so. She felt that she could not let him use a tantrum as a way to get what he wanted, even if his anger was justified.

The fact that Tyrone was able to tell the class about his rough spot and verbalize what he could have done instead reassured Laura that she was probably striking the right balance with Tyrone. It felt to Laura that they had achieved a strong partnership—that they were working together to help him acquire the skills, understanding, and attitudes he would need for a successful life.

A few weeks later, this partnership was further confirmed.

> Tyrone and Gabrielle were in line in the hall, ready to go to lunch, and I saw him hit Gabrielle's hand really hard. It made a really loud sound, and she jerked her hand back.
>
> I said, "Tyrone, that's not acceptable here. You're not to touch the other students."

He ran out of the line and back into the classroom, yelling, "You're unfair. She hit me."

I walked over to where he was sitting and said, "Tyrone, I can't hear what you're saying because of how you're carrying on—all this screaming and yelling and running out of the line. If you have something to say, you can just say it."

So he said, "Ms. Ecken, I didn't hit her. We were both giving each other five. We were hitting each other five and that's why it made that loud sound."

I said, "Why didn't you just say that to me?"

And he said, "Because you said I hit her and I didn't."

I said, "That's what I saw, but you knew it was something different, so why didn't you just say, 'Ms. Ecken, we were both giving fives?'

"I could've heard that if you weren't running back in the room and saying I was unfair. It's really hard to listen to people when they're not calm or telling me something in a respectful way. What are you going to do next time somebody says something to you that's wrong and you need to explain?"

He said, "Talk in a respectful way to them so they can hear me."

Then he said, "Well, say it again."

And I said, "What? Say what again, Tyrone?"

He said, "Tell me I hit Gabrielle again so I can practice it."

So I said, "Tyrone, stop hitting Gabrielle! That's never acceptable and it'll never be acceptable here."

Then he just said, "Ms. Ecken, we were doing high-fives and we were hitting each other together."

I said, "Oh, well, you two need to cut that out because somebody might get hurt."

And, you know, we do that, we practice that kind of stuff.

Both of these incidents with Tyrone happened in the spring of the second year. Laura and he had been together for nearly two years; they trusted each other. And by this time, Laura was generally able to provide Tyrone the levels of support and challenge he needed.

o

Laura, like most teachers, sometimes became angry and punitive with her students, but she fought against this tendency in herself. She knew that the most seriously misbehaving students in her classroom had experienced plenty of punishment in their young lives and that it had neither helped them become caring and responsible nor had it kindled their love of learning. Instead, Laura sought to engage each of her students in a partnership with her—a partnership for academic learning and a partnership for behaving in kind, fair, and responsible ways. She believed that her students wanted to learn and wanted to have a positive, nurturing relationship with her and that it was her job to provide the structure, guidance, and support necessary for them to do so.

Once Laura believed in her students, even her frequently misbehaving students, she was able to view student misbehavior in the light that she viewed mistakes in academic learning. Mistakes call for teaching, not punishment. Thus Laura applied the principles of good teaching to develop her approach to classroom discipline or to responding to misbehavior.

She structured the environment to make it manageable, and she tried to provide each student with the scaffolding or support he or she needed to be successful. If the student failed, she made adjustments and tried again. She exercised clear authority, but she also worked to respect her students' need for autonomy. She explicitly taught her students important emotional skills,

Key Points: Managing Mistakes and Misbehavior by Taking a Teaching Stance

- Create and discuss with students procedures for handling routine activities (such as leaving the classroom for lunch, gathering for class meetings, using the restroom).
- Decide on structures that will keep the classroom calm and productive.
- Allow enough freedom to provide sufficient challenge for them to grow in self-management.
- When students are engaged in an unproductive disagreement or appear unwilling to comply with a reasonable request, try to figure out what's wrong and provide the help they need.
- Help students anticipate the social or emotional challenges they are likely to face in an upcoming activity and discuss ways they might meet those challenges.
- Provide opportunities for students to practice and reflect on their use of social and emotional skills.

such as how to regulate their emotions and guide their behavior through self-talk, and she provided opportunities to practice and reflect on those skills. However, creating a manageable environment, scaffolding, and teaching her students social and emotional skills were only part of Laura's overall approach to managing misbehavior.

As she worked to develop students' social and emotional skills, she also worked to build their empathy and their moral understanding. For although Laura had to exercise considerable control in the classroom, her goal for her students was autonomy—moral autonomy as well as intellectual autonomy. In the next chapter, we'll see how Laura worked to build her students' capacity for empathy, restitution, and moral reflection. We will also see some of the practical methods she used when teaching and reminders were not enough.

6

MANAGING MISTAKES AND MISBEHAVIOR

WHEN TEACHING AND REMINDING AREN'T ENOUGH

Tralin has a friend in the room who's almost like a cousin, a new little girl, Ella. When we were lining up in the cafeteria to go outside, Ella got in line and Tyrone was next. But Tralin was trying to rush so she could stand by Ella, and she just shoved Tyrone out of the line.

Tyrone came up and told me what happened so I went back and said, "Tralin, we don't treat people like that in this classroom."

She called Tyrone a liar, and I said, "No, it's his place in the line, so get in line. We're heading outside."

Before we could get all the way outside, she was screaming at Tyrone, "Your mom uses crack cocaine! Your mom's a crackhead!"

SOME MISBEHAVIORS, while disruptive, cause little or no obvious harm to anyone other than the misbehaving children themselves. Others result in clear harm. As we saw earlier, when Laura reflected at the end of Year 1, she decided that she needed a stronger response to hurtful behavior. In Year 2, she stopped such behavior immediately. Sometimes she just gave a very firm reminder or command to stop, but more often she tried to help the misbehaving child see and understand the harm he or she had caused and firmly requested that the offending child think about and find a way to repair the harm. Laura used such incidents to develop her students' capacity for empathy and moral reflection and to build their understanding of the moral obligation to repair any harm they might have caused, as well as to signal how very important being kind was to Laura and the community.

Empathy, Restitution, and Moral Reflection

Helping children see the distress they have caused another and encouraging them to feel remorseful is a common parental response to their children's aggressive or inconsiderate behavior. Martin Hoffman (1978, 2000) has called this approach to misbehavior "induction." His research has shown it to be far superior to punishment in fostering prosocial behavior.

Early in the second year, when Tralin lost her temper and told Tyrone his mother was a crackhead, Laura made sure Tralin thought about how she had made Tyrone feel, as well as how to make it up to him.

> I asked her to just step aside so we could talk. I asked her why she had called his mother that, and she said, "Because she is and he lied on me and said I pushed him out of the line and I didn't touch him."
>
> I said, "You know, Tralin, you're lying to yourself. I saw you push him out of the line. You wanted to be with Ella, and so you shoved him out of the way. You know I'm not going to allow that, and I'm not going to allow you to call his mother names. Can you imagine how painful it is for Tyrone to know that about his mother, to suffer all the pain from that, and then to have to be at school and have you make his pain even worse? That's just not right."
>
> I asked her if she thought that maybe we ought to call Granny and let her know that this is what she's doing in school, but what really needed to happen, I thought, was for Tralin to make it up to Tyrone in some way. I said, "You know, you said some ugly things to Tyrone and I think it'd probably be best to take care of that."
>
> She just looked at me, so I said, "When you have a plan, just find me and let me know, but I think that you should take care of it before the day's over."
>
> About an hour later, Tralin came up to me and kind of stood there, so I asked her if she had a plan.
>
> She said, "I need to tell him that I'm sorry and that I didn't mean any of it. I was just mad and that's why I said it."
>
> I asked her if she wanted him to come out in the hall so she could tell him that privately, and she said, "Yeah, but first I need a drink."
>
> I told her, "Listen, you go get a drink and I'll tell Tyrone you want to talk to him in the hall."
>
> When Tyrone came back in, he was happy and so was Tralin.

She told me, "He said it was all right."

I said, "You know, next time you get mad about something, tell the person why you're mad. That's your best course of action. So they understand why you're upset."

I couldn't have asked for a better response. After I told Tralin that she was lying to herself and that she should think about that, she did. And I had nothing to do with that thinking. She came to the understanding that she acted that way because she was really mad. And I think that's pretty powerful for her to be able to figure out that she's doing things because she's really mad. Not because Tyrone deserved to hear about his mother.

But, you know, that's a year of experience with Tralin. I'm not going to get in power struggles with her, or anybody, for that matter. There's no learning that takes place in those things. And probably more than 50 percent of the time you lose that power struggle. So why get into it?

Laura could respond as firmly as she did with Tralin because she actually saw what happened between the children and because she knew both children well and had a secure, positive relationship with them. Laura might have taken the two children aside when the initial pushing incident happened and asked them to settle their problem peacefully. But she was in a rush to get her class out of the cafeteria so the next group of children could come in. She thought she could put a stop to the problem by simply giving Tyrone his rightful place in line.

Laura, like most teachers, sometimes tried to handle a problem herself so the class could get on with its activities. This time that didn't work and Laura's solution made the situation worse, leaving Tralin angry and precipitating a more egregious act on Tralin's part. At that point, Laura's goal was no longer just to make the problem go away. Now she felt she needed to help Tralin understand the harm she had caused Tyrone, her culpability, and her obligation to try to repair the harm. She didn't give Tralin a choice about whether to repair the harm—she told her she needed to. Laura's direct instruction to Tralin is very like the kind of direct instruction that caring parents provide their children when they violate important family values (Hoffman, 2000; Noddings, 2002).

Laura was invoking a moral principle and helping Tralin understand that in a caring community it is a moral obligation to repair as much as possible any harm you cause. But, as was characteristic of Laura, she left Tralin to come up with her own plan. By so doing, she conveyed her trust in Tralin and maximized Tralin's autonomy in a situation involving required compliance. Laura wanted Tralin to feel empathy for Tyrone and to act from a sense of care and moral obligation to repair the harm she caused. Tralin rose to Laura's expectations.

In Year 2, making restitution was almost always a part of Laura's response to misbehavior that involved clear harm. Laura consistently sent the message by her words, her requirements, and her own behaviors that there is a moral obligation to repair harm you have caused, insofar as that is possible.

Laura's students did not resent her requests that they think of a way to put things right with the person they had harmed, whether that person was another student, Laura herself, or another teacher. The students were not always able to think of a way to repair their harm, but when they needed suggestions, they readily accepted Laura's help.

> Louise, in computer class, did about everything the substitute told her not to do. If the teacher said, "Put the earphones on and plug them in so we can't hear the volume on your computer," Louise took them out and turned the computer up as loud as it could go. When the substitute told them to sit on the floor and listen to directions, Louise got up and went over and started a computer—just started working on one. She was clearly out of line.
>
> When I picked them up, the teacher asked Louise to tell me what she had done. The teacher kept prompting Louise until she told me all the things she did. I asked Louise why she did them, and all she could say was, "I just did it."
>
> I said, "Well, you know how to take care of it. I want you to have a seat right here while I walk the class downstairs. And when we're out of here, I want you to take care of it."
>
> She came down to the classroom a few minutes later and said, "I apologized and said I was sorry."
>
> I said, "Okay, how are you going to make it up to her?"
>
> She just looked at me.
>
> I said, "You interrupted the class. You wouldn't do as you were told. Don't you think you need to make that up to her?"
>
> She said yes but that she didn't know how.
>
> I asked, "What does the teacher have to do at the end of the day before she leaves?"
>
> She said, "Turn all the computers off."
>
> I said, "Do you think maybe that's something you could help her with?"
>
> And then Louise was real happy and she ran back upstairs. When she came down, she said, "The teacher said that was good, that I could come up at three o'clock and turn the computers off for her."

Louise remembered on her own, because I forgot. At three o'clock she just said, "I'm going up."

Eventually, most of Laura's students got to the point where they could recognize and admit their wrongful actions and accept the moral obligation to make reparation, as Louise did in remembering on her own to go and help the computer teacher.

Laura wasn't always aware of her students' hurtful actions, and she didn't always have enough energy or resolve to help them repair the harm they had caused. When her students, on their own initiative, began trying to make reparations, Laura knew that they were beginning to internalize this basic moral principle.

Tangela had trouble all week long, didn't want to come to group, didn't want to sit down and work. On Thursday she wouldn't come into the group to talk about how the lesson went.

I said, "Tangela, you need to get up here with the rest of us."

So she pulled her chair closer, but she wouldn't get in the group. She sat a foot or two away. I started the sharing and all of a sudden she just picked up her chair and turned it backwards.

I went over and talked to her. I didn't ask her what was going on, which was a very big mistake. I said, "You need to be part of this. You have things to say that the class needs to hear. And you also need to hear what your classmates are saying. You can't be in the conversation when you're not even looking at us."

She didn't turn around.

I went on with the meeting and we talked about successes. I said, "What went well?"

People said things like, "We got to work on time." "We got finished because we got to work on time." They started talking about how good it feels when you just do what you're supposed to do.

Then I said, "Any rough spots?"

Lana raised her hand and said, "Chantelle just keeps making fun of Tangela, and then when Tangela was sitting back there paying attention to you, Chantelle leaned over right in her face and went 'boo!' and that's when Tangela turned her chair around."

I said, "Chantelle, what's going on?"

Chantelle said, "I don't like her looking by me."

I said, "Here I am thinking that Tangela doesn't want any part of our group and doesn't want to be a serious learner, and it's not that at all. It's that you're harassing her.

"I have a serious problem with this. You know what else? I'm thinking about the very beginning of school when you screamed out that you

> had no friends in here, and Tangela is the one who stood up and said, 'Yes, you do, I'm your friend.' I'm just sitting here thinking how hard this must be for Tangela to be treated like this by you."
>
> Then I dropped it and we went on to other people who had rough spots.
>
> All of a sudden Chantelle started screaming. She wasn't saying anything, just crying in a scream.
>
> I said, "Chantelle, what is the matter with you?"
>
> She yelled, "I need to talk to Tangela in the hallway!"
>
> I said, "Tangela, would you mind going out in the hallway and talking to Chantelle?"
>
> So they went out in the hallway. When they came back in, Chantelle had quit crying and Tangela joined the group.
>
> Later, we were on our way to lunch and Chantelle said, "I want to tell you what I said to Tangela. I told her I was sorry and that she was my only friend at one time and that I was going to try and make it up to her."
>
> I said, "I think that was a good thing to do. How do you think that you can make it up to her?"
>
> Chantelle said, "By not bothering her or making fun of her."
>
> They were fine Thursday afternoon, and then Friday afternoon when we were painting, after Tangela got finished with her painting, she went and sat by Chantelle and they talked about what Chantelle was painting, and Tangela, who is very talented, gave her some ideas about how she could do it.

Despite Laura's efforts to take a nonblaming stance toward her students, she had blamed Tangela for not coming to the meeting. Laura thought that Tangela was not trying hard enough to regulate her emotions, and she believed that encouraging Tangela to join the group would solve the problem. When it didn't, she decided to let Tangela stay with her back to the group and go on with the meeting. Fortunately, Lana helped Laura understand what was happening to upset Tangela. Surprised and now upset with herself and Chantelle, Laura helped Chantelle see the harm she had caused Tangela and the injustice of it. But at that point Laura didn't know what more to do. It was Chantelle who had the moral feelings and the moral courage to seek to make things right with Tangela.

Reminders and Written Reflections

Not all of Laura's responses to misbehavior involved careful scaffolding, instruction, or reflection and reparation. In fact, most did not. Frequently, Laura's students misbehaved because momentarily they lost focus or let their self-interest get the better of them. Then Laura would just remind them to pay attention, be considerate, quit fooling around, or stop whatever they were doing. That was it, just a reminder or a request to "get back on track." And that was usually enough; they knew what they needed to do.

However, when a reminder wasn't enough or when the particular behavior was not harmful or interfering with the rest of the class, Laura would generally do one of two things. She would frequently ignore the behavior when stopping it wasn't worth the disruption. At other times, she let the behavior go, believing that the child's need to do what he or she was doing outweighed the transgression or that eventually the child would pull him- or herself together. For example, one day Denise, it seemed to Laura, needed to stay at the cookie-decorating table even though her turn was over.

> Last week, I brought in cookies for them to decorate. I went to the bakery and got three sugar cookies for each one of them, and I brought in icing and different kinds of sprinkles. Kids love that kind of stuff, and I don't think many of them get to do it very often.
>
> I set up the cookie-decorating table for four people to work at a time. The rest of the class was reading or doing other work. People would just come back as the seats emptied and take their turns.
>
> After Denise finished her cookies, she couldn't bring herself to leave the table. She just kind of stayed there. I said, "Denise, why don't you pick out some books and go sit down and read with somebody?"
>
> And she did—for about a minute. Then she was back. She was asking the other kids, "What do you think you want to put on that cookie? I'll hand it to you."
>
> Or if she saw someone struggling because they were trying to spread the icing too thin, she'd repeat what I had said to her when she was having trouble with the icing. She'd say, "Why don't you put some more icing on that knife? You don't have to use just a little bit. Miss Ecken doesn't care if you put a lot on there."
>
> I asked her twice to go read, and then I didn't get into it because I saw that it was important to her to stay there. It seemed like she couldn't get enough of being there with those cookies. So, she helped everybody do theirs, without taking over or anything like that.
>
> She was the only one that really was hanging around, so I let her be.

It's often difficult to know when to give a student room to not follow our instructions. The more we trust in the goodwill of our students, the more likely we are to give them leeway to manage themselves, even if they aren't doing just as we instructed, so long as they aren't causing harm or disruption. Laura was sometimes restrictive because she feared losing control, but far more often, she trusted students' goodwill. When, on the other hand, a student was being disruptive or discourteous or inconsiderate, and a gentle reminder was insufficient to get the child to stop, Laura's standard practice was to ask the student to go to a quiet place in the room or out by the hall monitor or to another classroom and write a reflection. Sometimes she asked the students to write about what they should have been doing. Sometimes she asked them to write about what she might be thinking about what they were doing. And sometimes she asked them to write from the point of view of their classmates or someone else who witnessed or experienced the brunt of their behavior.

> Martin and Leonard laughed at Kenny when he couldn't count by two. I stopped to talk with the whole class about how we want to be as a class, and still those two kept after Kenny. So I asked them to write, "Why do you want to be in a class where people can make mistakes and not be laughed at?"
>
> Martin wrote: "I am sorry for making fun of you Kenny and laughed at you because you didn't know your 2s and 5s and laughed at you when you was crying. I do not want to be in a class where people mistreat each other."
>
> Leonard wrote: "We should not laugh when some people do not know how to count by 2 because it hurts their feelings. I do not want to feel bad."

In this instance, Martin and Leonard each had a chance to take Kenny's point of view. Leonard went one step further and recognized that it feels bad to him if someone's feelings are hurt.

When Louise refused to cooperate with her tablemates, Laura asked her to write what she should have done and what her tablemates probably thought about her behavior.

> Louise wrote: "I should of listened to Leonard and Yolanda and Janice. I should of not kept on pounding my paper like I was doing. I shouldn't of did that to them three. But I did it. I should of stopped like they told me to. And Kenny told me to stop too and I didn't listen to him neither.
>
> I think Janice doesn't like me anymore and Leonard too. I think Yolanda is mad at me. I think Kenny doesn't like me to."

In her reflection that she "shouldn't of did that to them three," Louise recognized her responsibility to her tablemates, as well as her role in getting them angry with her. Her reflection is both heartbreakingly simple and complex, coming from a student who struggled to make friends.

Laura also used reflections when the whole class needed to understand the impact of their behavior. In the beginning of Year 1, when it seemed that the entire class was having difficulty listening to Laura and one another, Laura asked the class to write about what it feels like to be listened to and why it is important to listen when others are talking. The students' responses varied widely. Some students, like Brian and Janice, picked up on the importance of treating others the way you want to be treated. Others, like Rebecca and Kenny, focused on apologizing for their own behavior.

> Brian wrote: "It feels good to be listened to. When someone is talking you should listen to them like they listen to you."
>
> Janice wrote: "It feels good to be listened to. Because they will not listen to you and you will want them to listen to you."
>
> Rebecca wrote: "I am sorry Mrs. Ecken and I am sorry I was talking when you were talking to us and when you were working with us. I was talking over you and I was talking and I am really sorry."
>
> Kenny wrote: "I think the class cannot work. I got to be good. I want to be good. I love Mrs. Ecken."

When Laura first described her practice of asking students to reflect in writing about their misbehaviors, I worried that the students would perceive this as punishment and that it would dampen their enthusiasm for writing. I didn't mention my reservations to Laura. I had a lot of confidence in her ability to treat her students with care, so I decided to see how the practice actually worked before assuming that it would be negative. In fact, the note writing sometimes felt like a punishment to Laura's students, and sometimes when she asked them to write, the frustration in her voice added to this perception. However, the writing was meant to help her students reflect on their behavior and internalize the language and concepts related to self-control and proper school behavior. Further, each student's written statement served as a support for Laura and the student to talk about the misbehavior in a calmer moment. The students could write as much or as little as they wanted, and Laura generally followed up with a one-on-one conversation.

Even when Laura asked in a sharp or punitive way that a child write about his or her behavior, the conversation that followed the writing usually prompted Laura to think about ways to be more supportive to the child. Overall, writing about misbehaviors seemed to work in positive ways.

One of the unintended outcomes of the reflection writing and evidence that some of Laura's students recognized the writing as an aid to their understanding, was the number of spontaneous apologies some of them began to write.

> The room was in an uproar when I came back. The poor student teacher was just being abused. So we had a class meeting to talk about what had happened and how we could keep it from happening again.
>
> While the meeting was going on, Tralin was writing something. I didn't stop her because she was participating at the same time.
>
> Partway through the meeting, she got up and handed a note to the student teacher and sat back down.
>
> When I was cleaning up the room Friday afternoon, I found the note. It said: "Mrs. Smith, I'm sorry I called your husband ugly. I really don't think he is ugly. I was just saying it."
>
> Tralin did that on her own. She obviously didn't feel good about what she had done earlier.

It was encouraging to Laura that Tralin accepted responsibility for her actions and on her own initiative wrote the student teacher an apology. Laura remembered that in March of the previous year, Tralin would not even admit her part in the ransacking of the classroom and had to be cajoled by Laura to help repair the damage.

A few months later, Chantelle, who was having a lot of difficulty getting along with her classmates but was trying to behave better and make friends, began extending her reflection writing into notes of apology and reconciliation.

> Chantelle had just led to lunch, and it was time to go to special area. The system they worked out at their table meant that it was Paul's turn to lead. But Chantelle just pushed in front of him.
>
> Paul said, and he's very quiet, "It's my turn. You led to lunch." And he got in front of her.
>
> She pushed ahead of him.
>
> And so he got back up in front of her, and he said, "Chantelle, it's my turn. You led to lunch."
>
> She said, "I'm leading!" And she got in front, and he just shook his head.
>
> I saw all this, so when I walked the class out I said, "Chantelle, did you lead to lunch?"
>
> She said, "Yes."
>
> I said, "Is it agreed at your table that Paul leads to special area?"
>
> She said, "Yes."
>
> So I said, "Then why are you leading?"

She said, "I don't know."

And I said, "Well, I think that maybe you were bullying a little bit, because I saw Paul ask you twice, and you refused to give up the line."

She just said, "Oh."

I said, "What do you need to do if you've already had your turn and it's somebody else's turn?"

She said, "Give it to him."

I said, "Yeah, I think maybe if you just sit down for a few minutes and write about that before you go on upstairs to computer, that would be good."

So she wrote this little note and handed it to me: "To Mrs. Ecken, When someone tells me nicely I have already been first, if I forget, I could say in a nice way, 'No I haven't.' And they say, 'Yes you have.' And I should say, 'Oh yes, I have forgot.' I should not bully people around."

Then she said, "And, here, I wrote this for Paul."

I didn't ask her to do that, but she wrote to him: "To Paul, from Chantelle, I am sorry for trying to bully you around. Do you accept my apology? Well anyways, if you do, give me thumbs up. Now I think I know what it feels like to be bullied around, and it does not feel very good. If I don't want people bullying me around, I should not bully other people around. Signed, by Chantelle. Finished."

So she gave it to Paul, and Paul gave her the thumbs up and let her know that he was okay with her apology.

Perhaps because Laura really read what the students wrote and discussed their writing with them, the students took the writing seriously and seemed to use it as a vehicle to reflect.

The ability to cognitively represent and guide one's behavior is one of the important emotional skills children need to develop. It's likely that the writing helped Laura's students think about and monitor their behavior rather than just react to the world. And by asking students to write about their behavior and then conferencing with them in a supportive way, Laura was also able to continue building her students' trust—one of her most consistent goals.

Work Folders, Referrals, and Suspensions

Occasionally, Laura sent students from the room, usually when they were doing something harmful to the class's learning or well-being and refused to stop when asked. This was a discipline technique Laura learned as part of the Assertive Discipline training she had received in her teacher education program, and she used it when she couldn't find another alternative. Her goal was to temporarily remove the student from the situation and give the student time to reflect and pull him- or herself together. More often, she asked the student to go to a quiet place in the classroom or out by the hall monitor, but sometimes she chose the classroom next door. However, Laura explained to the students that the purpose was to give them some time to reflect and regroup and told them that they could return to the classroom after they had written about the problem behavior and whenever they were ready. Most important, she followed up with a personal conversation focused on helping the student behave better in the future.

However, Laura felt that some behaviors were so serious that she sent the student out of the class for the rest of the day with a folder of work, or referred the student to the office where the principal would either conference with the student or take the student home.

Unless Laura was unusually stressed, work folders as well as referrals to the office were reserved for serious misbehaviors like striking or flagrantly disrespecting Laura or cruelly taunting or physically harming another child. As much as Laura wanted her students' positive internal motivations to drive their learning and behavior, there were times when she found the threat or experience of unpleasant consequences to be necessary. But whenever Laura resorted to punitive action, she also followed up to reestablish her relationship with the student and continued to work on developing the student's ability and internal motivation to do the right thing. Martin, whose violent outbursts got him suspended more than once, is a case in point.

> Martin and Jennifer were in the cafeteria line. Martin somehow got out of the line, and then when he tried to get back in, Jennifer said, "No, you got out. You can get behind me."
>
> By this time, I was back in the room eating with my Wednesday group and Mack was in charge of the class.
>
> Apparently, Martin grabbed Jennifer's fork off her tray and she took the milk and hit him with it in the arm. Then Martin took his fist and swung at her twice. The first time he just barely hit her nose, and the second time he hit her with all of his might in the jaw.
>
> Mack brought Martin back to the room and told me, "Laura, Martin hit that little girl like he would hit a man."
>
> When Martin, who was already crying, heard Mack say that, he just started screaming, "She hit me with her milk! She hit me with her milk!"
>
> I asked Martin if she hurt him, and he said no. I asked him if he hurt her, and he said, "Yes, I popped her in her face."
>
> I said, "That's right, and you're going to the office. You're not staying here."
>
> He refused to go to the office. However, the principal was in the hall, and I told her what happened and she took him home. The whole time, he was screaming that Jennifer had hit him first with her milk and that it wasn't his fault.
>
> I went down to the lunchroom to talk with Jennifer. She refused to eat or lift her head up off the table. But from what I could see, her face wasn't swollen or cut.
>
> After lunch, when she came back in the room she put her head down again, and she wouldn't lift it up off the table.

The next morning, Martin came in before school the way he usually does and started to take the chairs down.

I said, "Martin, we need to have a talk. We need to talk about you hitting Jennifer."

He got real mad and just screamed, "It was her fault!"

I said, "Martin, let me ask you this. Did she hurt you?"

He said, "No."

I asked, "Did she make you hit her?"

He said, "No."

"Whose fault is it that you slammed Jennifer in the face?"

He said, "It's mine."

I said, "Yes. What could you have done when she hit you with the milk?"

He said, "Nothing. Just told her to stop."

I said, "Yes, that's something that you could've done. Is there anything else?"

He said, "I could've gotten away from her."

Then I asked him to think about what he could do to make this up to her, but he couldn't think of anything.

I said, "Well, you need to sit down a little while. I want you to think about how you can make it up to Jennifer for what you did to her yesterday. Martin, she laid her head down for over an hour, wouldn't even lift it off the table. You hurt her badly, and you hurt her feelings, also."

Well, he couldn't think of anything except to tell her that he was sorry. I asked if I could help him think of something more and he agreed.

I suggested that he could offer to get her book box for her every day when it's time for book boxes.

He said, "Yeah, I can do that."

And so I said, "What are you going to say to her this morning?"

He didn't know, so I said, "Let's think about it. She's going to be in here soon, and you sit right at her table. What are you going to say to her?"

He said, "I'm going to tell her I'm sorry."

I said, "Anything else?"

"I'm not going to do it again."

I said, "What about the plan that you're going to make it up."

He said, "I'm going to tell her that I'm going to get her book box for her."

I said, "Okay, let's practice. Pretend I'm Jennifer."

This was really difficult for him. He just stood there.

So I said, "How about, 'Jennifer, I'm really sorry I hit you in the face and I won't do it again'? Go on and say it. Act like I'm Jennifer."

And he said, "I'm really sorry I hit you in the face and I won't do it again."

Then I said, "What else are you going to tell her?"

And he said, "I'll get your book box for you at book box time."

That morning, after they got through doing the math problems, I saw Jennifer get up and get her book box. So I said, "Martin, I thought you told her you were going to do that for her."

He said, "I did, but she told me she didn't want me doing anything for her."

So I came over to the table and I said, "Jennifer, Martin feels really bad about what he did and he wants to make it up to you. And we came up with getting your book box as a good way to do it."

She said, "Okay."

I said, "Martin, what are you going to do tomorrow when it's time to get the book boxes out?"

And he looked at Jennifer and he said, "I'm going to get it out for you."

I talked to Jennifer's mother, and she said that she was shocked that it was Martin of all the people in the room who would hit Jennifer. He lives right down the street, and she talks to him all the time.

When I told Martin that Jennifer's mom was really upset, I said, "You might want to think about talking to the mom. What do you think you could say to her?"

He said, "I can tell her that I'll never hit Jennifer again."

I said, "She might feel better about Jennifer being in our class if you could let her know that."

And Martin never did hit Jennifer again. But the very next day he threatened to hit Leonard.

We were cleaning up the manipulatives. Martin finished with his and he went over to Leonard and he said, "I'll help you."

Leonard said, "I don't need any help."

Martin said, "Too bad," and he started grabbing some of the pieces to put them in the bag.

Leonard pushed Martin's hands away and Martin took a swing at him. Fortunately, he missed him.

I immediately said, "Martin, move away right now."

He said, "I'm going to steel him in his face next time he touches me."

I said, "Martin, he told you he didn't need any help."

Martin said, "He didn't have to shove me."

I said, "He pushed your hands away."

Martin said, "I'm gonna steel him in his jaw next time."

I said, "No, we're safe from that in here. Mary-Sue Larson [the principal] told you yesterday you'd be suspended for five days if you hit anyone again. Now you make your choice."

He said, "I'm not going to hit him."

I said, "Right. That's the choice to make. You cannot stay here and hit people." It was over then.

But Laura didn't let it end there. She knew that Martin needed some help controlling his temper. So on Monday of the next week, when Laura was scheduled to eat lunch with Jennifer, Martin, and Gabrielle's table, she decided to have Martin practice not hitting.

We just practiced. Jennifer picked up her milk and she hit Martin with it.

I kind of pushed him in the arm.

And we practiced how to tell people to stop without losing your temper and just jumping back and hitting them.

The next week, Martin antagonized Gabrielle and she retaliated by pulling his chair aside just as he was sitting down. Martin landed hard on the floor.

Well, he fell and hit his head. I had to put ice on it, so it was pretty serious. But he didn't do anything except run up to me in a rage.

He said, "She pulled the chair out from under me. She kicked it when I was trying to sit down."

I asked Gabrielle to come up and talk with us.

She lost total control of herself, and she just screamed as loud as she could, "I didn't do anything to him!"

I said, "Well, he thinks you did."

This may have been pretty dumb on my part, but I said, "Look, you two can talk it over."

They didn't get anything accomplished. Martin sat and sulked, and Gabrielle sat down on the carpet and cried. After a while they calmed down, and I talked with them.

I said, "Gabrielle, why did you do that? Tell me what was going on."

After she described the scene, I said, "What could you have done?"

She said, "Nothing."

I said, "Could you have said anything to him?"

She said, "Yes. I could've told him I didn't like it."

I said, "Yeah, you could've done that. What's the problem with what you did?"

She said, "He got hurt."

I said, "You know what? You need to make it up to him."

So she thought for a while but she didn't know anything to do. Later she came up to me and said, "I can help with his work for the rest of the week."

I said, "Well, you go talk to him and see what he thinks about it."

Martin said that was fine, and a little while later those two had their heads together and she was helping him.

Later that day, on our way down to lunch, I said, "You know, Martin, you didn't hit Gabrielle. I just want to tell you that this is an instance where you kept yourself under control. I want you to think of what you did, because if you can think of what you did, then you can do it again."

He said, "I don't know what I did."

I said, "No, this is important. You've got to think about what you did to keep yourself from getting up and knocking her off that chair and slamming her in her face like you did Jennifer. Because whatever you did, that's the kind of thing you need to do when somebody does something to you, so that you just don't jump up and react to it."

He said, "Well, I just said to myself, 'If I hit her I'm suspended for five days,' because Mary-Sue Larson told me that she'd kick me out for five days if I hit somebody else."

I said, "Okay, that's called self-talk. You talked to yourself. That's something to do when somebody does something to you."

Then I asked him if our practicing helped, and he wasn't clear on that. He really just thought it was the principal, Mary-Sue Larson, telling him he was going to be suspended.

Even though Laura referred Martin to the office, knowing that he would be suspended for hitting Jennifer, she continued to work to help him control his behavior and to let him know that she still cared about him and believed that he wanted to do the right thing. Laura was pretty disheartened when Martin tried to hit Leonard the very next day. But in both instances, Laura focused on building Martin's empathy and sense of obligation to a friend, as well as his ability to control his anger and his tendency to strike out.

A week later when Martin refrained from hitting Gabrielle, Laura saw some progress. She would have preferred for Martin to tell her that the practicing rather than the threat of suspension kept him from hitting Gabrielle (and perhaps it did help), but at least he had controlled his behavior. Laura made sure that Martin understood that it wasn't just the threatened suspension that had kept him in check but that he had a way to control himself—with "self-talk." And even though Martin was usually the aggressor, in this instance when he was the victim, Laura helped him experience what it's like to be harmed but to have someone make up for it.

Problems with Substitutes and Student Teachers

Laura's responses to student misbehavior and her overall approach to classroom management were aimed at helping her students internalize prosocial values such as kindness, fairness, respect, and responsibility and teaching her students the skills and understandings needed to use those values to guide their behavior. She wanted her students to become autonomous moral agents—to choose to do the right thing because they understood it to be right, not because they feared punishment or sought personal gain. And as long as Laura was running the classroom, her students appeared to be making steady progress toward true moral agency. However, when substitutes or student teachers were in charge, the students' behavior frequently degenerated. A stunning example was the looting described at the beginning of this chapter. The students refused to obey the substitute and ended up ransacking the classroom. Laura was embarrassed and confused by this event and other examples of her students' misbehavior with substitutes and student teachers. If her students had truly internalized the classroom values, why didn't they behave well when other people were in charge?

Attachment theory helps answer this question. According to attachment theory, children develop in the context of relationships. They depend on the support and guidance of their caregivers—their attachment figures—to meet the ongoing social and emotional challenges of daily living. Their ability to be successful, to behave at their best, depends not only on their own efforts but also on the support of their caregivers.

As Laura struggled to help her students control themselves with substitutes or student teachers, what she failed to realize was how much her students depended on her supportive presence to "hold themselves together." They were used to Laura. They came to depend on her ways, her guidance, and her predictability. They unconsciously trusted her. A rough day for a substitute teacher and her students' reflections on the day helped Laura better understand this.

> I had two different meetings with the kids to prepare them for having a substitute. The first meeting was to tell them that I wouldn't be there the next day and to explain what would be happening.
>
> When I told them I wasn't going to be there, Tralin and Leonard were really angry about it. They both said that they weren't going to come to school. So we had a talk about that. I said, "School's going to go on whether I'm here or not. You really need to come. Everybody's going to be here besides me, and you can do this."

Then at the end of the day, I had a meeting and talked about what would be expected the next day. I asked them to think about what they would need to do to make it a successful day. Basically, people said they'd have to listen and work together and that sort of thing.

But it wasn't a successful day. Apparently they were loud and they wouldn't do what they were asked to do. The substitute left a list of names that included just about everyone in the class for having misbehaved in some way or another—yelling across the room, distracting others, playing instead of working, hitting, changing seats, talking out, throwing paper across the room, talking during sharing time. That was just the morning.

We had a meeting about what went on. I said, "I don't want to hear anybody's name. It looks like it was a rough day. I just want to know what went on."

Lana said, "Well, we were really mad because most of us weren't doing nothing and he made us all write."

Apparently, they had to write a definition of "silence" ten times.

I asked them what they thought about that and they said, "It's not fair. Why didn't he make the people that wouldn't be quiet in the hall write?" That was the general consensus.

Then they said that in the morning he gave everybody whose name wasn't on the list a Jolly Rancher [a kind of candy]. They told him that's not the way we do things here but he wouldn't listen.

They told me, "We didn't like it. That wasn't right. If he was going to give somebody something, he should've given everybody something."

And then they said that he screamed at them. Chantelle said, "You don't treat us like that. You talk to us."

Ella jumped in on that and said, "We're not used to being treated like that. You're nice to us and you listen to us."

And so I said, "What do you think caused all this stuff to go on?"

There was dead silence.

I said, "Let's talk about that. What do you think caused the day to be so rough?"

They were pretty honest about it. They knew they did things they shouldn't have done.

Louise said, "Ms. Ecken, nice people know when it's time to be quiet and they know what to do."

I said, "I hear what you're saying, Louise. Every one of you all know how to act, and you know how to listen, and you know how to stay in your seat, and you know how to walk to and from lunch quietly. I know

> some things went on that didn't feel good to you. But the bottom line is you all know how to act and that's what you need to do."
>
> Then Tralin said that during the day she started crying. She said, "I just don't like it and I don't want to be here when Ms. Ecken's not here. I'm used to her."

Although Laura continually tried to impress on her students that they were responsible for themselves, it became clear to her how important her support was to their success. Still, Laura kept working to help them increase their ability to hold themselves together on their own. A few weeks after the incident just described, Laura told her students that she would need to be out of class at the end of the week. She planned familiar lessons for the students, and to provide extra support she had a class meeting in which she and the class planned for the substitute. Together they wrote a letter to the substitute telling about the class and how they wanted to be treated, and they made a list of things they could do to keep themselves from getting out of control, including ways they could support one another.

Laura hoped that her plans and the letter to the substitute would help the substitute maintain a familiar environment for her students. She also hoped that explicitly planning with her students ways to maintain self-control and ways to help one another maintain control would create the supportive context her students would need in her absence.

Unfortunately, the substitute never showed up and Laura's students were dispersed into other teachers' classrooms for the day. However, a week later Laura's students had a substitute in computer class and seemed to apply their earlier preparation to their behavior with her.

> With the exception of Louise, they were wonderful. At the end-of-the-day meeting I asked, "What happened today with the sub? What happened that you were able to do so well?"
>
> Nikki said, "I think it's because we had that meeting about a sub with you."
>
> Cindy said, "I think it's because we made the wish this morning that we would do well in computer."
>
> Tyrone said, "People remembered in computer how you taught us about the sub. And people love computer."
>
> Tralin said, "She started telling us directions and we listened."
>
> Rebecca said, "I got the attitude off my face."
>
> I said, "Well, how did you do that, Rebecca, so when other people have attitude on their face they can do the same thing?"
>
> She said, "I don't know. I just did it."

Then Mary said, "I told myself I'll need to be good so I can be on the computer for a long time."

Ella said, "Well, maybe we didn't want to be writing about how to do for a sub when we got back."

And Tangela said, "I said it in my head."

I said, "Well, how did all that feel?"

Gabrielle said, "I felt happy because no one acted up."

And then they all basically said, "Yeah, we felt happy to do it."

I said, "Look, you've done it now. You've had a sub. You've talked to yourself. That's what people do. They talk to themselves in their head. You told yourself you could do it. You told yourself what you needed to do and you did it, so we'll just keep working on it."

It's clear that a number of factors led to the students' success with a substitute teacher in computer class; it was only for a fifty-minute period and the kids loved to work on the computers. But they had failed to be successful with a substitute in computer class in the past. It seems likely that their reflections on how to work well with a substitute provided the extra support they needed to be able to hold themselves together and focus on their learning. Laura's hard work had paid off. Her students did not have any more substitutes for the rest of the year, and even though Laura had been terribly disappointed when the substitute she and the class had carefully planned for did not show up, she was grateful that her class had the opportunity to successfully put their skills to the test with a substitute in computer class.

The Difficulty of Discipline and Classroom Management

Structuring the environment and establishing expectations that are sensitive to our students' capabilities are key to managing mistakes in the cognitive domain and misbehaviors in the social and moral domains. In Vygotsky's terms, we need to create environments and set expectations that match the children's "zone of proximal development"—the area where they can be successful with our help and guidance. In more familiar terms, we need to keep our expectations reasonable but high. Although this may seem obvious, what is not obvious is how easy it is to have expectations that are at first too high and then too low, especially in classrooms in which the students vary greatly in their academic and social knowledge and skills.

It is not uncommon to inadvertently set off a downward spiral of failure if our students cannot meet our initial expectations. We are apt to decide that they cannot learn and change our expectations from too high to too low. This downward spiral in the academic domain has had devastating effects, particularly for children in disadvantaged communities, making it necessary for us to constantly remind one another that "all children can learn."

In the social, emotional, and moral domains—the domains of classroom discipline—this downward spiral is even more pernicious and less recognized. Because children's basic cognitive capacities are not completely dependent on their interactions with their primary caregivers, they will progress cognitively, even if they do not have a secure attachment relationship with their caregivers. They will not progress as well, and they may not acquire some of the specialized language and information needed for success in the school setting, but through interacting with their physical environment and their peers, children will progress through the various stages of cognitive development. By age six or seven, virtually all children will be able to manage the basic logical operations that characterize what Piaget labeled the "concrete operations stage."

In the social, emotional, and moral domains, however, children are more dependent on the help and guidance of their caregivers. As we have already noted, some have virtually no ability to trust, and some are not able to balance their need for autonomy with their need for adult guidance. Some children have no ability to regulate or communicate their emotions; they do not know how they should feel in various situations, and they cannot keep their behavior organized in the face of strong emotions.

Adjusting our expectations to our students' social and emotional abilities is an even harder task than adjusting our instruction to the level of their academic skills and knowledge. When we try to get children whose social and emotional skills are at the infancy or toddler levels to behave like school-aged children, we and they will fail. They do not have the capacity to behave as we wish. We need to back up, match our demands to their capacities, and begin helping them develop the skills and understandings that they lack.

If instead we try to control their behavior with rewards and punishments, we will end up in a perpetual battle. Our level of external control will escalate, and that will feel oppressive to them and to us. If ever-increasing levels of control fail, eventually we will declare our students incorrigible. Or, if we manage to gain control, maintaining control will be an ongoing struggle; in the end, we will have reinforced their lack of trust and justified an adversarial approach to the world.

However, all children can learn to trust; they can learn to balance their need for autonomy with their need for guidance, and they can learn to regulate their emotions and monitor their own behavior. But to teach these skills, we will need to begin where the children are and painstakingly build their trust in us while we work with them to acquire the social and emotional skills basic to forming collaborative and supportive human relationships.

Because elementary schools and the academic curriculum were designed for children who already have well-developed social and emotional skills, we will need to redesign the classroom environment and the curriculum to explicitly support children's social, emotional, and moral development. We will need to drastically redesign our approach to discipline as primarily a process for building supportive relationships and teaching social, emotional, and moral skills and understandings. This is a difficult process, made more difficult by the fact that the students who need our unconditional care and careful teaching the most will be the most likely to resist our efforts.

Laura constantly struggled to come up with the right response and to balance the needs of individual students with the needs of the class as a whole. She also struggled with her role and her own human needs. She tolerated situations and behaviors that are unimaginable to many teachers because she knew that she needed to work with her students as they were and not demand that they be what they were not and could not immediately become.

The process of helping her students become caring, self-regulating people and serious learners was slow and bumpy. Until her students were able to trust that she cared for them and found them to be worthy no matter what they did, they were not able to admit even to themselves that they had behaved badly. Until they could make such an admission, they could not really join with Laura in a partnership to improve their behavior. Once they began to see Laura as their partner, once they came to trust her and she them, their work together was highly rewarding for both Laura and the children.

It wasn't until Year 2 that Laura began to feel confident with her handling of misbehavior. She needed to figure out when and how much to use her authority to control situations and how much autonomy to give the students. She needed to understand her students—their contexts, beliefs, skills, and understandings. She needed to build trust, and she needed to figure out how to make the classroom a more supportive place, given her students' developmental levels.

One aspect of classroom life that Laura changed substantially in Year 2 was the degree to which her students engaged in competitive activities. By Year 2, Laura came to believe that competition was a pervasive source of misbehavior in her classroom. The demands of competition were well beyond her students' emotional abilities, and she decided to eliminate it. This was a bold step on Laura's part, and to this we turn in the next chapter.

Key Points: When Teaching and Reminding Aren't Enough

- Encourage students to feel empathy and, if necessary, help them think of ways to make reparations for harm they have caused.
- Encourage and give students time to think about the causes of their actions, and challenge their efforts to blame others for their own misdeeds.
- Assume that students want to behave well, and remind them or redirect them in a spirit of helpfulness.
- When students don't change their behavior following a helpful reminder, consider ignoring the behavior if further action would be more disruptive. Other possible actions are reassessing the situation, directing students to a quiet place for reflection, discussing the situation with the student at a later time, and reaffirming your commitment to them.
- For extremely volatile students or in situations that feel out of control, seek help—for example, from the school psychologist, principal, or a special education teacher.
- If it's necessary to ask students to leave the room, consider preparing meaningful work for them to do while out of the classroom.
- Be sure to reconnect with students when they return and discuss ways to make it possible for them to remain in control and in the classroom.
- Prepare students for substitutes and student teachers. Remember they have come to depend on your support to cope with classroom challenges.
- Hold a class meeting after the class has had a substitute or student teacher to discuss successes and rough spots.

7

COMPETITION IN THE CLASSROOM

We were playing kickball. Louise started to run to second base, but everybody yelled at her to get back because it was a foul ball. They were screaming at her in the ugliest way you've ever seen.

When she finally started back, first she got hit with the ball, then Kenny wouldn't let her on the base, so she kind of pushed him so she could get on, and he started hitting her with his fists as hard as he could.

Louise started crying and the whole class attacked her for being a crybaby. They thought she was crying about getting hit with the ball. Most of them didn't see the hits Kenny gave her.

I couldn't get them to stop yelling at Louise. They were like an angry mob. I was saying, "Now listen, guys, let me explain what happened."

But it didn't matter what I was saying. I was trying to get everybody to settle down and get Louise taken care of, and they were just in her face and in my face. And they wouldn't stop.

So then I said, "Let's go in."

Well, that made it a hundred times worse, but we went in. I told them to get their journals out, so then they started screaming about that. I said, "Look, get your journals out. You can write about anything you need to. The class needs a break."

They did get their journals out and started writing. And then we had to move on. We had another lesson to do.

THE STUDENTS IN Laura's class loved kickball. They loved competitive games of all sorts, but the games almost always ended up in hurt feelings, tears, or even physical fights unless they were closely supervised and vigorously refereed. The incident with Louise happened at the end of the first year, one week before school let out. It was hugely disappointing to Laura and she blamed herself.

> You've had them for nine months and they still don't know how to act. How can you not take it on yourself?

Year 1: Competition Looks Ugly

Ironically, Laura had worked very hard all year to eliminate competition in her classroom. She assiduously avoided comparing her students with one another; she never praised or showered affection on one student in order to get other students to behave better; she had her students work in collaborative partnerships daily, and she worked hard to build her students' sense of community. She realized that they had made substantial progress in their ability to engage in the give and take of cooperation when it was carefully structured, yet, at the end of the year, she believed that overall she had failed to alter her students' competitive orientation to the world.

Laura did not see competition as evil, but she did believe that the competitive way that most of her students approached life was unhealthy and likely to interfere with their academic learning as well as their ability to form friendships and play games and sports. All during the first year, her students took every opportunity to turn their classmates into competitors. They were constantly on the lookout for ways to be one up or look better than their classmates. At their worst, they would laugh at classmates' mistakes, make fun of their clothes, try to make them look bad by reporting any wrongdoing, and set their classmates against one another.

Their approach to competitive games was simply part of this wider confrontational approach to life, which, in turn, was related to their basic mistrust. They feared that unless they were ever-vigilant they would be abandoned or harmed and that they might not be good enough—might not be worthy of love.

Even though she understood their larger problem, Laura's initial approach to students' behavior in situations designed to be competitive was to try to teach them how to participate without disintegrating or becoming mean-spirited. Accordingly, in preparation for the school's field day, a few weeks before the incident with Louise described earlier, Laura took her students outside to practice relay racing.

> Before we started, we talked about whether they wanted to enter the field day games and races. I asked them if it really was something they

wanted to do. I wanted them to recognize that some teams were going to be faster and some teams were going to lose, and to think about whether that would be too painful for them. They said no, they really liked to race. So we decided to try some relay races.

We divided into two teams. When Kenny and Leonard took off, they stayed right even going out, but on the way back Leonard got ahead a little bit, and Kenny completely quit running. He just completely quit running and started yelling and screaming and throwing this little fit out on the field.

I said, "Kenny, this is just for fun. We're just out here having fun, running back and forth on these relay teams, getting ready for field day. If Leonard beats you, it's no big deal. It's just a game. It doesn't mean anything."

Well, that was dumb of me to say, because it really does mean a lot to them.

The very next relay, the same thing happened with Martin. He and Ed were running backwards. Ed's really fast, I mean, he is a really fast backward runner, and he started beating Martin. Martin took the marker [that he was using for a baton] and he flung it across the field.

I asked him and Kenny to sit by the fence, and when they thought they could join us and be part of the teams to come on back over. Martin came back after a little while, but Kenny didn't.

Competition is so difficult for them. Just in that short time, two people weren't going to play unless they knew they were going to win. They just totally took themselves out of it.

With Laura's help, most of her students eventually enjoyed the relay races, and the class participated in the school field day with relatively few problems. However, competition continued to be an issue through the remaining few weeks before school ended.

Rebecca brought in a bingo game and asked if we could play it. So about twenty 'til three we played bingo at our tables instead of going outside. When Tyrone won the first game, they were kind of ticked because they thought he was going to get something for winning. They were fine when I said we were just playing the game, there weren't any prizes.

But then what ended up happening was my kids who need to make an issue over who wins, who doesn't win, they found a way to do it. Even if *they* didn't win, if somebody at their table did, they'd start harassing or fussing with the other tables, like, "Our table beat your table. We've got a winner."

We talked about it a little bit, and they stopped it as best they could, but they were still giving each other the look.

As the year drew to a close, Laura's biggest problem with competition didn't occur in the context of games but as she engaged students in a variety of activities to help them remember and bring closure to their year. Always looking for ways to honor her students' need for autonomy and to involve them in decision making, Laura held two class meetings to decide on a product for remembering the year. The students turned this into a rancorous competition.

> In the second meeting, we were still trying to get consensus about whether to make a class book or class quilt. People had staked out pretty strong positions the day before, so I asked them to talk about the advantages of each one.
>
> Denise listened to someone's reasons for the book and changed her mind from the day before. She said she'd rather have a book. Yolanda and Tralin were big-time for the quilt, and they had counted Denise on their side. These two started screaming out, "Reading's stupid! I don't want to read no book!"
>
> People started shouting stuff like, "I don't care what anybody says."
>
> It was impossible. So I came up with a plan where we'd make both, so everyone would get a photograph of the quilt and everyone would get a copy of the book. And still I had some people saying no. We couldn't even get consensus that we'd make them both.
>
> And, you know, that was a very hard thing to deal with. The meeting was just unbelievable. They were all screaming, and somebody would say they wanted this, and be explaining it, and people who had already talked would yell out, "I'm not making no book" or "I'm not making a quilt." It was like they would be giving up their very lives to have to go with something different than what they said at the beginning. A lot of it seemed to be, "This is what I said, and these other people said it, and we're gonna stick together, and we're not going to change."

Despite this trying meeting, Laura and her students actually enjoyed making both the quilt and the book. All of the angry feelings seemed to disappear, and the class became calm and friendly again. The kids brainstormed a long list of things they wanted to remember and then signed up for the things that they wanted to draw and write about for the quilt and the book. When it was time to assemble the books, the class recognized it as an opportunity to collaborate.

> It was real interesting when we were trying to put the book together. It's got forty or fifty pages that had to be collated. So we took the

chairs and put them all down the middle of the room, and the kids were just going to go along and pick up their pages. After one person tried it, he said, "Can somebody help me?"

So then we did the whole thing in partners, and it was so sweet. One child walked down the row picking up the papers of the book and handing them to a partner who walked alongside. Then they changed positions and went down the row again.

They have grown in so many ways. It's just very hard for me when, all the same, they can still be so unkind to each other.

Regardless of how disappointing her students' bad times were to Laura, once they were over the students recovered quickly. They did not seem to hold resentments toward one another or toward Laura. And, equally important, Laura did not hold resentments toward them. In a manner quite similar to toddlers, Laura's students quickly returned to an even keel once their strong emotions had subsided, and, like a sensitive parent, Laura expected and accepted their recovery. She saw her students as struggling to grow up and their misbehaviors as resulting from their immaturity. And she saw her job as one of helping them build the skills and understanding they would need to manage life's tasks successfully.

Year 2: Eliminating Competitive Games

When Laura reflected on the first year, one of the big problems she decided to address in the year ahead was her students' lack of ability to play together with a cooperative spirit. She had taught them how to work together, but she had left their play to them, and it was frequently competitive and destructive. Laura began the second year with a resolve to remove as much competition as she could from their games and to teach her students to enjoy one another in play.

In the Kentucky school day, there is no official recess. Teachers, at their discretion, take their students outside to play or provide some informal play time in the classroom. Thus Laura was in a position to structure her students' play time as well as their work time. She decided to begin the year by outlawing competitive games like kickball and teaching her students how to play cooperative games. With Terry Orlick's book, *The Second Cooperative Sports and Games Book*, as a resource, Laura introduced the idea of cooperative games.

I said to them, "Your parents send you here with the thought that you're going to learn a lot and also that you're going to be safe. And

> this doesn't mean just being safe from getting hit in the parking lot or the school bus running over you. It also means that you're going to be safe from being ridiculed or humiliated. Your parents expect that, and that's the kind of place we want to have here."
>
> I told them that as I looked back over last year, I realized that games like kickball and Man from Mars were things that didn't feel safe, that we didn't feel good about. People got too upset over winners and losers.
>
> I was just cut and dried about it. I said, "It's my obligation to make this a place where everybody wants to be and where it feels safe. We're not going to be playing kickball and Man from Mars anymore."
>
> Then I went into how we're going to do some new games where people can cooperate and have fun, and we're not going to have winners and losers, where people get so upset."

Laura did not engage her students in a problem-solving process here because she believed that they would not agree to abandon their competitive games. Too much was at stake to offer students a choice. Laura decided to structure their recreational games cooperatively because she believed this was necessary for their well-being and for the smooth running of the classroom.

Her students responded well to the cooperative games. By the end of the first month of school, Laura could see dramatic changes in the feel of the class and in her feelings about the class.

> Last year when I took the kids out, we would play games like kickball and it would never end well. They'd fight over what the score was and whether they were really out and who was it.
>
> It was difficult last year, trying to run the classroom a certain way and then going outside and doing things that were really not part of what I was doing inside. Now we're doing these cooperative games and it makes more sense.
>
> The big one they love is Frozen Catchers. Four out of the twenty, a table group, are it. They run and try to freeze everybody, while the other ones try to unfreeze everybody. It only lasts for a couple minutes, and then I'll call the next group to be the catchers. It's working out really, really well because everyone is important. They're yelling to be unfrozen, and you can just see it doesn't matter who comes. If you're frozen, you'll call on anybody who can unfreeze you.
>
> We have not really had many rough spots out there. Martin, though, on Friday, was frozen, and Mary ran by and unfroze about three or four people near him, but not him. He just stormed off the field.
>
> His feelings were so hurt because she is very popular. He said, "I was frozen and she didn't unfreeze me."

> Well, she heard him, and she walked over and said, "Martin? I didn't even see you."
>
> And just that quick he went, "Oh, okay," and ran back out.
>
> That's a big deal for him to even agree with her when she said she didn't see him. I would have expected him to say something like, "You know you saw me!"
>
> Last year after we'd go out, it would take me three or four days to maybe forget all the rough spots before we'd go back out again. They'd want to go out and I'd always say, "Listen, you guys can play at home. I have to teach." But it was really that I was afraid to take them out, because I knew what it was going to be like. Now we go outside every single day.

Whereas the introduction of cooperative games made a huge difference in Laura's classroom, it did not happen without some struggles. Toward the end of October, once the students became accustomed to the games, some of them tried to turn them into competitions. Laura held a class meeting to talk with them about what was happening.

> I said, "You know, I really have a problem with going outside and playing Frozen Catchers with you all because it's turned into a big competition of who can catch four or five of the fastest people in the room. People get in their mind that they're only going to catch those people. People are getting shoved and pushed down. And people are running right by people and not even bothering to catch them. I want to know what you all think about what I'm seeing out there, and what we can do to make it better."
>
> Tyrone started off. He said, "If people think they can chase just the people they want to, the people who don't get caught will think they don't have any friends. And that's not fair."
>
> Chantelle said, "When people get knocked down, they should stop and help people up."
>
> Rebecca said, "I think if they push somebody down they ought to sit out for five minutes."
>
> Leonard objected. He said, "That's a long time. We're not out there that long."
>
> Tyrone said, "They should only sit out five minutes if they push somebody down on purpose."
>
> I said, "Wait a minute. If somebody pushes somebody down on purpose, then they're not going to be part of the game at all. I'm making this call as the teacher."
>
> So Leonard said, "Well, what if it's an accident? You didn't mean to push them down, but you run into them and you push them down?"

> Brian said, "If you sit, you'll know not to do it again."
>
> Rebecca said, "That's right. If you sit out, then you'll be more careful, and you won't be running after people knocking other people down."
>
> Leonard wouldn't give up. He said, "Five minutes is too long. We're not out there but about ten minutes."
>
> So I asked them, "How many of you think people should sit out if they knock somebody down?"
>
> Everybody except Leonard agreed. And so I said, "What about this? What if you sit out one rotation? If you accidentally knock somebody down because you're being too rough, then you sit out that one time." Everybody said that would be okay, even Leonard.
>
> After we settled that, Tyrone said, "We shouldn't say, 'I'm gonna shake you.'" That's what Martin does all the time.
>
> Then Martin and Leonard started hollering at Tyrone and saying, "There's nothing wrong with saying that, and you say it too."
>
> Tyrone said, "I know I say it too. And I'm just saying we shouldn't say it because it makes people mad."
>
> I said, "Well, class, what do you think about the people who are playing and say, 'I'm gonna shake you'?"
>
> The gist of it was people said, "It's not nice, and it's like they're saying they're better runners than us."
>
> So I said, "Well, here are three things coming out of this that we said we want to try to do. We want to chase everyone—don't pass people up, don't try to go after just a few people, because then it's not a class game. Don't push people down. And don't say you're gonna shake people."
>
> I asked did anybody have any comments on that, and everybody thought it was fair and that they would try those three things.

By this time in the year, Laura had enough confidence in her students to involve them in problem solving about the games. Although there was no negotiation about pushing someone down on purpose, the students were very involved in the decision about accidentally pushing someone down and the general politeness rules that should govern their game playing. Tyrone even surfaced a problem Laura had failed to notice: people taunting others with the phrase, "I'm gonna shake you."

Reflecting on the way they were playing Frozen Catchers helped the class consolidate their understanding of the meaning of kindness and consideration and highlighted the fact that playing with a collaborative spirit results in more fun for everyone. Yet even after this meeting in which the class reached consensus about how they *should* play, the problems didn't immediately go away.

The next time we went outside, I said, "Now, remember, we want to be careful and we want to chase everybody."

I didn't remind them of all three things, which was a big mistake on my part. The first thing that happened—before the game even started—Martin said, "I'm gonna shake you."

So I said, "And we're not going to say, 'I'm gonna shake you.' Remember, we settled on that."

Martin started stomping his feet.

Leonard said, "He needs to sit out."

And I said, "No, we haven't even started. We're reviewing the meeting."

So Leonard said, "If you're not making him sit out for saying it, I'm saying it," and he started screaming, "I'm gonna shake you!"

I said, "Listen, I'm not getting into this with you guys. Here's the way it is. If anybody says, 'I'm gonna shake you,' from this point on you're sitting out."

So they played the first little rotation. Everybody had a good time, and just before we started the second rotation, Martin said, "No one caught me."

I called them together. "Guys," I said, "I want you all to listen. If you say, 'No one caught me,' you're out. Because that's like getting into somebody's face and saying, 'Ha, ha, ha, you never got me,' and that's not what this is all about."

Martin was mad that I said it, but then as soon as they started playing again, he was fine and they all had a ball.

When we went back to the classroom, I said, "Okay, what went well? How did you feel about the game today?"

Somebody said, "We all chased each other, and only one person got pushed down, and it was an accident. We all played. Nobody passed us."

And they were like, "Yes!"

So I said, "Well, that's what we're trying to do—find something that everybody can play, that's a lot of fun, and that everybody feels good about."

When she needed to be, Laura was clear with Martin and Leonard about her authority, but she orchestrated the situation to help both boys find a way back into the game. And when Martin said, "No one caught me," Laura could have engaged the class in a discussion to discover for themselves that it violated the spirit of their agreement about "I'm gonna shake you," but they had already spent a long time talking and only a short time playing. She chose instead to deal with the situation directly and get them back to playing.

Laura introduced additional cooperative games, and, as she did after nearly every lesson or unit of study, she engaged her students in reflecting on their learning and on how they worked together, signaling to her students that how well they played together was as important as how well they worked together. During one such reflection session, Tralin recognized a way she was growing.

> We were playing with the balls at the tables because it was just a mess outside. They were making up ball-passing routines and practicing them. At the end, after the tables showed some of the routines they had invented, Tralin said, "When I kept messing up, I wanted to scream and blame it on somebody else, but I told myself not to scream. It'll hurt their feelings, and they'll think that I hurt their feelings. And it wasn't their fault; it was mine when I couldn't catch the ball."
>
> Tyrone and Martin both yelled out, "Take a bow!"
>
> I thought it was good that they realized Tralin did some powerful thinking and told herself what to do.

The cooperative games were allowing Laura's students to enjoy one another in a whole new way. They were having fun together without the threat of failure or humiliation hanging over their heads. And although playing these games required them to regulate their emotions—for example, to take occasional disappointments in stride or to keep from getting so excited that they went out of control—their growing emotional skills were generally up to the task.

A More Collaborative Spirit Emerges

As the students began enjoying the cooperative games, and as Laura held very firm in her efforts to make the class safe for all the students, an atmosphere of collaboration began to emerge. Incidents of anger and uncooperative and inconsiderate behavior still occurred, but now they occurred against a background of harmoniousness rather than the other way around. By early November, Laura was thrilled with her students' growing cooperative and considerate behavior and the friendly atmosphere in her classroom.

> The class was studying animal habitats, and partners were doing research. Leonard and Tralin were studying the leopard. I was helping with the reading because it was pretty hard for them. When I got to a part about how the leopard mother immediately teaches the cubs to

climb, because that's one way they stay safe from lions and other animals that eat them, Leonard interrupted, right in the middle.

He said, "Can I have that book for a minute? I've got to take this to the lion people and let them know that leopard cubs are one thing they eat."

So he went and showed the lion people, and later when everybody shared something they learned, the lion people told the class that lions eat leopard cubs.

Two weeks later, the class started on its second research project, this one on water and weather. Laura described another incident that let her know students were becoming more sensitive to one another's needs.

After the partnerships had their topics, I started giving out research books. I would hold up a book and say, "Who needs this?"

Well, Tyrone and Lana had a topic that overlapped with Cindy and her partner, who was absent. When I held up a book that either one of their partnerships could use, Tyrone was kind of taking every book. At the end, when we got ready to put the books in folders for each partnership, Tyrone saw that Cindy hardly had any books, and he and Lana had like eight. He just walked over and gave her some. I was getting ready to suggest that maybe her group needed a few more books, but he took care of it on his own.

A couple of weeks later, Laura gave students an activity to use an atlas and fill in the names of the states on a blank outline map. She had intended for this to be an individual activity, but to her surprise, most of her students turned it into a collaborative one.

They're working away and Martin starts calling across to Chantelle. So I said, "Martin, don't be screaming back and forth across the room." He told me he and Jennifer were working on the map together.

I told him, "I don't have a problem with that at all, but I do have a problem with you interrupting other learners when you're minding Chantelle's business and not your own."

When I was walking around, Chantelle and Rebecca were also working together. They were drawing arrows to states where the name wouldn't fit.

I said, "This is a really interesting way to do this. In my mind, I thought of abbreviations, like putting NH for New Hampshire, but you all have drawn arrows and written it out where you have room to

> do it. It just shows there are different ways to do things, that people don't have to do things the same way."
>
> I was about to leave, and Rebecca said, "Well, Ms. Ecken, I didn't think of it. Mary taught me how to do it." And I just thought that was sweet that she was giving Mary credit when she didn't need to.
>
> Paul was the first one finished. When he told me he was done, Martin heard that and yelled to him, "Well, come on over here and help us."
>
> Paul asked if that would be okay, and I said, "Sure, if you want to, go on over and work with them. I'll just keep your map with me."

By January, even Laura's students were commenting on the shift away from the fierce competitiveness that characterized so much of the first year and the beginning of the second year.

> The partnerships had all been reading a book about Martin Luther King. Chantelle and Lana were sharing their ideas with the class, and John whispered to Paul and Derek, "We were thinking what they were thinking."
>
> Chantelle overheard, so she said, "John just whispered that they were thinking what we were thinking."
>
> I said, "Well, how did that feel?"
>
> And she said, "Good."
>
> When I asked her why, she said, "Because we're thinking alike."
>
> John piped in and said, "We usually get mad and say somebody stole our answer, and now we're glad we're thinking the same thing."

There are several possible explanations for this shift in atmosphere and spirit. Laura was very firm in insisting that the students treat one another with respect, the students' reading and writing skills were improving significantly so they were feeling better about their academic competence, and the elimination of competitive games removed a source of stress from the classroom. It's likely all of these contributed to the harmony in the classroom, primarily because they contributed to each student's feelings of safety and competence. Their trust in Laura and one another was growing. As their trust grew, their need for an adversarial stance lessened. They gradually stopped seeing one another as competitors, and they trusted that Laura could protect and help them. From the perspective of attachment theory, they were more secure in their relationship with their teacher or caregiver and more trusting of the world—at least of the world in their classroom. They were beginning to change their working models of caregivers, themselves, and relationships.

As we have seen, the progress toward harmony was not smooth, but it was steady and Laura was continually reassured that her students were learning, were learning to work well collaboratively, and were finally learning to be friends and to treat one another with kindness and respect throughout the day, not just in activities carefully structured to foster cooperation.

Competition in a Learning Environment

By eliminating as much competition as possible from her students' school experience, Laura took a position that is unusual in American schools. Competition is often described as the American way, and it is certainly a fact of life in American society. Generally, our schools abound in competitive activities—honor rolls, art contests, awards assemblies, and the pervasive efforts to control student behavior by offering rewards to students or classes who perform best. Was Laura doing her students a disservice? Was she sacrificing their ability to survive in a competitive society for the short-term goal of a more harmonious classroom?

Although many people believe that immersing children in competitive situations is the best way to prepare them to succeed in our competitive society, there is no evidence to support this belief. Quite the contrary. Numerous studies have documented both the facilitative effects of cooperation and the deleterious effects of competition on conceptual and procedural learning, motivation, friendly feelings, self-esteem, helping, and even motor learning and performance (Kohn, 1992; Johnson and Johnson, 1989; Nicholls, 1989; Stanne, Johnson, and Johnson, 1999). For example, in their 1989 review of 185 studies comparing the effects of cooperative versus competitive task structures, Johnson and Johnson found that cooperation led to more learning, longer time on task, more frequent use of higher-level reasoning strategies, increased creativity, and greater transfer to new situations. Although it may seem counterintuitive, competitive learning environments do not help children be better prepared to succeed in future competitive situations.

When we try to motivate students to higher levels of performance by comparing their performance with their fellow students, we run several risks. First, the students who usually win such competitions may focus on winning, taking shortcuts in their learning or failing to explore novel lines of thinking. Competition may limit rather than foster the learning of these students.

Second, in competitive learning situations, students are likely to form premature notions of what they're "good at" and to turn away from areas of perceived weakness—at a point in their development when we want them to continue building their skills and understanding in all areas of instruction. Some students who see no hope of winning—students who are learning disabled or whose skills are simply less well developed than their classmates—may not try at all, because if they don't try they can't be perceived as really losing (Nicholls, 1989).

Third, competitive learning situations make it hard for students to develop stable self-concepts because they are continuously comparing themselves with others. Students' self-confidence depends on having stable self-concepts that are based on achievements relative to personal, internal standards.

Fourth, the students who cannot control their emotions may find the threat of losing so overwhelming that they fail to keep their behavior organized; they may freeze or disintegrate into tears. Laura's students Kenny and Martin, for example, fell apart when they saw they were about to lose a race. A competitive learning environment may prevent such students from learning anything at all.

Fifth, competition in the classroom divides students and undermines bonds of care and respect. Students who lose feel inferior to and thus resent students who win. Students who win feel superior to and thus lose respect for those who lose.

Finally, competition as a motivator can undermine students' trust in the teacher. By publicly recognizing the performance of some students over others, the teacher may be perceived as valuing some students over others. All students may get the message that their teacher's commitment to them depends on their performance, and the students who usually perform poorly may get the message that their teacher does not care for them at all.

Using competition to motivate students will undermine our students' sense of belonging, their self-esteem, and their competence. Furthermore, it's likely to foster unfriendly feelings and a conflictual, uncollaborative stance in the world. For a much fuller discussion of the harmful effects of competition, see *No Contest: The Case Against Competition,* by Alfie Kohn (1992).

This is not to imply that all competition is always bad or counterproductive. Many people enjoy playing competitive games and sports with their friends and believe that these competitive activities contribute to their friendship. Athletes frequently report that engaging in a competition brings out the best in their performance (Stanne, Johnson, and Johnson, 1999). However, the conditions of such competitions are quite different from the conditions of classroom learning. These are competitions in the realm of performance, not learning. And they are entered into by choice.

In the classroom, students are primarily learners, not performers. Nor do they generally have a choice about participating in the academic competitions that we may use to motivate engagement in learning tasks. If we structure such competitions, our students, by virtue of the class roster, are automatically enrolled in the contest. Their only choice at this point is whether to try.

Furthermore, as we saw in Laura's class, competition can create problems in the classroom even when it has no direct relationship to student learning. The games students play on the playground and in physical education are often competitive. Although these games may seem harmless, when played by children who have little control over their emotions and fragile self-concepts they can generate angry, hurtful behavior. Such behavior is likely to undermine peer relationships and students' sense of trust and belonging.

Because competition is a fact in the world outside the classroom, many parents fear that if we don't run competitive classrooms, their children will not be tough enough to survive. If we downplay competition in our classrooms, some parents worry that we are undermining their children's chances for success. What might we do to prepare our students for a competitive world without perpetuating that world, and how can we reassure our students' parents?

First, we can point out that the ability to cooperate is even more important than the ability to compete. We can help parents see that to be successful in life, their children will need to be able to cooperate not only with friends and family but in the workplace. We can also point out that learning and performance have consistently been found to be superior in cooperative learning environments. We can further point out that our goal is to prepare our students to be able to compete when competition is called for but not to instill or encourage a competitive attitude. In other words, we do not want our students to view their peers and others as their competitors, and we don't want winning or being better than others to be their measure of success. In fact, those attitudes are likely to get in the way of their success.

Preparing Children for a Competitive World

Most of our students, unless they choose a sports career, will meet only occasional competitive situations. When they do, such as when applying for a job or a promotion or for acceptance into college or graduate school, they will need to be able to do their best work under the extra stress of competition. If they lose a competition, they will need to be able to objectively analyze the reasons why, figure out whether they have a chance to win in a new competition, and, if so, prepare themselves. They will need the psychological reserve to stay focused and perhaps the perseverance to shore up their skills.

Success in a competitive world requires having the self-knowledge, self-confidence, and judgment to choose appropriate competitive venues; the relevant knowledge and skills; the emotional control to do one's best under stress; and the perseverance to remain focused in the face of failure that can reasonably be overcome. We can help our students develop all these qualities without the use of competition. If we give our students honest feedback and provide them with opportunities to share their learning and display their skills, they will develop self-knowledge and judgment. If we set appropriately high standards and help and encourage our students to set high standards for themselves, they will develop needed skills and knowledge. And if we encourage and support them through the inevitable experiences of failure, we will help them develop emotional control and perseverance.

Consider the following situation with Martin. Laura had asked the students to write about their ambitions for their lives. Her goal in giving her students this assignment was to help them begin to make connections between their current lives and the future. After the class had been writing for a while, Laura checked in with Martin and discovered that he had misunderstood the assignment and was writing about his "ambition" to become a whale.

> I asked Martin to read me what he had written so far. He read that he wished he could be a whale so he could dive and swim.
>
> I said, "Martin, this is supposed to be about your hopes and dreams, what you want to do with your life and your future. You were born a person; you can't be a whale."
>
> "I wish!" he said. "I said I *wish* I could be a whale." Then he kind of pushed his chair back and folded his arms.
>
> I felt bad because I knew that he was trying to do the assignment, and I knew that he was very upset.
>
> At one point, as I was trying to explain about ambitions, I said, "Martin what do you want to do with your life?"
>
> He said, "Jump in the river and die."
>
> I had to get him going somehow, and all I could think of was his love for football.
>
> I said, "Martin, you and Damian [Laura's son] talk about being football players and getting big and playing for the Pittsburgh Steelers.

Let's get that started. How do you want to get it started?" I'm there with the pencil in my hand, ready to take dictation for a sentence or two, to get him back on track.

This whole time he's sitting back, he's got his head in his hands, and he's very, very upset. When he saw that I was going to help him get started, he finally took his hands down and began to brighten up.

I said, "When serious learners get behind, they have to work twice as hard to catch up. Tell me, how do you want to start?"

He said he wanted to run the ball and play quarterback for the Green Bay Packers. I wrote it down, but I had to say, "Now, Martin, you just can't walk up to the Green Bay Packers and say, "Here I am, I'm your quarterback." You have to have a plan. What are you going to do to get to that point where the Green Bay Packers would want you?"

We started talking about school, and he said, "If you don't have good grades, they're not going to let you play, so you've got to work really hard in school."

I said, "Yes, you can write about that. So keep going and get it done." Then I just kind of walked away, and he picked up the pencil and ended up with a pretty nice little piece. In the end, he was successful and could stand up and read his piece with pride to the rest of the class.

At first, I had thought about leaving him alone and letting him write about being a whale, but then I thought, no, that's going to be humiliating when all the kids start reading about being singers and dancers and teachers and managers and principals, and he's talking about being a whale. So I pushed a little and got him to come around and really think about something that maybe he could do.

There are many other ways Laura could have handled this situation, including letting Martin turn the assignment into a flight of fancy. She chose to require him to begin again for a variety of reasons. She knew that Martin was capable of completing the assignment. She wanted Martin, like all the others, to have something he could read to the class. And she believed that it was important to her students' eventual success in school and in the world for them to begin thinking about their future lives.

Fortunately, Laura knew Martin well enough to remind him of one of his ambitions—an admittedly childish dream of becoming a football player. She got Martin to think about some of the things he would have to do to have a chance of reaching this goal, she stayed with him, doing part of the writing to help him overcome the frustration of having to start over, and she labeled him a "serious learner." In the course of this short interaction, Martin was helped to see himself as a serious learner, overcome his frustration, keep his behavior organized, and persevere at the assigned task—important qualities Martin will need to succeed in a competitive world.

Every classroom presents countless opportunities to encourage and support students to keep trying in the face of mistakes or failure. Such situations are opportunities to develop in students the skills often cited as justification for competition in the classroom—the skills to withstand disappointment and overcome the frustration of losing.

Although our students don't have to have competitive experiences in school to be successful in a competitive world, we do not wish to argue that competition has no place in school. It seems unrealistic and unwise to try to take competition entirely out of our students' lives. In *The Challenge to Care in Schools,* Nel Noddings (1992) offers three conditions that need to be satisfied for competition to be healthy or positive: (1) the activity must be enjoyable, (2) the participants need to be able to take some pleasure in the victories of others, and (3) the performance or products must be improved by the competition.

Like Noddings, we are arguing that students shouldn't have to compete with one another for grades or for our care, attention, and esteem and that learning activities should be primarily cooperative and conducted in a classroom atmosphere that encourages and supports cooperation and helpfulness. Furthermore, any competitive activities should be carefully designed to stress fun and learning over winning and to allow all students an equal opportunity to win. We are also arguing that students shouldn't compete with one another before they have the social and emotional skills needed to manage the emotional experiences of winning and losing.

Once we are confident that our students have acquired sufficient ability to regulate their emotions, we can orchestrate or help our students orchestrate competitive situations in which the teams are fair, no one is harmed, and learning, trying hard, and enjoying the game are seen as more important than winning. Our goals in these instances should be to help prevent students who perform poorly from withdrawing from competitive activities, to teach students how to handle disappointment and persevere in the face of failure, and to teach them positive and graceful ways to handle inevitable experiences of losing and winning.

By the end of November, Laura was so pleased with her students' progress in handling cooperative games and in treating one another with respect that she introduced some simple competitive games of chance. Her hope was to teach her students to handle the experience of competition and the principles of good sportsmanship. Here she experienced a bump in the road.

We're working on place value, and we're doing some little games. I modeled how to play by playing me against the class. At the end of each game, we added up the points. The winner depended on a spinner that came up "More" or "Less." If the class had more points and the spinner landed on "More," they won. If it landed on "Less," then I won.

When they won I would say, "Congratulations, you all played a really nice game."

Then I'd prompt them: "What do you think maybe you could say to me?"

Thank goodness I lost the first two games. They were able to say, "Well, you played a good game, too." So that was our pattern for that game.

Then we played a game for two partnerships to compete by rolling cubes to get to a mat of 100 and then come back down to 0. The teams began fussing back and forth with each other. Some of them were high-fiving and carrying on when they got a good roll, and so I stopped everyone and said, "I really don't like what I'm seeing, and I don't like what I'm hearing. I see a lot of people getting in people's faces when they have a good roll. And I see you laughing at people when they're not having a good roll. I don't like to see the class treating each other this way, so let's talk about what can we do."

Somebody said, "We can do what we do when we play against you, and say, 'Congratulations, you had a good game.'"

When we started again, they went back to our model from the place-value game and said, "Congratulations, you played a good game." And then the people who won said, "Well, you played a good game, too."

Then as we played further, they thought of different things. Sometimes the losers would stand up and shake the winners' hands, and go, "Congratulations, you played a good game." And some of them were giving fives to the other team when the game was over, not like they were doing before but just having a ball. It was a really good feeling.

After four or five rounds, I stopped and said, "Okay, how do you all feel right now?"

And people just started laughing. They were having a lot of fun and it felt good.

I said, "Yeah, and how did it feel before we stopped and talked about it?"

People generally agreed it wasn't fun to get in people's faces.

It was pretty powerful for them to see that what they had been doing didn't feel good and then to have the experience of how good it

(back of illustration continued on following page)

> really did feel when the ugliness was gone. It wasn't like I was trying to set that up—or even knew it was going to happen. Honestly, I was hoping that we had done enough modeling of how to talk ourselves through these games so that we wouldn't have problems. But since when we did have problems we went on and talked about them, on the whole it might have been good for them.

Laura continued to engage her students in competitive games in which winning and losing were determined by chance. She was able to progressively relax her control over the games as her students incorporated the value of winning and losing gracefully into their play and gradually developed the skills to do so.

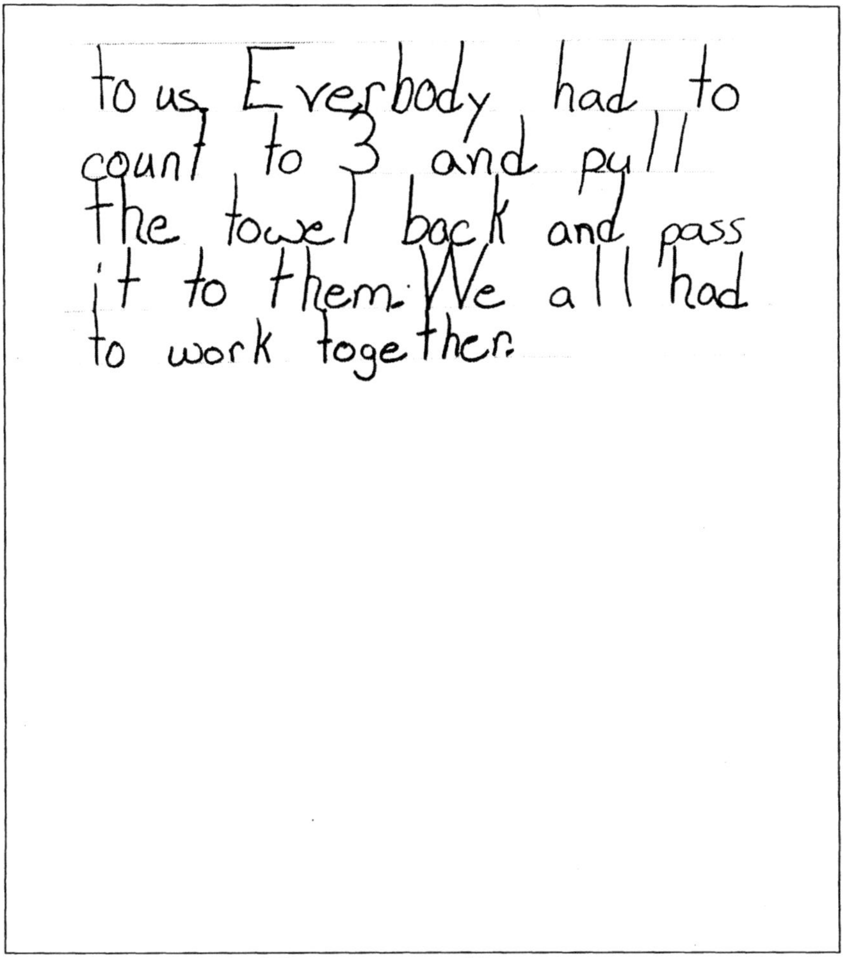
to us. Everbody had to
count to 3 and pull
the towel back and pass
it to them. We all had
to work together.

(back of illustration continued from previous page)

It was the cooperative games, however, that remained their favorites. At the end of the year, two students wrote about the cooperative games for the class book. It was clear that they had internalized the collaborative spirit that the games were designed to engender.

FROZEN CATCHERS
BY JENNIFER

Whenever it's sunny we go out and play
Frozen catchers. Frozen catchers is a game
where you have to run around and freeze people
and then another person comes and unfreezes them.

> Our class plays frozen catchers by tables like
> Monday, Tuesday, Wednesday, Thursday, and last but not
> least Friday. And if we have enough time we will
> take a long mile walk or run. And when we go
> outside it doesn't matter who won or lost the only
> thing that matters is that we're having a good time.

> BALLS AND TOWELS
> BY TARA

> Sometimes we would go
> outside and play with the
> balls and towels. We
> would pass the ball to
> the people next to us and
> they would pass it back
> to us. Everybody had to
> count to 3 and pull
> the towel back and pass
> it to them. We all had to work together.

At the end of Year 1, Laura realized that a competitive spirit still pervaded her classroom. Two contentious meetings to decide whether to capture class memories in a book or quilt forced Laura to recognize that a number of her students continued to see their classmates as competitors, despite her many efforts to eliminate competition from her classroom. For example, she did not place grades on papers; she did not single kids out for special rewards; she encouraged her students to help one another; she never compared them, and she made every effort to let her students know that she cared for them equally. Still, some of her students saw threat everywhere.

Competitiveness and mean-spirited behavior often surfaced on the playground. When they played the common games of childhood, many of Laura's students became much too excited about winning and much too dejected about losing. Their lack of skill regulating their behavior in the face of strong emotions caused them to become abusive or to disintegrate when they lost; winning caused them to celebrate too vigorously or to tease and belittle their opponents.

Laura believed that these repeated unpleasant and confrontational experiences on the playground kept the competitive ethos alive in her classroom. She decided to begin the second year by completely eliminating competition on the playground and teaching her students how to play together cooperatively. Although she had to sometimes insist that her students play the cooperative games cooperatively, they embraced them, with huge dividends as a result in the classroom as well as on the playground.

Because she knew that competitive games and sports were part of her students' lives outside of school, Laura also introduced some simple competitive activities in an effort to help students handle the emotional highs and lows of competition and to teach them good sportsmanship. But she structured these competitive activities to minimize the likelihood that they would engender hurt feelings or ill will; winning and losing were controlled by chance, so she was able to downplay the importance of winning and stress that the goals of the games were to have fun and to learn. Competition with these characteristics has been shown by research to have the least harmful effects on students' self-esteem, helpfulness, and friendly feelings (Stanne, Johnson, and Johnson, 1999). Yet even in these activities, Laura's students initially responded by "being ugly" to one another. With her help, they were able to see that playing even competitive games with a respectful and cooperative spirit was more fun.

The negative effects of pervasive or unguided competition are present in most schools and classrooms. Such competition limits some students' access to learning, contributes to a competitive or unfriendly spirit, and

Key Points: Competition in the Classroom

- Avoid competition in learning activities.
- Refrain from trying to motivate students by comparing them to better-performing or better-behaving classmates.
- Engage students in cooperative games and sports.
- Monitor student play and help them play even competitive games cooperatively.
- Discuss the value of working and playing cooperatively, and engage students in reflecting on their play experiences.
- Help students see that having fun is more important than winning, and teach them how to win and lose gracefully.
- Help parents see the value of teaching their children to be cooperative.

interferes with one of the major tasks of middle childhood—the development of a stable, positive sense of self. Laura's approach to cooperation and competition was fashioned to meet the cultural and developmental needs of her students, both as a means of creating a nurturing learning environment and as a means of preparing her students to face the challenges they would inevitably meet in life—challenges that would most often call on their skills of collaboration and perseverance.

Laura's goal was to prepare her students for life success as well as academic success. To this end, she wove lessons for life into all aspects of the classroom—into class meetings, into her responses to student misbehavior, and into the curriculum. In Part Three, Putting It All Together, we will see how Laura's many lessons focused on one common goal: showing her students how to compose good, successful, and happy lives.

PART THREE

PUTTING IT ALL TOGETHER

8

SHOWING STUDENTS HOW TO COMPOSE A LIFE

> We did a list of things we've gotten better at since the beginning of the year [Year 2]. It was the most interesting thing. People wrote their own list of things they feel they've gotten better at, and then we came together in a meeting to share. The first nine or ten people shared things that were strictly academic, like "I've gotten better at doing the times," "I've gotten better counting by threes," "I've gotten better at reading my words," "I've gotten better at spelling."
>
> When it was Martin's turn, he said, "I've gotten better at making this a safe place."
>
> So I just wrote that down on the class list, and I said, "Yes, you have, and that really feels good."
>
> After Martin said that, then other stuff started coming out.
>
> Jennifer said, "I've gotten better at keeping myself together when I'm ticked." And people had to talk about that a little bit.
>
> And a couple people said they've learned to work with partners and talk to people and tell people things that are on their minds.
>
> They're starting to really think about something that I like to say to them: "School's not just learning how to read and write and do math, but it's also learning about how to live your life. You're learning things that can help you the rest of your life—to have a happy life, to get along with people."

LAURA SAW her job as helping her students become good and successful *people* as well as good and successful *learners*. She saw herself responsible, in her role as teacher, along with parents, ministers, and others, for helping her students develop the knowledge, skills, understandings, and values needed to lead happy, productive, and good lives. In everything she did, she was aware that she was helping her students to, in the words of Mary Catherine Bateson (1990), "compose their lives."

To succeed at composing fulfilling lives, Laura's students would need to construct concepts of themselves as good and capable people, understand that they are in charge of their lives, and be able to exercise control over their behavior when they meet obstacles or temptations. Also, they would need to know something about the possible lives they might compose. For many, these prerequisites were lacking. Laura set out to address each one.

Helping Students Find Their "Real Selves"

A major implication of attachment theory is that a number of children in every classroom—those with a history of insecure attachment—will have a negative view of themselves and will believe or fear that they are unworthy of care. A central part of helping these children learn to trust involves helping them believe that they are worthy.

Pointing Out Strengths

Laura consciously set out to help each of her students see the good that was in them—the "real you." She did this in ways that were realistic and that were consistent with real strengths she saw in the children; her students began to believe her.

> On Friday we took a two-mile walk. The whole school did. We took a walk up a hill to a lake where we were going to have lunch. Tralin was walking with me, and she said, "Look at this Mrs. Ecken, it's just like Martin Luther King when he marched."
>
> And I said, "You're right, Tralin. It does look like Martin Luther King when he was on one of his walks."
>
> And then I said, "You know, you're really becoming a serious learner because serious learners connect things that they learn with things in their lives, and they start seeing that things are related. Like this walk is, in a way, similar to Martin Luther King's walk, people all together on a march."
>
> Then we walked over an overpass with a creek and a little bit of a waterfall below. In class we had been talking about the mountains and the streams, how when the snow melts it becomes a river. They were

like, "Look, it's one of those waterfalls where the water is coming down off the big hills."

So I made a point of saying, "This is what serious learners do. The things they learn in school they notice out in their lives, and they make connections."

These comments about students' strengths were a natural part of Laura's interactions with them, whether acknowledging something privately to a child or to the entire class.

Assuming the Best

When a child misbehaved or did something that appeared to be misbehavior, Laura tried hard to attribute the best possible motive to the child or to give the child time to rise to his or her best and do something to address the problem.

Tyrone's history of taking things put Laura in a difficult position in the second year when yet another book was missing from the classroom and Tyrone was the likely culprit. For example, in the first year Tyrone had taken a little pilgrim doll that belonged to one of his classmates. When Laura confronted him, he said simply, "I want it. It's so nice." Several other things that disappeared from the classroom were found to have been taken by Tyrone.

Then early in the second year, Tyrone took some things from the play-therapy room where he went once a week.

> On Tuesday when Tyrone went to Seven Counties Counseling, he took some of the counselor's things. Miss Jill saw him put them in his pocket. She gave him every opportunity she could to put them back, and he didn't. So after she walked Martin and Leonard back down to the room, she had a talk with Tyrone and told him that she knew that he had her things. She said that she was going to trust that he would do the right thing, and she asked him to walk back into the room and put them back where they belonged. She didn't go in with him.

Laura decided to talk with Tyrone's new foster mother about the thefts. What she learned only raised her concern for Tyrone.

> I talked to Ms. Jewell, and she told me that Tyrone had been going to the store and stealing.
>
> She told me that when she confronted him he said, "It's what we do. It's how my family gets things." I mean, he was just so open about that.

> Ms. Jewell said that she told him, "This is your family now, and it's not what *we* do, and it's not how *we* get things."

A week later, Tyrone took a favorite class book home and claimed that he didn't take it. However, the book was nowhere to be found and his tablemates were sure that he took it.

> I bought this book for the class, *Amelia's Notebook*. They loved that book so much that I bought four more, a copy for each table to share. Tyrone took the copy for his table home on Tuesday, and apparently he took another book home as well. On Wednesday morning, he met me in the hallway on his way to breakfast and asked me to put his book bag with his book in it in the classroom for him, which I did.
>
> Well, in the afternoon when it was time to get out the book bags and give the Amelia books to new people, there was no Amelia book for Tyrone's table. Everyone at the table claimed that Tyrone had taken the book.
>
> Here's what Tyrone said: "Uh-uh, I don't have the book. I brought my book back, and Ms. Ecken saw me bring it back."
>
> And so I said, "Yeah, Tyrone brought a book back. It was *Hansel and Gretel*. I don't know what to tell you. You say Tyrone took *Amelia's Notebook*. Tyrone's saying that he only took *Hansel and Gretel*.
>
> So they're furious, and no one from that table got to take an *Amelia's Notebook* home Wednesday night.
>
> On Thursday, when it was time to give out the books again, the other kids at Tyrone's table were really mad at him again.
>
> I said, "I am so sorry this has happened, but, you know, we don't have any extra books. The other groups are bringing their books back, so new people at those tables get to take them."
>
> And all of a sudden, Tyrone looked up and said, "I do have that book. I found it on my dresser."
>
> I said, "Well, would you mind if I called your house to see if Ms. Jewell can bring it over?"
>
> He said, "No, you can call."
>
> So I called, and she ran it right over.
>
> That was a big move in the right direction for Tyrone. I'm really glad that I didn't make an issue of it early. I knew that eventually I would have to call Ms. Jewell and see if the book was there. I'm glad I waited long enough for Tyrone to do something on his own.

For about two months, there were no more problems with Tyrone trying to steal anything. Then in early December he took another favorite book home and failed to bring it back.

> When Martin wanted to check out the NFL football book, I said, "You can't because Tyrone didn't bring it back."
>
> So Martin said, "Go ahead and put me down for it. I'll walk home with Tyrone after school and get it."
>
> I said, "Tyrone, is that okay with you?"
>
> Tyrone agreed, but when Martin went over to Tyrone's to get the book, Tyrone couldn't find it.
>
> Martin came back the next day in a huff because Tyrone's got this very popular book and no one else can use it.
>
> So I said, "Tyrone, that's a book that everybody wants. And it's a really big responsibility to bring that book home. It needs to come back because people are lined up to check it out at night. Now you've had it for two nights, and people can't check it out. I'm just letting you know, I have a serious problem with this."
>
> The next day, before he went to breakfast, he brought in the book. "Look!" he said, and he was real happy about it.

Even though Laura believed that Tyrone had succumbed to temptation once again and was hoping to keep the football book, she didn't accuse him of stealing. She let him know that she had a serious problem with his behavior, but she did not threaten him. Instead, she appealed to the best in him—to his sense of responsibility.

Then a month later, it again appeared that Tyrone had taken a book home and was trying to keep it for himself.

> We have this book about NBA sports that both Martin and Tyrone really like. Martin had the book in his book box, and Tyrone borrowed it to read during book box time. When it was time to pack up the book boxes, Tyrone asked Martin if he could borrow it for overnight. Martin agreed.
>
> I told the class to put their books for home in their book bags and take the bags out to their lockers. Usually we do the book bags at the very end of the day and don't bother with the lockers.
>
> So Tyrone was signed up to take the NBA book home. Well, the next morning he came in and said, "I never took the book home. I never got out of the classroom with it. I don't know where the book is."
>
> I said, "That's okay. If you forgot to take it home, it's here somewhere. Just find it."
>
> He looked all over; they all did, but the book was nowhere in sight.
>
> So first I was thinking, "He's stolen the book, and he's not going to bring it back, and he's swearing he never took it home, but it's not here so he must've taken it home." But I didn't say anything to him and I said to myself, "Laura, you don't know. Don't open your mouth."

> He went on and on saying he never took it home. I felt sure that he did. I had a picture in my mind of him walking out of the room with it. I didn't know what to do. And so I just looked at him and I said, "Tyrone, if you left the book here, it'll turn up." I was kind of letting him know that if the book wasn't here because he took it home, it wasn't ever going to turn up.
>
> A little while later, while we're doing something else, I thought, "Oh, my goodness, they took their books out to their lockers yesterday."
>
> I said to Tyrone, "Why don't you run out and look in your locker?" Well, there was the book.
>
> I want to tell you, I really did think he stole it.

In situations like these, there's a fine line between affording children the benefit of the doubt and being unrealistic about their motives. However, given how easily Laura's students took offense and how easily they dissolved at the thought of being misjudged, Laura tried to be very careful about making accusations. But she let students know when the issue was serious and still on her mind.

Pointing Out Inconsistencies with Their "Real Selves"

Because Laura's students experienced her as caring, they wanted to live up to her positive expectations—they wanted to be the real self that Laura believed was inside them. They were aware that Laura had confidence in them, even when she was disciplining them. Once when Denise refused to stop disrupting a lesson, Laura asked her to write about what she, Laura, was thinking about Denise's behavior. Denise wrote,

> You think, "Where did you come from? Where is the real Denise? This is a ghost. I don't see this. I want my real Denise here right now."

When one of Laura's students misbehaved and it was clear that the child intended harm, Laura would often talk with him or her in a calm moment, after the incident was well past. In these conversations, Laura's hope was to let the child know that the particular misbehavior was out of character, inconsistent with the real child.

In the following example, Ella had created a huge uproar by telling her mother that she was mistreated by a student teacher while Laura was out of the room. Ella's mother threatened to call the school board. Ella also convinced Tralin to say, untruthfully, that she, too, had been mistreated, and Ella tried to get the whole class to back up her story. The class refused to go along. Rebecca even took Ella outside to tell her she was wrong to do what she was doing. When Tralin saw the trouble she and Ella were causing, she admitted that she had lied. Eventually, Ella's mother withdrew her threat to call the school board. There's no question that on Ella's part this was a serious misbehavior, intended to cause harm to the student teacher. The following week when things had calmed down, Laura had a talk with Ella.

> Carol [the student teacher] went back to the university to take methods classes. She'll be back in three weeks. So I spoke to Ella. I didn't speak to her at length but just a beginning conversation.
>
> I said, "You know, Ella, you're doing so well in this class now. You get along with people and you're very respectful to me and very helpful, and you're respectful to the other children.
>
> "I remember when you first came to this class, how difficult it was for you. I think it may have been because I was new to you, somebody that you didn't know. I'm seeing a little bit of that with Ms. Jackson.
>
> "So I just want you to remember to be who you are, because look at the good and helpful person that you are. The disrespectful, nasty stuff, that's not you. That's not about you."

Laura conveyed a deep sense of respect to Ella in this example and to her students in general without accepting unacceptable behavior. She trusted that they were good people. Perhaps their goodness was deeply hidden or camouflaged by momentary behaviors, but she believed that it was there. And her students gradually realized this and they tried, with many mistakes, to become the real selves that Laura saw in them. Laura, for her part, worked to provide them with the skills and understandings that would enable them to be their best.

Teaching Students to Take Charge of Their Lives

Most of Laura's students needed to develop a variety of skills and understandings in order to successfully direct their own lives. They needed to learn to regulate their emotions and control their behavior in the face of strong emotions, but they also needed to know how to set worthy goals and how to cognitively guide their behavior in accord with their goals.

Modeling and Rehearsing Successful Behavior

In November of the first year, Laura asked her students to assess how they were doing at following their class norms and to suggest things they needed to get better at as a class. Her goal was to then have students practice ways to be more successful with things that were causing problems.

Eight issues came up when we revisited the norms:

- Talking out when someone else is talking
- Having a conversation when Ms. Ecken is teaching or someone is sharing with the class
- Unkind reminders
- Not listening to reminders
- Playing during work time
- Name calling and saying mean things
- Laughing at people
- Helping in an unkind way

I added one: Not getting started on time. They really do have a problem getting started. Like if we leave the reading circle to go do a partner activity, some of them have to walk around the room for five minutes before they can sit down and do something.

We began with not getting started on time and modeled what it looks like *not* to get started on time, and then what it looks like when we do. I was really pleased because later, after we had modeled it, they really were better at finding a place in the room and getting to work.

They want to do the right thing, but in a lot of cases they haven't been taught. We might think they don't need to be taught something like not playing during work time, but maybe they do. And maybe they need to be taught how to start on time.

On Friday, we moved on to why talking out makes it difficult for learning to occur. They were supposed to do role-plays about talking out, so first we talked about how to keep from talking out. They really didn't know, but then what they came up with was kind of like talking in their brain, literally talking to themselves: "I need to raise my hand" or "I need to wait until they're finished saying this, then I can say what I want to." They had about ten things they could tell themselves, and I listed them.

Then we talked about them. These are the things you can do when you really want to say something and it's not your turn to talk or you're going to interrupt what is going on. These are things you can say to yourself in your mind that will help you work through this.

This was Laura's students' first introduction to the process of "self-talk"—talking to themselves to control their own behavior. As the year went on, Laura reminded them over and over again about this way to help themselves do the right thing, but it was not until the second year that they clearly began to use self-talk. In the meanwhile, as they were developing their abilities to control their emotions and their behavior, Laura continued to provide as much assistance and structure as she believed they needed.

Making Opportunities to Set and Monitor Personal Goals

In January of the first year, Laura introduced personal goal setting. She asked her students to write goals on little strips of paper each week and tape them on their tables so they would be reminded of them. Most students willingly complied, but when Denise refused, Laura understood her well enough not to push.

> When we set the goals on Monday, Denise wrote for her goal, "I don't need to work on nothing."
>
> I said, "Oh, Denise, you know everybody needs to work on things. I need to work on things all the time. I have goals for myself" (which made me think that I need to start writing them just like they're doing).
>
> Anyway, I said to her, "If you can't think of something right now, that's fine. When you do, just put it on your list."
>
> It wasn't one minute later that she wrote down something. It was that quick. I think it was about not fighting with people.
>
> It was real interesting. In my mind it was like she was trying to set something up with me, to make me tell her she had to write a goal or to tell her that she had all kinds of stuff she needed to be working on. When she could see I wasn't going to make an issue out of it, then she was like, "Fine, I can do this. I've got stuff I need to work on."

The kind of testing Denise did is consistent with what would be expected from a child who has not yet learned to trust. It was as if Denise, having learned to like Laura, needed to see if Laura would show her lack of respect or tell her somehow that she was a bad child in need of improvement. But Laura envisioned goal setting as a skill to teach children, not necessarily as an opportunity to tell them how they should improve. Her response to Denise reflected this, all the while taking into account Denise's own tenuous trust of her.

Laura's willingness to give students time to come up with authentic goals meant they could approach their goals seriously.

> On Monday when we were writing goals, little Jennifer told me, "I can't think of anything."
>
> I said, "Well, you know, whenever you do, that's fine."
>
> Tuesday afternoon we were talking about getting new partners. We went over some of the things we do to let people know we want to work with them.
>
> When the activity was over, I was near Jennifer's desk and she said, "Miss Ecken, look. I'm working on this." She had put down for a goal, "Greeting a new partner." It is something she has trouble with. So it wasn't like she was just going to throw anything down on the paper. She waited until she thought of a goal that's really real to her.

Of course, Laura's students weren't always serious in approaching their goals, but in some cases it was because they didn't yet really understand the point of goal setting. Sometimes their misunderstandings were quite funny. The following incident occurred a little over two weeks after Martin had set as his goal that he would not hit Deshawn, a new boy in the class whom he had beaten up one day after school.

> When we got back from special area, where Martin had given Deshawn such a hard time, I said, "Martin, for two weeks you've been working on not threatening or hitting Deshawn."
>
> Just as clearly as he could, he looked at me and he said, "I'm not working on that this week."
>
> So I said, "Well, a lot of times people work on things for a while and then decide that they've accomplished them. They're able to say, "I can move on now because I know that I don't need to work on this anymore."
>
> And then I said, "But if you feel like you're still having a problem with hitting Deshawn, you can still work on that. You can keep it as a goal and add it to your paper."
>
> A little while later, we were all sitting in a circle in the chairs and we were going to share about the reading lesson. I said, "I want to talk to you all first a little bit about setting our goals. If you find as you go through the week that maybe what you're working on is okay, but you really need to work on something else, it is okay to add it. You don't ever want to be in a situation where you're trying to work on five or ten things; it's just too difficult to concentrate on that many things. But it's certainly fine with me if you're going through the week and you see that you need to add something to your goals."
>
> The next day, I saw Martin pick up his pencil and write on his goals that he was going to work on not hitting Deshawn.

Laura was able to help Martin understand that when you're serious about working on a goal, you don't "opt out" just when the goal gets most challenging.

Allowing Room for Goals to Work

Gradually, Laura's students began autonomously to use their goals to guide their behavior. Early in the second year, Jennifer, who frequently withdrew and refused to speak when she was angry or upset, announced that she had the goal of "putting myself back together when I'm ticked." A few months later, she pointedly put her goal to use.

> In the computer room on Wednesday, Jennifer was mad because somebody touched her computer and then she couldn't get it to do what she wanted it to do.
>
> When we were coming back to the classroom, she said, "Do you mind if I sit in the hall? I'm ticked, and I've got to get myself back together."
>
> I said, "No, no, that's fine."
>
> So she sat out there. After a while, I walked out and I said, "Jenny, is it anything you want to talk about?"
>
> She said, "No, I think I'm okay now," and she just walked back in.

Laura not only respected Jennifer's goal, but by letting her stay in the hall she allowed Jennifer the autonomy to decide on a strategy for achieving it.

Expanding Students' Goals

In the second year, Laura didn't have her students write weekly goals, but she frequently talked with them about goals and periodically had class meetings in which the children, and sometimes Laura, shared "things we have gotten better at."

In one such meeting (the meeting that introduces this chapter), Martin declared that he had gotten better at making the classroom a safe place. Laura was delighted, both because it was true and because helping Martin achieve this goal was one of Laura's own primary goals for the year. Laura saw Martin's recognition of the significant progress he was making as an opportunity to push him to expand his goals.

> After we got through with that class meeting, they were reading in their book boxes and I called Martin over. I said, "You know, Martin, you really have gotten good about helping this be a safe place and not name calling or laughing and making fun of people. But I've noticed

> that I'm giving you a lot of reminders for silly stuff, like laughing and playing instead of doing your work. What do you think we can do about that?"
>
> Well, he didn't know anything he could do about it. So I said, "What about if we have a goal, like we did for it to be a safe place? If maybe we could have a goal that you're going to work on being a serious learner."
>
> And he said, "Oh, okay."
>
> We talked about it a few times during the week. At times when he got right to work, I said, "You know, I can see that you're working really hard on being a serious learner." And then a couple times when he was fooling around, I said, "Martin, don't forget about being a serious learner." And it was helpful. I didn't spend nearly as much time reminding him.

Laura helped Martin set a goal that he might not have come up with on his own. She didn't communicate that he was a "bad" child with much to improve but that he was a capable child who was already making great progress. As with her handling of Denise earlier, she weighed Martin's own psychology and her relationship with him in deciding to push him to take on a new goal.

Teaching Skills of Self-Control

Living up to their goals wasn't easy for many of Laura's students. They needed strategies for exercising control, which Laura worked to teach them. And they also needed help understanding both the limits and range of their ability to use their control in the different parts of their lives.

Teaching Self-Talk

Self-talk was an extremely useful tool for Laura and her students. She taught them to analyze situations and to talk to themselves and give themselves instructions about how to behave rather than act without thinking. Self-talk helped her students realize that they were in charge of their own behavior and, on a practical level, it gave them a way to pull themselves together and do what they really wanted to do. Tralin was a student who was able to verbalize the power of self-talk in her own bouts with self-control.

> We were going to line up for lunch, and it was just a mess. So I had them do it again. Later that day, we needed to get together on the car-

> peting for reading, and that was a mess. I stopped them and said, "No, now listen. Let's just do this; let's practice it and get it right."
>
> Tralin was like, "I hate this! I hate this school! You're always practicing stuff!"
>
> I said, "Look, drop the attitude. We need to get this right, so we can do it in a calm way."
>
> Tralin was a little bit grouchy over that, but we practiced, and got set up, and I read some of *Shoeshine Girl* to them.
>
> Later, Tralin was working and I was in her vicinity. She came over and she said, "You know what I'm doing? I'm saying in my mind, 'If you make up your mind, you can do anything.'"
>
> She was letting me know that she was trying, that she had a plan, and that she was not going to show that attitude.

Later that year in summer school, Tralin was able to teach what she was learning about self-talk to another student. It thrilled Laura to see how valuable this strategy for self-control had become to Tralin.

> We were teaching the kids about Kentucky, and we had spent all morning in Shakertown, where they have restored the village and they have people making brooms, doing leatherwork, and weaving and washing and ironing clothes in the old-time way. As you go through Shakertown, you see all these things.
>
> After lunch we went on to Fort Harrod, which was the first settlement in Kentucky.
>
> When we got to Fort Harrod, Kenny started to whine and cry, "I'm so tired, I don't want to do anything else."
>
> Tralin said to him, "I'm tired, too, Kenny, but I'm just saying in my mind, 'We're going to see stuff here and let's go do it.'"
>
> I asked Tralin, "Do you really feel like you want to whine and cry right now?"
>
> She said, "Yes, I'm really tired, but I'm telling myself not to do it."
>
> I said to Kenny, "What Tralin's doing, that's something you can do when you're really tired but you still know that you've got stuff to do."
>
> It must have made sense to him. He recovered himself and we had a really nice time.

One reason self-talk was so successful for Laura's students was its concrete simplicity. A student really could "tell myself in my mind." It was a first line of defense against going out of control.

Helping Students Understand Their "Territory"

Even while Laura's students were learning to take control of their lives in school, a number of them felt frustrated and out of control in their lives outside of school. Not infrequently, their frustrations showed up as misbehavior in the classroom. To counteract the helplessness her students sometimes felt about their lives, Laura worked hard to give them control in the classroom.

When Leonard's life outside of class became chaotic, with repercussions in the classroom, Laura eventually helped him focus on making the classroom a place where he could maintain control by himself. Laura's first response, however, was to control Leonard.

> Leonard's having problems at home. The phone's disconnected. The mom's been to court. The dad didn't come home.
>
> This week he started up that screaming he used to do, just screaming out as loud as he can. And he was smarting off all the time to the other kids, and to me, too.
>
> I talked to him Thursday afternoon, and I said, "Leonard, I hate to say this to you, but I can't run this class with you doing that. It's just not going to work. It's hard on everybody when you're constantly trying to egg things on, and get into things, and get smart with me about what we're doing or what I'm saying.
>
> "It's not going to work. And so, I'm going to ask that you stop it."
>
> To me there wasn't any point in talking about it, in saying, "What do you think you can do?" Because it's so obvious he needs to stop.

Three weeks later, it was clear that things hadn't improved at home and that in the classroom Leonard needed Laura's help, not just her expectations. This time Laura took an approach that helped him understand better his ability to take control over at least some parts of his life.

> I had a talk with Leonard. I told him I knew a little bit about what's going on at home, and I told him that I was really sorry that he's having a difficult time, but I said, "You know, you may never be in a situation where things just go smoothly in your life, where there aren't things that are out of your control. But when you come in here, you do have control over what you do and how you act. And even though things are really, really rough, you can be a success. You just have to find it within yourself to do what's right, and remember that what you do affects the people around you."
>
> The next day after we had that talk—and it probably had nothing to do with it—I noticed him coming down the hall in much better spir-

its. I was standing out in the hall watching them all come down from breakfast in the auditorium. He passed Yolanda from last year, and he gave her five, and as he passed Mary, going to her locker, he gave her a playful pinch on the ear and laughed. And, you know, it's just obvious he's so happy to be here at this school, because there are so many things going on in his life outside that he can't control.

A few weeks after Laura encouraged Leonard to be in control of his life in the classroom, he provided an impressive example of doing just that.

When we were inside playing the cooperative ball game on Friday, they had trouble at Leonard's table. Tangela wanted to pass it and everyone else wanted to roll it. I went back and talked to them and said, "Why don't you try it both ways?"

When I was walking away, I heard Leonard say something like, "I'm going to smack you, Tangela."

And so I walked back and I told him, "You are leaving now. You're going over to Ms. Minyard's room. You're not going to sit here and threaten somebody in this classroom just because she wants to play the game in a little bit different way than you do. I will not have it." And I walked away to another group.

So he got up and came over to me and said, "Mrs. Ecken, I didn't say I was going to slap Tangela. I said, 'There you go slapping it again, Tangela.' You just, you didn't hear what I said."

I realized right away what he meant, because if the ball comes at Tangela too fast, she doesn't try to touch it, she just slaps it. And that's why they didn't want to throw it with her.

So I said, "Oh, please forgive me for just jumping to conclusions like that. I thought you were threatening Tangela."

He said, "I wasn't saying that at all."

Then Tangela looked up and said, "He was just saying I was slapping the ball, Mrs. Ecken."

So after the ball activity, when we were wrapping up about what went well and what didn't, I brought up what happened with Leonard. I said, "When I accused Leonard of threatening to slap Tangela, I was wrong. I misunderstood what he said. But he came up to me in a very nice way and explained what happened, so it was very easy for me to listen to him. If instead he had jumped up and started screaming at me—because I had treated him really unfairly and accused him of doing something he didn't do—it would've been very hard for me to listen to him, or even believe him. But, you know, he was very calm and he just

> told me in a nice way. When people talk to you in that way, it's very easy to listen and hear what they have to say."
>
> That whole incident made a big impression, I think. The next week, one of the kids mentioned it in relation to something else that was going on. They said, "Remember how Leonard tried to talk in a nice way."

It's not always possible to know whether or how we, as teachers, have made a difference in our students' lives. But it seems likely that Laura's ongoing efforts to put words to the problems her students faced and her encouragement for them to exercise control over their lives did help them see the world as a more manageable place, at least the world of the classroom.

Highlighting the Crossover from Classroom to Life

Although Laura focused on teaching students how to be in control so they could succeed in school, she never doubted that she was teaching them life skills. The goal of all of Laura's teaching—about academic subjects and about getting along with others—was to help students make more and more connections and to apply their learning to their lives. For her students living in the housing project across the fence, learning to use their self-control to avoid the kind of trouble that would come looking for them was one of the most important lessons Laura could teach.

> We were in the morning meeting and Tralin said, "Last night I was out on the porch and Ella and I were putting grease in each other's hair and these girls walked by and said, 'Your hair's all going to all fall out.' And then they started telling us we were ugly.
>
> "We didn't say anything to them. I looked at Ella and said, 'Don't say nothing to them or they'll start an argument or a fight.' And so we just walked."
>
> I said, "What do you mean?"
>
> She said, "We just got up and went in the house. We could tell they wanted to start something with us."
>
> I said, "Here we've got two people that are taking stuff that we've done in school—like just moving your partnership when you can see that the people near you want to mess with you—and they're using it at home. That's what learning is."

Modeling a Future

In addition to accepting responsibility for their lives and developing the skills to set and reach positive goals, elementary-school-age children begin to look to the future and to imagine their future lives. Erik Erikson called this the "age of industry," and he described the main developmental task of this age to be gaining a sense of competence through the successful acquisition of the tools of one's culture (Erikson, 1963).

Toward the end of the first year, it became clear to Laura that her students had very limited and even somewhat pessimistic views of their future. She knew that many of them would need to overcome significant obstacles on their way to composing happy and productive lives. Thus she planned to weave throughout the second year a focus on biographies and possible adult professions. She wanted her students to understand that many people face obstacles, that there are many paths to a successful life, and that they should begin dreaming about and planning for their futures now. She wanted both to expand their knowledge about possible jobs and professions and to instill in them a sense of hope for their future lives.

This focus on their future began with students interviewing each other about what they wanted to be when they grew up. It continued throughout the year with the use of biographies across the curriculum. And it was punctuated with visits from local professionals whom the students interviewed about their jobs and work lives.

Using Biographies to Acknowledge Challenges

The class library included many biographies that students could choose for their book boxes or take home to read. Laura also read biographies aloud to the class—biographies of contemporary figures such as naturalist Jane Goodall, astronaut Mae Jamison, and Martin Luther King Jr. And toward the end of the year, students worked with a partner to study and report on a significant person in history.

As with their science research projects, students had a limited choice of topics and several sources for information. For about an hour each day the student partners read, took notes, and discussed. Then, as was customary when they did research, they gathered as a class to share something new they had learned. Laura facilitated this sharing, occasionally drawing the class into a deeper discussion of particularly interesting or important points. On the fourth day of their research, Louise and Tralin reported on the harassment Elizabeth Blackwell, the first woman doctor, suffered when she tried to go to medical school.

> When it was Louise's turn, she told that Elizabeth Blackwell was called names like "crazy" and "bad."
>
> Tralin, who was her partner, tried to explain. She said, "They called her that when she walked into the hospital. When she started to go

into these classes the men called her 'crazy' and 'bad' because they knew she was going to be a doctor."

For the other kids, it still wasn't clear why she should be called names. I said, "Well, what was going on there?"

Tralin said, "She started going to classes with men and there were only men doctors."

Tyrone asked, "Why can't a woman be a doctor?"

Tralin said, "Well, there were only men doctors and it was the law. They didn't have any women doctors and she was the first."

I said, "Yes, it was a different life then, and that's why there are books about Elizabeth Blackwell, because she was the first woman doctor and she had to overcome all these obstacles and hardships to be there."

I asked the class, "Is anyone else reading about a woman who wanted to do things but it was hard for her because she was a woman?"

Tangela said, "Amelia Earhart, she wanted to be a pilot and she was a tomboy."

And Lana, who's Tangela's partner, said, "When she told her sister she wanted to be a pilot, her sister said, 'Good,' but her friends called her 'pilot girl' and stuff."

Then I asked, "Is anyone else studying someone that had to endure hardships?"

Tyrone said, "When Thomas Edison was little, his friend drowned. And he got a whipping in the square of the town and his dad said anyone could watch if they wanted to. And you know when he went to school, they probably said"—and then Tyrone sang it just like a kid would sing it—" 'Thomas got a whoopin', Thomas got a whoopin'.' "

I said, "Yes, you know, Tyrone, that's probably something that did happen and that he had to overcome and just go on with his life."

It was Tyrone who opened up this conversation with his, to our adult minds, naive question, "Why can't a woman be a doctor?" Tyrone's question provided Laura with an opportunity to bring up an issue she addressed whenever she had an opening—that becoming successful usually involves overcoming obstacles.

Laura was well aware that her students faced more than their fair share of obstacles, but she wanted them to see themselves as children with many gifts, who could use their gifts and their education to overcome those obstacles. She wanted them to feel a kinship with Fredrick Douglass, who had to fight to get an education; with Elizabeth Blackwell, who had to withstand derision to pursue her dream of becoming a doctor; and even with Thomas Edison, who had to overcome the humiliation of a whoopin' in the town square.

However, like many of the most dramatic lessons in Laura's class, this one wasn't specifically planned. The opportunity arose and Laura seized it.

> It's really interesting to me that focusing on the hardships in the lives of the people we were studying wasn't initially in my plan. Initially, my focus was just to help my students see what kind of jobs were out there and how people made their lives and made successes out of themselves.
>
> As they started studying, they saw that many of the people had a lot of hardships and obstacles to overcome. It was so important because these kids have all kinds of hardships in their lives, unbelievable things that they're going to have to overcome to be successful. And here they are studying successful people and seeing that they, too, met roadblocks, that they, too, sometimes had to overcome things that seemed almost impossible to overcome. Here were examples of people who found a way to contribute to the world because they were able to say, "This is what I want to do and I'm going to do it and I'm not going to stop. I'm going to go out there and I'm *not* going to worry about what people are going to think or say about me. I've got a dream and I'm going to fulfill it."
>
> That's probably one of the most important things that we've done this year—for the kids to see that people do have hardships and still they can be successful.

Laura's students were sensitive to hardships, and by recognizing them in the lives of the people they were studying, it opened the way to an important discussion in their consideration of how to compose a life.

Bringing in Local Visitors to Demonstrate Success

Over the year, Laura brought into the class people from the community to talk about their jobs—as a football coach, a dentist, a technical writer for the Louisville Water Company, and the owner of a small business. Before each visit, Laura had her students generate a list of questions they would like to ask the person about his or her job.

> Before Mr. Odell Henderson came in, I explained that he was in the landscaping business and what that meant. So the kids talked at their tables about what they wanted to add to the list that they ask all their visitors: What is fun and interesting? What skills are needed? What are the

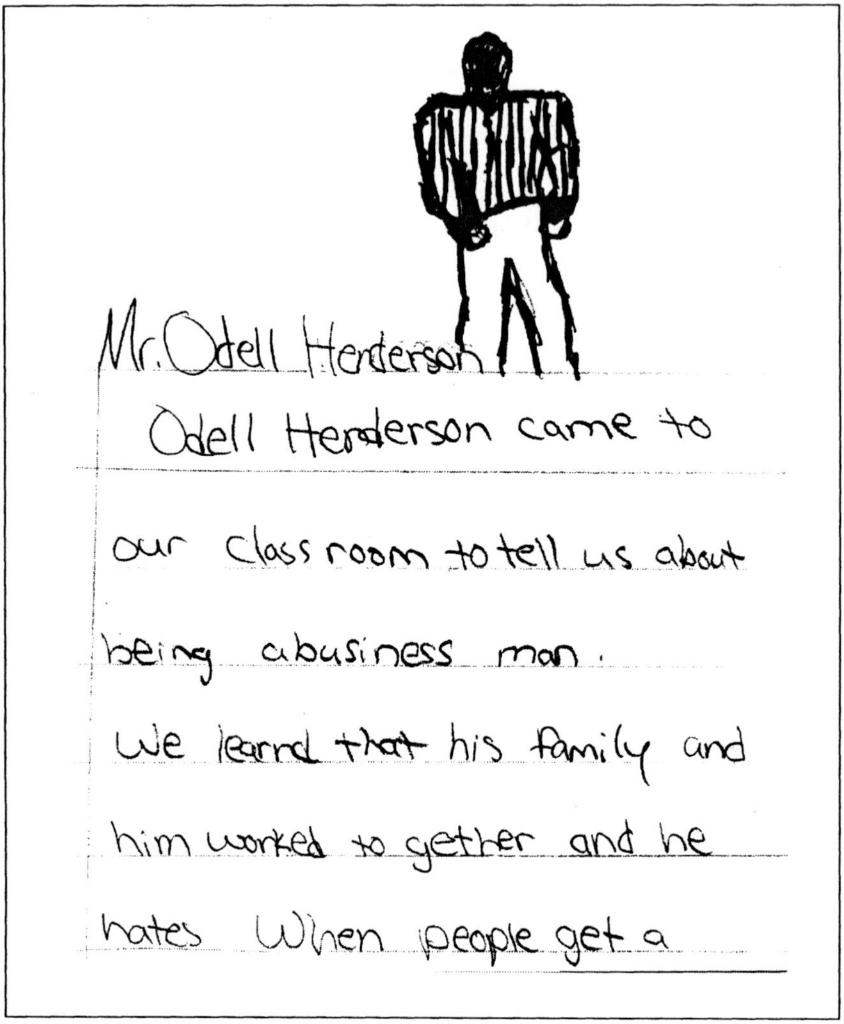

benefits to society? What things can you learn while doing the job? They came up with quite a few new questions:

- How many houses do you go to each day to plant the flowers?
- Is your job fun?
- Do you like the people you work with? Louise came up with this. I thought it was interesting because she has a lot of trouble getting along with the kids and getting the kids to like her. So I guess that was important to her that you like the people you work with.
- How old were you when you started?

an attitude. He likes to be with people that respects him very well. He works hard.

- What grosses you out about your job?
- Do you have to work on Saturdays and Sundays?
- How much does your equipment cost?

When Mr. Henderson came, the questions were on a bulletin board on the side of the room. I wanted the kids to have a conversation with him, not just read off questions, but I told them, "If as you're talking about things you need some help thinking of a question, you can look over and use these questions as a guide."

Mr. Henderson was very comfortable with the kids and he started by saying, "I want to tell you all a little bit about myself."

He told them that he grew up in Louisville, that he started out in public housing, that he went to Iroquois High School, which is the area high school that they'll go to and that a lot of their brothers and sisters go to.

Then he told how he went to Moorehead State University on a scholarship and was a receiver on their football team. He told them that he was a really good player and felt sure he would have a career in the NFL. Then he tore up his knee in practice and that finished his career.

He told them how upset he was and that he even thought about quitting college and going back home. But what he decided instead was to finish his education since it was something that no one could ever take away from him and the only way he was really going to make it in this world. So he went ahead and finished college.

After this introduction, he invited the students to ask him questions.

Gabrielle asked him how old he was when he started working. He told them he was in third grade, just like many of them, when he started a little shoeshine business. His father was in the military in Germany at the time, and I guess lots of people in the military were needing to have their shoes shined. He also told them he started his landscaping business when he was about thirty-five years old.

Tyrone asked him what was fun about his job. He said, "It's the ability to work for myself and set my own goals and then to reach my own goals."

Then he added, "What's really fun about it is seeing what the landscaping looked like when you first came and then seeing how beautiful it is when you get finished. And seeing that the homeowner is satisfied, and that you're satisfied. And that you get paid—that's really fun when you get paid!"

Tralin picked up about living in Germany and asked him what he liked about Germany. He told her he liked the totally different culture there and he liked learning the language. So then she asked him to count to ten, which he did.

Then Louise got right back on the subject and asked her question, about whether he likes the people he works with. He said, "Yes, I do, because basically it's my family and a few of my friends. And the reason I like them is they're dependable. They come to work when they say they're going to come. And they're responsible—they do what they say they're going to do."

I was really pleased by how clearly Mr. Henderson was holding up some of the same values I have been working on with the kids. I was also pleased at how nicely the kids were doing. I thought, listening to

> them, "This class has come a long way." For example, when they were asking their questions, some kids asked Mr. Henderson a question that someone else had originally said they wanted to ask. It didn't seem to bother anyone. No one said, "That's my question." Believe me, a year ago they would have. They just really wanted the questions answered and it didn't matter who asked them.
>
> Then Tom asked about his hours. He said that he gets up at 5 A.M. and is out the door by 6:30. Rebecca chimed in, "Just like my grandma."
>
> Martin asked about the kind of equipment he used, and Mr. Henderson told about his truck and trailer, the little backhoe, the shovels, and all that kind of stuff.
>
> Then he talked about his advertising. He explained that he has a mission and he wants to do a really good job and have his customers be satisfied. He showed how he had written about all that in his first advertising brochure, which was printed in black and white. Then he pulled out some color brochures and explained that when his business got better, he went to color to attract more customers. The kids loved seeing that concrete measure of Mr. Henderson's success.

Laura's students were literally on the edge of their chairs during this interview. Here was someone from the projects who had a successful business and a rewarding life. Here was someone who thought he would be a professional ball player but instead had to rely on his education. Odell Henderson conveyed to Laura's students strong messages of hope, self-respect, determination, and the value of education. He provided a model of success that too few of Laura's students had experienced. Not surprisingly, at the end of the interview with Mr. Henderson, when he offered his business card to anyone who wanted it, every child in the class was pleased to accept and admire this small token of a promising future.

o

The hardships that many of her students faced sometimes took Laura's breath away. She, like most teachers of children in poverty, wished she could do more to better their lives outside of school. However, what she could and did do was important, powerful, and likely to affect her students' lives even after they left her classroom. She made their lives in the classroom as positive as she could by creating a classroom community that met her students' basic needs for autonomy, belonging, and competence. She helped them become aware that they were, in fact, composing their lives, and she taught them the academic, social, emotional, and moral skills and understandings they will need to compose happy, productive, and good lives. Finally, she gave them hope for the future as she nurtured in them the understanding that they are in control of their lives and that they have the capacity to compose successful lives, even in the face of hardship. As we will see in the next chapter, she was striving to create conditions for success in their lives, and in her life with them.

Key Points: Showing Students How to Compose a Life

- Help students build a positive self-concept by frequently pointing out their real strengths, assuming the best, appealing to their sense of fairness, responsibility, or empathy, and helping them see that their momentary misbehavior is inconsistent with their "real selves."
- Teach students to take charge of their lives by modeling and helping them rehearse successful ways to solve problems and set and monitor personal goals.
- Directly teach skills of self-control such as counting to ten and using self-talk.
- Provide students with enough space to take charge of their lives in the classroom, and help them see that they have the power to do so.
- Talk with students about how the life skills they are learning in the classroom can be used in their lives outside of school.
- Help students envision their future, understand that there are many ways to construct a successful adult life, and see that successful lives involve challenge and opportunity.

9

FINDING THE CONDITIONS FOR SUCCESS

On Monday, Leonard and Tangela were getting into it at their table. Tangela was kind of bugging Leonard, and Leonard said, "Shut up, you ugly thing."

Even after I said, "Leonard, we don't talk to people like that in here," he did it again.

He said, "Tangela just keeps saying stuff to bother me."

I said, "Leonard, we don't talk like that. If Tangela is bothering you, just tell her."

He said, "Well, you won't do anything to her."

I told him, "You're absolutely right. I'm not going to 'do anything' to anybody in this class. I don't ever want to. Not you. Not Tangela. Not anyone. What we're trying to do is just set up a class where we're all respectful to each other. I don't ever want to be in a position where I'm 'doing something' to somebody."

And you know, he looked at me like it clicked. He nodded and then he just went on back to work.

LAURA OVERSTATED her unwillingness to control. In fact, of course, she exercised a good deal of control in the classroom. But her goal was not to control through punishment. Her goal was to help students understand the consequences of their behavior and acquire the skills to control themselves. Laura conveyed this message over and over in different words, at different times, to different students. Gradually they came to understand, they began to take responsibility for their own behavior, and they became her allies in creating a harmonious and productive community of learners. They became a source of support to Laura, not simply her challenge.

Many of the traditions, structures, and common practices in education serve to undermine rather than support the development of nurturing relationships with our students. Building such relationships is hard work even in the best of circumstances, and few of us teach in the best of circumstances. Generally, we have too little time, too many children, and insufficient resources and support. However, there are a number of things we can do to improve our circumstances and increase our chances for success.

Relationships Take Time

Relationships take time to build. As we have emphasized earlier, this is particularly true for children with a history of insecure attachment or whose backgrounds, customs, or cultures differ significantly from ours. We can gain time with a class by keeping them with us for more of the school day and for more than a single year, and we can gain time with individual students by working to keep class sizes small.

Keeping Students for Two or More Years

One way to increase our chances of building nurturing relationships with our students, especially the ones we find difficult, is to keep students for two or three years. Some teachers do this by teaching a multigrade class, and some do it by looping—moving up a grade or two with their students. If your school does not have a policy of moving teachers up with their classes, it can often be arranged on a case-by-case basis. Some teachers have found partners who also want to keep a class for two or more years, and they work out a trade. However you manage to do it, the single most important step you can take to increase your ability to build nurturing relationships with your students is to stay with them for more than one year.

Nel Noddings (1992) has argued forcefully for the importance of continuity in education, and she and David Flinders (Flinders and Noddings, 2001) have outlined in a clear and succinct pamphlet the research and the many benefits likely to result from teachers and students staying together for more than one year. For example, teachers are more satisfied, as they are better able to see the results of their efforts; students see their teachers as more caring and they have more confidence in them; discipline problems are lessened, and group cooperation is increased.[1]

Laura taught in a school that had an ungraded primary, so it was natural for her to have her students for more than one year. However, because of enrollment swings, even in an ungraded primary some years bring an almost completely new class. This was the case for Laura in Year 1; only two of her students were returning from the previous year. Again, as sometimes happens, this class of almost all new students contained an unusually large number of students with a history of learning and behavior problems. Laura struggled mightily to build trusting relationships with these students. Although her relationships improved throughout the first year, it wasn't until the second year that she felt she had established enough trust to really push her more difficult students to strive for higher standards in their learning and behavior. Also, the second year was more pleasant and productive for Laura herself; she was able to see the progress and reap the benefits of her efforts during the first year.

ALLOWING TIME FOR TRUST TO GROW. Although Laura was able to build a mutually trusting relationship with some of her students early in the first year, with her more troubled students it took much longer. With some, she was still working on building her relationship with them well into the second year. As late as December of the second year, Rebecca worried that Laura's response to conflict might be "mean."

> Rebecca and Tyrone got into a big fuss over their crayons. They were sitting next to each other coloring, and Rebecca accused Tyrone of taking her yellow. She grabbed it away from in front of him when they were cleaning up and put it in her zip-lock bag. And then she took another one she thought was hers. Later, while the class was doing cursive handwriting, I asked Rebecca and Tyrone what had been going on, because they both had really gotten upset.
>
> Rebecca said, "They were mine. I could tell by the way they looked."
>
> Tyrone said, "I know the yellow was mine because I dropped it and chipped it, and the one she took had the little chip in it."
>
> I said, "Rebecca, do you see the problem here? Tyrone is positive it was his, and you're sure it was yours. Since you all sit so close together, let's try to work this out so it doesn't happen again. What's an idea?"
>
> Tyrone said, "Well, try to keep them in front of you."
>
> I said, "Rebecca, what do you think?"
>
> No answer. Nothing.
>
> So I said, "Well, can you think of a way?"
>
> She said, "No!"
>
> So I suggested that after they unzip their bags, they take out only the crayons they're using, instead of dumping them all out on the table.
>
> Tyrone thought that would work but Rebecca said "No!" again, and then put her head down and wouldn't say anything.

> When we started the reading lesson, she was still pouty and wouldn't cooperate with her partner, so I had to ask her to go to the table in the back of the room and do the work by herself, which she did.
>
> When it was time for lunch and I was asking people to line up, Rebecca motioned me to the back table.
>
> She said, "Well, I want to tell you what I thought about the crayon plan. I think it's a good plan."
>
> I asked her, "Why didn't you let me know before, when we were talking with Tyrone?"
>
> She said, "Cause I thought you were going to be mean to me."
>
> I said, "Rebecca, have I ever been mean to you?"
>
> She started laughing, and she said, "No."
>
> I said, "Well, we've been together for two years now. That should be a clue that I will never be mean to you."
>
> And then she started laughing again and said, "Okay."
>
> This happened at 11:30. About 2:00 she walked up to me and said, "Aren't you glad we got those crayons worked out in a fast way?"
>
> To myself I'm like, "I can't believe this," but I said, "Yeah, it didn't take us long to agree on a plan once we could talk about it, did it?"

Laura was surprised that after all their time together, Rebecca could still mistrust her. But because this was Laura and Rebecca's second year together, Laura could also recognize the progress Rebecca had made. As a result, instead of this incident ending in anger and frustration for both of them, it allowed Laura and Rebecca to continue building confidence in their abilities to solve problems and trust each other.

ALLOWING TIME FOR COMMUNITY NORMS TO COALESCE. By January of the second year, although a few students remained mistrustful, Laura's class was generally so harmonious that new students clearly benefited from being surrounded by classmates who trusted their teacher and who had internalized a spirit of cooperation and a desire to learn. The atmosphere in the class seemed to accelerate new students' ability to trust Laura, and her experienced students actively socialized new students to the class norms.

> I have this new little boy, Derek. His mom brought him in this morning, so when she was leaving I stepped outside with her and told her I was glad to have Derek join our class. I asked her, "Is there anything about Derek that you think would be helpful for me to know?"
>
> She said, "Yes, he's hyper. He won't do what his teachers ask him to do, and he's got a really bad attitude. I'll probably have to come up

here a couple times a day to make him do what he's supposed to do, so I'll be in later today to check on him."

What I noticed right away was Derek surveying the classroom—looking around and figuring out who he was going to like and who he wasn't going to like. When it was time for lunch and I asked them to line up, he was working with Brian. He said to him, "Get in line, fat boy."

Well, Mary and Ella were just horrified that he had called Brian that. They came running up and said, "Derek called Brian 'fat boy.'"

Brian said, "It's okay. It's okay. We're just kind of talking."

I thought it was good that Brian didn't go over the deep end, but you could tell he was embarrassed.

I said, "Derek, this is a classroom where everyone is safe, and they're safe from people calling them names. That won't be tolerated here."

Then we went on down to lunch. It was Tuesday, so Tyrone's table was going to bring their trays back to the classroom to eat with me. Tyrone asked if Derek could join us, since Derek's turn wouldn't come up until the following Monday, and I said, "Sure."

During lunch, Tyrone was clearly trying to win Derek's approval. The two of them got into a bunch of fooling around that Tyrone knew was out of line. But it seemed that if Derek was going to be loud or run down the hall, Tyrone was determined to be right there with him.

Even though Tyrone did his best to befriend Derek, Derek chose to establish his place in the classroom by making fun of Tyrone, causing Laura to deliver Derek's second explicit lesson in the norms of the classroom.

On Friday afternoon Tyrone came up to me and said, "Ms. Ecken, I've tried to solve this myself. I've asked him to stop a couple times and he won't stop. Derek keeps saying that I'm wearing a girl's belt."

I said, "Derek, is that true?"

He said, "Yeah."

So I said, "You know, that's just a plain, blue leather belt. There's nothing girl about it. It's just a belt."

I asked Tyrone how Derek's comment made him feel. Tyrone said, "It makes me feel like he's making fun of me."

I said, "Derek, we're not going to have that here. You need to take care of it."

I walked away and didn't hear what he said, but he must have told Tyrone he was sorry because Tyrone said, "I accept."

Derek also had some difficulty understanding and adjusting to the academic norms of the classroom. The class was doing partner work with a

Martin Luther King biography. Laura had Derek join an existing partnership of two hard-working students. She hoped that these students would help Derek get a sense of what partner work was like and that they would provide a good model for Derek of serious learning.

> I asked Derek to join John and Paul's partnership, but he said, "No, I want to be Leonard's partner."
>
> I said, "Well, I just think it would be better if you work with John and Paul."
>
> In this activity, first they're supposed to read the captions under the pictures and talk about them. Then they go back and read the chapter together. Finally they talk and write about the question, "Why do you suppose black and white people were not treated equally?"
>
> When it was time to talk about the question and do the writing, I overheard Derek say, "How much do we have to write down?"
>
> John said, "Well, as much as we can think of."
>
> Derek said, "You're kidding!"

After the students had talked in their partnerships and written about the question, they gathered as a class to share their thinking, which Laura recorded on chart paper. Laura then asked the class to reflect on how their partnerships had gone. Here again, Laura's students helped Derek get a sense of the norms of kindness and hard work that had come to characterize the class.

> After people talked about things that went well in the partnerships, I asked them if there were any rough spots.
>
> Tyrone said, "It's really not a rough spot like a fight. I didn't understand that the little words under the pictures were the captions. Brian kept telling me that I wasn't doing the assignment right, and then he showed me the little bitty words that are the captions."
>
> Because Derek was there I made a big deal of it. I said, "Now, you all got that settled because you talked about it. And Brian explained it and you understood it. That was a good thing to happen."

Derek was not accustomed to the kind of class Laura ran and might well have been very disruptive. He was embarrassed by her affectionate way with students and unused to classrooms where academic work was willingly engaged in. In striving to be dominant, he belittled and teased several of the other students. Earlier in the year, such teasing would have escalated into fighting, but by this time most of Laura's students had learned to ignore mean comments or to seek her protection when they needed it.

> When I got back from the fifth-grade classroom on Thursday, Martin said, "Ms. Ecken, Derek is making fun of me. He's making fun of Tyrone. We've asked him to stop and he won't quit."
>
> Apparently, it started with Derek making fun of Gabrielle because she was having trouble making her Qs and Martin telling her to ignore him.
>
> So Derek started talking about Martin's mom, and Martin tried to ignore him. Martin said, "I turned around and started talking to Jennifer about a program on TV so I couldn't hear him [a strategy Laura taught the class to help them ignore taunting]."
>
> And then Tyrone said, "I was going up to use the restroom and Derek goes, 'Look at how he walks, and his mother's ugly, too.' "
>
> Martin said, "I walked over to Tyrone and I said, 'Just ignore him.' "
>
> And, you know, they didn't get into it with him.
>
> I had a talk with Derek. I told him, "Derek, people don't put up with teasing in this classroom. They're not going to just sit and be afraid because you're making fun of them and saying stuff about them. They're going to ask you to stop, just like Tyrone did the other day. They're going to confront you about what you're getting on them about, and if you don't stop they're going to ignore you. And then if they can't take it anymore, they're going to come to me. So I just want you to be aware of how this classroom works."
>
> Then I said to him, "I know you can do this, Derek. I've seen you get along and do what you need to do. So come on." That was the end of the conversation, and actually he did fine the rest of the day.
>
> He really is getting better. He has trouble academically, and I think that's one reason why he does so much teasing. But one thing I've noticed, when he first came he wouldn't get near me and now he comes up and hugs me and he does what all of them do. So he's coming along; he just needs more time.

Derek was in many ways a dear child, but he was also difficult. Part of Laura's optimism that Derek would adjust and become a contributing member of the classroom stemmed from her success with the class. But she also realized that her students would help her help Derek.

Laura continued to be affectionate with Derek and continued to stop him whenever he hurt or tried to dominate another child. By March, despite his mother's warnings, Derek was beginning to become an eager and cooperative student.

> Derek and Brian are partners on the animal research project. At the end of the first lesson, when we were talking about successes and rough

> spots, Brian said, "When we got our partners we didn't fuss about it. We just smiled. When we were writing, I wrote some of it and he wrote some of it."
>
> Derek added, "We got straight to work. Then we kept on getting in fights, and how we solved it, we talked about it and got right back to work."
>
> I said, "You know, Derek has only been here a few weeks, and he's already working out rough spots."
>
> And so Derek had to get up and take a bow. Everybody clapped and he was so proud.

By the end of the year, it was clear to Laura that Derek had internalized the friendship and learning norms of the class. Laura did much to help this happen—in the ways she welcomed him to the class and included him in displays the class had made earlier of family portraits and class graphs, by being available to help him adjust to their ways of doing things, by frequently commenting on his progress and telling him how glad she was to have him in her class, and by reporting his progress to his parents.

Yet, in Laura's words, "A lot of Derek's fitting in had to do with the class." By the time he arrived in January of the second year, just about all of Laura's students were serious learners and intrinsically motivated to treat classmates and Laura with kindness and respect. Thus Laura could spend more time helping Derek, and they could help him as well. At the end of the year, Derek wrote two pages for the class book about what he wanted to remember.

> WRITING NOTEBOOKS
>
> In our classroom we got to get
> out our notebooks and we got
> to write in our notebooks. We
> got to write anything in our
> notebooks and it was so fun
> writing in our notebooks.

These pages—written by a boy who entered the classroom expecting to master a dominance hierarchy and having no experience of students who willingly agreed to write "as much as we can think of"—indicate how thoroughly Derek internalized two important norms of the class: we are friends and we are serious learners.

These norms hadn't really coalesced until the middle of Laura's second year with her class. Pianta (1999) has argued that "when a child's contact with the same teacher is extended for more than an academic year, the intervention deepens and enriches the child-teacher relationship, increasing the possibility that this relationship will produce benefits in terms of student success" (p. 174). Laura's experience of having her students for two years—of being able to draw on her knowledge of them and her strong relationships with them to motivate their kind behavior and serious learning—is compelling evidence of Pianta's point.

Husbanding the School Day

In addition to staying with your students for two or more years, there are a number of strategies for increasing the time you have with students on a daily basis.

AVOIDING DEPARTMENTALIZATION AND PULLOUTS. Pullouts and departmentalization lessen the amount of time you and your students have together. Particularly for primary students, departmentalization can seriously reduce their ability to manage their lives at school and learn to understand and trust you. Likewise, the less time your students are in your classroom, the less time you have to get to know and understand them.

This does not mean that you should never send students to another teacher for instruction or never under any circumstances departmentalize instruction. It does mean that special support teachers should be encouraged to work with your students in your room, as much as possible, and that you should carefully balance the potential benefits of departmentalization or special-area teachers with the potential burdens. Although departmentalization allows the possibility of higher-quality specialized instruction, the opportunity to reduce your lesson planning, and the chance to have some planning or work time during the school day, it also means that children must adjust to multiple teaching styles and that you have less time to learn about them, less opportunity to connect their learning across curriculum domains, less insight into how different events in each child's day interrelate, and less opportunity to provide a consistent educational experience for your students.[2]

Laura's students went to a special-area teacher for one forty-minute period every day. Three days a week this worked quite well, and two days the students were unhappy or causing trouble (they begged not to go to the music teacher, and the physical education teacher could not control Laura's students with her extrinsic point system). Four students also met as a group with a psychologist for play therapy once a week, and one student, Leonard, had individualized reading instruction once a week.

The individualized reading instruction posed something of a problem because the reading specialist insisted on taking Leonard out of the classroom in the morning, during the time Laura reserved for class reading and writing instruction. This instruction period was also a time rich with class discussion about how characters (and people) conduct their lives. To allow Leonard to remain a full participant in the class's core experiences and thinking, Laura decided to move the reading period for the whole class to the afternoon.

MAKING LUNCHTIME SPECIAL TIME. Much has already been made of Laura's practice of eating lunch in the classroom with four or five students every day. The students loved this chance to have their teacher simply sit and talk with them. And Laura didn't mind giving up the thirty minutes because this relaxed time was such a powerful investment in the relationships she was building with each student.

Limiting Class Size

Common sense and research support the simple proposition that small class sizes lead to better educational outcomes for students and higher job satisfaction for teachers. For example, in the most carefully controlled study to date, Tennessee kindergarten through fourth-grade children in small classes (thirteen to seventeen students) outperformed students in large classes (twenty-two to twenty-six students), whether the large classes had a full-time classroom aide or not (Nye, Hedges, and Konstantopoulos, 2000). These results held for all types of schools—inner-city, rural, and suburban.

The researchers did not offer an explanation for why children in small classes perform better. However, Pianta (1999), in reviewing several smaller-scale studies, concludes that teachers are able to form more positive relationships with their students in smaller classes. "Across different grades, and across both special and regular education classrooms, when teachers have fewer children to teach, there is evidence that teachers respond more frequently and positively to children, interact with them in a more individualized manner, and can monitor their progress more carefully" (p. 153). In a longitudinal study of more than ten thousand students in English infant schools (children range in age from four to seven), teachers with small classes (fewer than twenty students) were "more easily able to provide effective scaffolding for [their] pupils in the form of individual attention, immediacy of feedback, sustained interactions, and flexible and effective questioning techniques" (Blatchford, Moriarty, Edmonds, and Martin, 2002, p. 128).

Although there is very little you can do about having too many students, it may be possible to influence how your school's discretionary dollars are spent. Some schools (the school Laura taught in was one) choose to limit the number of classroom aides and specialty teachers, preferring to use those funds to add additional regular classroom teachers and thereby reduce class size. It may also be possible by providing the union or school board with the research on class size to convince them of the importance of working to achieve smaller classes across the district.

Support Takes Many Forms

A relevant finding from research in child-parent attachment is that when mothers have a strong network of social support, including a spouse, friends, or other family members, their children are more likely to be securely attached (Crockenberg, 1981). Parenting is too hard a job to do alone. So too with teaching.

Every teacher knows that as rewarding as teaching can be, it can also be emotionally draining, especially when working with children who have a history of learning or behavior problems. To manage your class, do a good job of teaching the curriculum, and be a supportive presence for each student, you are likely to need support yourself. Certainly you don't need active opposition.

Several possible sources of support include your students' parents, your colleagues, members of the community, a mentor from your district or a nearby college or university, and even your students themselves. Your school's principal can be one of your most important allies.

Getting Your Principal's Support

An approach to teaching and classroom management that relies primarily on establishing nurturing relationships with students and a caring, harmonious classroom community is a major break from approaches that rely primarily on rules, rewards, and consequences. If you teach in a school with an established system of rigid rules and consequences and with a zero-tolerance policy that does not adjust for individual children and circumstances, it will be important to discuss your quite different approach with your principal and try to elicit his or her support.

Teachers in such schools, even first-year teachers, have gained permission to use a developmental approach to discipline by explaining to their principal the research base for it and the systematic approach to building trust, building motivation, and managing the classroom that it calls for. Even in seemingly inflexible schools, teachers have been allowed to forgo posting the otherwise required set of rules and consequences in their classroom and instead to work with their students to devise a set of norms to live by.

Many principals are unhappy with discipline systems based on ever-escalating rewards and punishments, but they fear that chaos is the alternative. At the same time, most principals believe in the goals of a developmental approach to discipline—fostering students' internal commitment to learning and to being good people. By assuring your principal that you will exercise firm control while reducing your use of rewards and punishments, you are likely to gain permission to try developmental approaches, if not outright support for your efforts.

At the outset, it will be important to help others understand that your students' behavior will be a bit ragged at first. You may need to explain that learning in the social domain, like learning in the academic domain, requires that students be allowed the freedom to make mistakes—not total freedom but carefully orchestrated freedom and more freedom than is usually allowed in discipline systems based on external control.

You will also need to help others see that when students make mistakes, problem solving with them and encouraging them to repair their mistakes is a strong and usually sufficient response. Even you, however, will find that when things go wrong, when students misbehave—as they inevitably will—the tendency to punish or at least cause them to suffer the logical consequences of their behavior is very strong. The belief, derived from learning theory, that children are only motivated by self-interest and thus must experience personal pain if they are to change their behavior is deeply rooted.

Even though Laura was fortunate that her principal and several of her colleagues shared her beliefs and goals, there were times when she had to fight against a systemic tendency to believe the worst, to over-control, and to punish. For example, significant damage to the school bathrooms began occurring at Laura's school. Frustrated and angered by this vandalism, the principal and the school governance team decided to prevent this behavior through external control rather than engage the students in a plan to stop it. In January of Laura's first year with her students, they required all teachers to escort their classes to and from the bathrooms. Laura, as we saw in Chapter Three, had already devised bathroom procedures designed to build her students' responsibility and autonomy. The new school policy was in clear conflict with what she was trying to teach her students about controlling their own behavior.

> My students and I had been following our plan for quite some time, and it was very apparent to me that I could not go back. So I explained our system to the principal and the hall monitor and pointed out that my kids don't wreck the bathrooms, that we have this plan and it works. I said that if they ever find that one of my kids does wreck the bathrooms, then we'll talk about it.
>
> It was a little ugly at first, because the hall monitor assumed that every student I taught would wreck the bathrooms. But it worked out.

If you are surrounded by a discipline system based on external control, it will be necessary to be clear about your goals, realistic about the amount of freedom your students can handle, and strong in protecting your students' opportunities to freely choose to do the right thing.

Calling On Your Students' Growing Abilities to Be Allies

There is nothing easy about a developmental approach to teaching and classroom discipline, but a perhaps surprising source of support for your efforts will be your students themselves.

This support will come gradually. At first they will resist you. They will see it as your job to control their behavior and that of their fellow students. They will want the familiar stickers and other rewards, and they will definitely want you to punish their misbehaving classmates. So don't expect their support in the beginning. In time, however, as they begin to gain self-control and pride in their accomplishments, they will become your allies in creating a harmonious and productive classroom. As we saw, it was Laura's students, most of all, who taught the new student, Derek, the class norms.

To gain this support you will need many conversations with your students to help them understand the difference between your approach and that to which they have become accustomed. Some of these conversations can occur in the beginning of the year when you are deciding with your class how they want their class to be. We saw some of the ways Laura did this in earlier chapters. These conversations also need to occur all year, many of them with individual students in response to specific situations.

Children who have experienced a lot of punishment often feel that any attempt to control their behavior is a form of punishment. And the more pervasive that punishment has been in your students' home and school lives, the more difficult it will be for you to build a relationship based on trust. These students will have learned both to mistrust adults and to expect adults to control them. They will have had little practice taking responsibility for their own behavior.

Because you will be striving not to punish misbehavior but to problem solve, educate, and only when necessary control behavior, don't be surprised if initially your students, as well as many of your colleagues, see you as failing to really deal with misbehavior. Many people—teachers, parents, and even students—believe that there are only two responses to misbehavior: punishment or nothing. Because having a conversation, teaching a skill, and encouraging reflection and reparation are not punishments, anyone accustomed to punishment or logical consequences is likely to see your alternative approaches as "doing nothing." It took Laura's students quite a while to see that she was indeed "doing something" in response to misbehavior.

Rachel didn't come to school on Wednesday. Her sister, who's in the fourth grade, came in and told me that Rachel was home sick.

Then she said, "Leonard and Kenny were throwing rocks at us when we were trying to go home yesterday, and Kenny picked me up and threw me on the ground."

She said, "Rachel told me not to even tell you. She said, 'Don't tell Mrs. Ecken. She won't do anything about it except talk to them.' "

This was in March of the first year. It surprised Laura that Rachel saw her as doing nothing about misbehavior except talk. Still, talk is what she did.

I had a talk with Leonard and Kenny and I said, "Rachel's sister is going to come back down here this afternoon and we're going to talk about this."

About fifteen minutes later, I was collecting math papers when I saw Kenny go out in the hallway and call Leonard to come out.

I finished collecting the papers and walked over to the door. I heard Kenny say, "Let's tell them we didn't do any of that stuff."

Leonard, though, called Kenny a liar and said, "You know we threw those rocks at them."

Leonard never ceases to amaze me. On the one hand, he's so streetwise and open to the gang stuff, but he's also not willing to be a liar, or even to tolerate another kid wanting to lie. He's got a rough way to go, but he's got a lot of gifts. In his own way he's trying to work out being a decent person. He wants to be cool, but he also wants to be decent. And he hasn't figured out how to be both yet.

Well, I had a meeting with all of them. Leonard apologized to Rachel and said that he wouldn't do it again. I asked him how would he make it up, and so he started walking her home and making sure nobody bothered her. It was a nice thing because he was trying to do what was right and that was what he could think of.

I also met with Rachel. I wanted her to understand why I think talking to people is so important. I told her, "I'm not here to control anybody or to punish people. The only way I know to help people control themselves is to talk to them."

Having Another Classroom Where a Student Can Regroup

Even in the best-managed classrooms, where there is just the right balance between autonomy and structure, reminders and redirection will sometimes fail to stop serious misbehaviors. While students are coming to understand a cooperative approach to relationships and learning to control their emotions and take responsibility for their behavior, it may sometimes be necessary to ask them to leave the room. If Laura's students failed to stop their disruptive or harmful behavior when asked, and she did not have time to deal with them in the moment, she asked them to go to a quiet place in the room or in the hall by the hall monitor until they felt that they could control their own behavior well enough to rejoin the class.

However, sometimes Laura felt that the misbehavior was so serious or the child so unlikely to regain self-control that he or she needed to leave the classroom. We have seen examples of this in vignettes throughout the book. For example, when Laura thought Leonard had threatened to slap Chantelle, she asked him to leave the class and go to Ms. Blanchard's room. Like many teachers, Sandy Blanchard and Laura had an arrangement that they could send students for brief periods to one another's room. Sandy's and Laura's approaches to discipline and classroom management were based on the same philosophical principles, and they talked together about their concerns and goals for their students. Whenever Laura asked a student to go to Sandy's room, it was understood by Sandy and the student that the student could return to Laura's room when he or she felt ready to do so.

Getting Help Managing Students with Serious Behavior Problems

Sometimes a student's misbehavior is so serious that you believe that sending the child to a colleague's class to calm down is insufficient. Initially, Laura sent seriously misbehaving students to the principal, along with a brief explanatory note—a common practice in many schools. Laura's principal shared her nonpunitive approach to working with children, and she usually dealt with the students who were sent to her in a serious but supportive way. After giving them some time to calm down and reflect, she, like Laura, talked with them. Eventually they were sent back to class. (In extreme cases, the principal walked them home.)

However, there is a problem inherent in this system. Because students are only sent to the principal on the occasion of serious misbehavior, it is difficult for the principal to develop a balanced view of the students who frequently misbehave. In time, having few counterbalancing positive experiences with these students, the principal's relationship with them is likely to become conflictual. Even the most seriously misbehaving students in Laura's classroom did many positive things and had many endearing qualities. Knowing these things helped Laura keep a positive relationship with them. The school principal did not have this advantage.

Laura searched for alternatives to sending seriously misbehaving students to the principal's office. She had two options open to her, and she used them both.

The county provided counseling for students if their parents consented. Four of Laura's students met weekly with a psychologist for play therapy. The psychologist worked closely with Laura, sometimes observing in the classroom, and the students enjoyed and looked forward to their group sessions with the psychologist.

Laura's school also had a classroom for students classified with behavior disorders. By the end of the first year, Laura was especially concerned about her ability to meet all of Martin's needs. She was unwilling to have him classified for behavior disorder placement and removed from her class, but she really struggled with how to provide him with the help he needed and still fulfill her obligations to the rest of her class.

> First of all, I know I'm in an area of service. I know that my job is to serve these children in any way that they need. And, I guess, here's where I'm having difficulty knowing what to do—Martin is having so much trouble.
>
> I have a goal to support him. So I can do that and get done what he needs, but it's usually at the expense of everybody else. I can take care of Martin and try to make situations that he can deal with and be successful in, but how much can I do that at the expense of the rest of the class?
>
> I know it's my job to teach that child, and I know it's my job to do anything and everything humanly possible to make him successful. But I'm at the point where all I do is think about him. He consumes me.

Before the start of the second year, Laura met with Lucille Wilson, her colleague who taught the children classified with behavioral disorders. Laura discussed her concerns with Lucille, and they developed a plan for Lucille to work with Martin when it was necessary for Laura to send him out of her classroom. Because Lucille only had six students, she would be able to give Martin extra attention and help him understand and build the skills to better control his behavior.

This was a difficult decision for Laura and one that many teachers face. She knew that sending Martin out of the classroom frequently would disrupt their relationship and reduce her chances of providing him with the focused help he most needed. At the same time, she feared that in trying to manage Martin in the classroom she was seriously jeopardizing the welfare of the rest of her students.

Initially, this arrangement angered Martin and he fought it. He refused to go to Ms. Wilson's room, and when he did go he did not complete his work folder assignments. What eventually helped was involving Martin in the decision making. Laura asked Martin to help her solve the problem of his disruptive and hurtful behavior and helped him see that she really wanted him to stay in her classroom. As the year progressed, Martin's self-control increased and his disruptions decreased. Laura found it less and less necessary to send Martin to Lucille's room and, as we saw earlier, Martin became proud of his ability to make the classroom a safe place.

In regular classrooms with twenty to thirty students, it is frequently difficult to do what's best for students with serious behavior problems while meeting the needs of the rest of the class. Often the only options are stopping regular instruction for everyone else and dealing with these students or sending them to the office, where they may be suspended. And suspension, while offering the teacher and the rest of the class a break from having to deal with the troubled child, is the last thing a child with serious behavior problems needs.

If you have other options—a school psychologist or a specially staffed classroom for children with behavior disorders—use them. If you can, also find a colleague who will accept your temporarily misbehaving students. The key is to find someone to whom you can send these students when you cannot manage them in your classroom—someone who will be supportive rather than punitive and who will keep them in school rather than send them home.

Enlisting Parents

Laura was not shy about meeting with a child's parent or guardian if she was having trouble with the child. If the problem was persistent misbehavior or defiance, Laura would usually engage the child's caretaker in helping her understand the child and the cause of the problem. If the problem was academic, she usually provided materials that the parent or guardian could help the child with at home, as she did when she met with Tralin and her grandmother about Tralin's reluctance to do the reading assignments.

Often when we simply inform parents that their child is misbehaving or failing to learn sufficiently, without providing some guidance about how they might help, parents end up feeling embarrassed, defensive, or angry—none of which is likely to improve matters. Laura was most often successful when she could offer specific suggestions for how the child's caretaker might help.

In a few cases, Laura learned the hard way that some parents could be so punitive that sharing with them any concerns she had for their child would seriously undermine the child's ability to trust Laura. In most cases, however, parents or guardians want to be helpful if you let them know that you really care about their child and see the child's strengths.

Sometimes the most unlikely parents can become genuine allies. For example, Kenny's parents had serious drug-abuse problems, and Kenny and his siblings had spent time in a foster home immediately before enrolling in Laura's school. The children's transfer back to their parents took place only a few days before Kenny joined Laura's class. From the very beginning, Kenny's behavior seemed to reflect the instability in his home life. He was inattentive and frequently refused to engage in learning activities. Laura noticed, however, that Kenny's father frequently came to school and seemed supportive of Kenny and his younger sister. She approached Kenny's father for help.

> I'm keeping a behavioral log on Kenny, and this week by Wednesday it was three pages long—a page for each day.
>
> Wednesday Kenny refused to work on his math problems. When I tried to explain how to do them, he turned his head away from me and wouldn't listen. I gave him the option of using the manipulatives. He took out the little place-value cubes and started building houses.
>
> I called his dad and explained that Kenny needs help with his math and that he had gone the whole day without doing any work. I said that I was going to send home some math and asked if he could help Kenny with it.
>
> This is the first time I've really initiated any kind of conversation with the dad, but he is often at school because the younger one has so many problems. When he's in the building, he always stops in to see how Kenny is doing, and Kenny is always better after his dad has visited.
>
> Well, on Thursday and Friday Kenny did really, really well. At the end of each day, I met with him and asked him how he felt about how the day went. And both days he said, "Happy."
>
> I asked him what he did that day that made him feel happy.
>
> And he said things like, "Well, I did my work and I didn't scream or yell out."
>
> From being all out of whack at the beginning of the week, on Thursday and Friday he seemed to come along, as he often does when his dad's been in.

Laura kept in touch with parents on a regular basis. She frequently sent notes home, often at the parents' request, telling them about their child's ongoing progress. Laura also made a point of letting her students know in a variety of ways that she was working in partnership with their parents to help them learn and become the best that they could be. When Tyrone was having a bad spell, Ms. Jewell, Tyrone's foster parent, asked Laura for a daily note about Tyrone's behavior. The extra attention from Ms. Jewell was just enough to get Tyrone trying a little harder in school.

> Ever since Christmas vacation, Tyrone's just been playing during every lesson, especially when we had things to write. In general, things started deteriorating with him. I talked to Ms. Jewell and she said, "Why don't you just send a note home and let me know how he's been?"
>
> So I've been sending a note home with him every day, and he's been fine ever since. I think he just needed that little push, that if he's not quite ready to do it on his own, he needs to be thinking, "Ms. Jewel's going to know how I've been and I need to hold this together."
>
> It's been really, really good for Tyrone. He's had a few fits, but on the whole he's done really well. And every day I am able to write to Ms. Jewell, "Tyrone did a good job today. He tried hard" . . . or whatever.
>
> On Tuesday he said, "How come I always get these good notes?"
>
> Before I could answer, John said, "Because you're a good kid." Tyrone just smiled. It was a nice moment.

Finding Partners and Mentors

When Laura decided to change her approach to discipline and classroom management from Assertive Discipline to Developmental Discipline, she had the advantage of participating in three years of the Developmental Studies Center's Child Development Project, with on-site professional development and support. The project goals immediately resonated with Laura, and she experienced considerable success; her students were better behaved and she enjoyed teaching more. When I began collecting examples of Developmental Discipline in practice, she and I began our almost weekly telephone conversations.

As mentioned earlier, these conversations became important as a source of support and encouragement for Laura, and they helped both of us deepen our understanding of Developmental Discipline. We cannot duplicate our learning experience for you, although this book is our effort to share with you what we learned. However, we can encourage you to find at least one partner or colleague to join and support you in your effort to implement a developmental approach to discipline in your classroom.

If your partner is another teacher at your school, it will be important to meet or combine classes regularly enough so that you will be familiar with the children in one another's classrooms and the ongoing challenges and successes each of you is experiencing. If your colleague teaches the same or a similar grade, you could plan joint class projects. You might even regularly share some curriculum planning to free up time for meeting.

Another option, if your colleague teaches two or more grades higher or lower, is to set up a buddy program of weekly or biweekly activities in which each older student works with a younger buddy on a variety of projects. Laura and her students met weekly with their kindergarten buddy class. A buddy program has numerous direct benefits for your students and provides you with a colleague who is knowledgeable about your class. It can build your students' sense of the school as a caring community and provide the older students with meaningful opportunities to be helpful and of service to their school community.[3]

You might also try forming a study group with several colleagues. Perhaps the school psychologist would be interested in joining your group, or you might ask a faculty member from a nearby school of education to meet with you. Many university-based faculty would be both sympathetic to your goals and interested in helping you realize them. Frequently university-based faculty are required to perform service to local schools, and often they are looking for research opportunities. Supporting and documenting your experiences would satisfy both of these needs.

You Don't Have to Be Perfect

An important condition for undertaking a Developmental Discipline approach to teaching and classroom management is understanding that you don't have to be perfect. Your goals—to sensitively meet each student's needs for autonomy, belonging, and competence—are hugely ambitious. They frame everything you want to achieve for your students, but they also mean that you are bound to fall short of them from time to time. When you feel you have failed a student in some way or your students fail to live up to your expectations, remember that mistakes are inevitable and almost always repairable and that, whatever your students' successes or failures, you are only part of the picture.

Reflecting on Mistakes

It's impossible to always know, let alone do, the right thing. As a teacher, many, many times in a day you find yourself making decisions quickly about one complicated situation while simultaneously managing several others.

Laura's quick decision about how to help one child recover a lost earring left the whole class upset. Laura thought offering a reward would be expedient; instead, it violated an underlying principle of running a classroom community, as the students made clear when time for the reward came around.

> Janice had just gotten her ears pierced two or three weeks before, and she was still wearing those special piercing earrings. We were starting to watch *The Boy King* about Martin Luther King's childhood when she realized she had lost an earring. I helped her look for it for about the first five minutes of the show, and then I said, "Janice, maybe we can find it later."
>
> About halfway through the movie she's still on the floor looking for the earring, but now she's crying.
>
> I said, "Look, we'll look for it after we watch this movie."
>
> So after the movie, I said to the class, "You know, we really need to find Janice's earring." But people were just kind of playing and this and that and not really looking.
>
> So I said, "We can only spend the next ten minutes looking and then we'll have to move on. So let's look really hard for the earring, and I'll have a reward." This was a big mistake, offering a reward.
>
> They're immediately asking what's the reward, so I said, "Whoever finds the earring can get out a bag of candy from the closet and everybody can have a piece, because we'll celebrate finding the earring. And the person who finds it can take two pieces."
>
> So everybody's thrilled about that, and they're all on the floor looking for the earring. Even my student teacher was looking for the earring, and Louise came over to her and said, "That's not fair for you to be looking for the earring."
>
> The student teacher said, "What do you mean?"
>
> Louise said, "You'll get the reward, and that's not fair that you should be doing it like we are."
>
> Finally, after a few minutes Rachel found the earring. So I said, "Let's all go over to the carpeting and, Rachel, you go to the closet and get the bag of candy."
>
> We went to the carpeting and before Rachel could even get the candy, the rest of the class was in a rage, complaining that it wasn't fair for her to get two pieces.
>
> I said, "What do you all mean? She found the earring and that's what we agreed to. What's the problem?"
>
> And they said, "We all looked. We were all looking just like she was. Why should she get two pieces and we only get one?"

I went around the circle and I asked everyone, "Well, what do you think?" Except for Janice and one other child, the whole class agreed it was unfair.

I said, "I'm hearing what you're saying." I looked at Rachel and asked, "Rachel, what do you think about what they're saying?"

She said, "I'm just going to take one piece."

I said, "Okay, well, that sounds like it will work out with everybody."

Then Martin said, "Forget it, let her have two."

Denise immediately agreed, "Let her take two if she wants."

But then Kenny said, "It's just stupid! It's just stupid that she was going to take two anyway."

I said, "Look, Kenny, I'm a human being just like you all are. I'm forty-four years old, but that doesn't mean that I don't make mistakes. I listened to what you all said, and I understood what you said, and we changed it. We're all going to take one piece of candy. It's over. I don't think you need to be sitting there calling it stupid, what I've done. I agree it wasn't the best thing to do and, you know, we're changing it. So can you get over it?"

So he said, "Okay."

Then Rachel gave out one piece of candy apiece and they were fine.

I was really lucky it was Rachel who found the earring, because she knew we were all in a no-win situation. She was able to say, "Yeah, I'll just take one piece."

Laura frequently did things that she later believed she shouldn't have or failed to do things that she later believed she should have. In various vignettes throughout the book, Laura has commented on some of these mistakes, and there were many others. She and her students survived these mistakes because they came to trust the goodwill of the other.

Trusting Your Own Best Self

Besides trusting the children, Laura had to be able to trust that, despite her mistakes, she, like the children, could come back to her own best self.

Laura didn't always make a clean recovery from mistakes or missteps, but she was usually able to reflect and recognize them. When Denise and Laura got into a strawberry milk showdown, it pushed all of Laura's buttons and took two of her other students to get everyone back on an even keel.

> We went down to pick up our sack lunches for field day. Going through the line, Denise said, "I don't want any of this milk and I'm not drinking it."
>
> I said, "Denise, they've got all the flavors. You love that strawberry milk."
>
> She said, "I'm not touching any of it!"
>
> I said, "Honey, nobody's going to make you take milk. But if you get thirsty that might be a problem."
>
> She grabbed a strawberry milk. I've seen her drink it a hundred times.
>
> About five minutes after we got back to the room, she came up to me and said, "I want to go trade this for chocolate."
>
> I said, "No, I'm sorry, you can't. They've got all those kids coming through that cafeteria. You picked out the strawberry. That's what you're going to have to drink."
>
> Denise took that whole carton of strawberry milk and poured it on the floor. All of it. And then she just looked at me.
>
> I said, "Denise? If you think you're getting back at me for not letting you get the chocolate milk, you're not. You've poured that on the floor, and now you can clean it up."
>
> She said, "I'm just really mad."
>
> "Look," I said, "until it's cleaned up, you're not going to the next field day event."
>
> She got down to clean it up, and she was moaning and groaning and carrying on. Yolanda and Cindy said, "Mrs. Ecken, can we please help her do that?"
>
> I said, "Sure. If you'd like to help her, I think that's nice."
>
> They got down and helped her, and then she was fine.
>
> But I'm going to be honest; it's things like that milk that drive me absolutely nuts. I could have said, "You little brat! What in the world's wrong with you?" Sometimes I just want to yell, "Are you an idiot, or what?"

Some of Laura's students were very challenging, and she sometimes resented them. When she had such feelings, she tried to use them as a cue to calm down and remind herself of the child's strengths or the hardships she knew the child was facing.

Laura did the best job she could of living up to her principles, and she usually succeeded. Overall, her behaviors were aligned with her beliefs, and because she regularly reflected on her practice, she often became aware of her mistakes. This allowed her to discuss them with her students and sometimes undo them. To be this open, she had to have as much trust in herself as she had in her students. She needed to give herself permission to make mistakes without thinking of herself as a bad teacher, just as she needed to give her students permission to misbehave without thinking of them as bad children.

This confidence in herself—in her competence and good will—kept Laura from being discouraged and allowed her to keep on trying.

As Laura looked back on the two years, she knew that she had succeeded in educating all her students not only for competence but also for caring. They would need lots more help from other caring teachers along the way. Many faced huge obstacles, and some might not make it. But she felt confident that

Key Points: Finding the Conditions for Success

- Remember: You don't have to be perfect!
- Find additional time to build trusting relationships with your students and between students; if possible, keep students for two or more years.
- Avoid or carefully limit departmentalization and pullouts; look for times during the day to spend time with one or a few students, and look for ways to limit class size.
- Share this book and your plans with your principal and one or more colleagues, and consider working together by, for example, establishing buddy classes or a study group.
- Share your plans and goals with your students, and ask for their suggestions and help.
- Communicate regularly with parents, grandparents, or guardians, and enlist their help.
- Contact a local teacher education program, teacher center, or staff development organization for support. Seek additional help managing students with serious behavior problems from, for example, your school's psychologist, special education teachers, and city or county mental health or social workers.

she had succeeded in helping each of them make real progress. Laura's success was the result of her hard work and unrelenting care, but it was made possible by the support she sought and received from her principal and colleagues, her students' families, and most of all from her students, who down deep wanted to be competent, caring, loving, and lovable.

NOTES

1. If your school does not have an easy way for you to stay with your students for more than one year, you might order the Flinders and Noddings pamphlet, *Multiyear Teaching: The Case for Continuity*, from Phi Delta Kappa to share and discuss with your principal and fellow teachers.
2. Nel Noddings, in *The Challenge to Care in Schools* (1992, pp. 68–70), offers multiyear teaching by a team of teachers with different specialties as an alternative approach to achieving the benefits of specialized instruction without losing the benefits of continuity.
3. *That's My Buddy* (Developmental Studies Center, 1996) outlines a number of engaging buddy projects and provides useful guidelines for running successful buddy activities.

EPILOGUE: BRINGING IT BACK HOME

TEACHING CONDITIONS vary greatly across the country and even across a single district. Each person's solution to eliminating or ameliorating any systemic barriers to building nurturing relationships with students will differ. However you manage to do it, increasing your time with your students, leveling with them, and enlisting their support will be keys to your success. In addition, it will be crucial to find supportive colleagues wherever you can, whether in the principal, other teachers, parents, community members, or nearby university faculty.

Remember that beliefs about children and their motivations run deep and are often unexamined. We have incorporated deep within us such conflicting messages as "Children are innocent and loving" and "If you give them an inch they'll take a mile."

Likewise, many of our emotional and behavioral responses to children are not reasoned but automatic; we become angry or hurt when children violate our trust, and we want to punish them when they defy us or persistently disobey. We are not accustomed to thinking of children as biologically designed to seek adult guidance and care or as having their own particular working models of adults, relationships, and the world. Nor are we accustomed to teaching our students to trust, to regulate their emotions, or to guide their behavior by reflection and self-talk.

Adopting a developmental approach to teaching and discipline often involves changing how we think and feel about children, how we interact with them, and what we are trying to teach them. Such profound changes happen slowly, and as they are happening they lead to a good deal of uncertainty, requiring reflection and patience. Allow yourself mistakes; be confident in your goodwill and competence, your ability to reflect on your practice, and your openness to learning from your mistakes. Give yourself time, and be sure to keep your eye on the many successes, both large and small, that happen along the way. As you struggle with the inevitable problems, uncertainties, and setbacks, these successes will provide the most sustaining support of all.

AFTERWORD

Laura Ecken

I loved this experience. It was exciting to think about the work we were doing and what it might mean to people. I think the thing I most enjoyed was talking to Marilyn on the phone and taking the time to reflect and try to understand what had gone on in my classroom. I liked thinking together about how I might improve things or how I could better meet the needs of the children. It was a great opportunity.

It was hard trying to describe in detail everything that had taken place in the classroom. So many things were happening, and I wanted to make sure that Marilyn got a true picture of it all. It was hard to take notes and to try not to miss anything and still keep on top of what was happening in the moment. I had little papers with me, and I'd write on them and stick them in my pocket. It certainly wasn't a very sophisticated system, but it worked.

The hardest part was being exposed. It was difficult knowing that people might see my mistakes and think I should have known better. But I didn't let that stop me. If I made mistakes or did things I shouldn't have, I still wanted to share all of that.

I love the book because I think it captures the struggles and the joys of children. It's real, and I feel like it can give hope to people who are struggling. I think it shows that perseverance works, that trust and respect are essential, that all kids want to learn and be part of the classroom, and that the rewards are enormous for all involved when serious learning takes place.

LAURA ECKEN

APPENDIX I
ATTACHMENT THEORY: A NEW WAY OF LOOKING AT CHILDREN

ATTACHMENT THEORY tells us that the nature of our early attachment relationships can affect the nature of our attachments throughout our lives. When a child thrives, the child's early relationship with his or her primary caregiver (usually the mother) has been responsive to the child's basic needs, and the child is securely attached to the caregiver. A securely attached child has learned to value himself or herself as someone worthy of care and to trust others to provide needed care. If, however, the primary relationship has not met the child's basic needs, the attachment will be insecure, and all of the child's subsequent relationships will begin from a position of devaluing the self and mistrusting the other. Research in attachment theory suggests that one aspect of the struggle facing children who do not thrive in our classrooms is the quality of their earliest relationships.

Understanding the implications of attachment theory for children's ongoing development in our classrooms means rethinking how we approach our relationships with all children but especially with those who are the most difficult and least likable—the children whose earliest attachment relationships appear to have set them on a course toward early failure. Research indicates that we *can* form supportive relationships with even the most difficult children *if we understand what they need.* Attachment theory research helps us understand these needs and provides useful guidelines for how to help children.

Attachment Theory in Education

Attachment theory is very different from the two theories that have been predominant in shaping most educational approaches to discipline and classroom management: (1) the behaviorist learning theory of Skinner, Thorndike, and Watson and (2) Freud's psychoanalytic theory. Most educators are inclined toward the view of children offered early in the twentieth century by John Dewey, who thought that children are socially oriented and that learning is an active, social process in which children construct rather than receive knowledge. In his time, however, Dewey's view did not substantially affect mainstream educational thought and practice (Bayles and Hood, 1966; Karier, 1986); his influence was limited to those in the progressive education movement.

In contrast, the Freudian conception of the child as a pleasure seeker who needed to be tamed by society was widely accepted. The learning theorists also struck a powerful chord with their conception of the child as a passive recipient of stimuli. They said children need to be shaped to perfection through a program of external reinforcements. Both views were diametrically opposed to Dewey's. Even though Dewey's views remain an important influence in schools of education today, Freudian conceptions of human nature have continued to predominate in popular American culture, and behaviorist or reinforcement learning theory has been central in shaping educational theory and practice (Karier, 1986).

However, even while behaviorist theory, with its view of human beings as blank slates on which experience writes and its view of learning as the passive receipt of stimuli, was becoming entrenched in mainstream American educational theory and practice, alternative psychological theories more consistent with Dewey's position were emerging. Piaget and Vygotsky, for example, in their investigations of children's thought and learning, documented both that children's thinking was controlled by an internal process of development and that conceptual learning was the result of children's active mental processes, not simply the product of reinforced associations. Furthermore, even though Piaget focused on the role of social relationships with peers and Vygotsky on the social relationships with adults, they documented the social nature of conceptual learning. Gradually, the psychological theories of Piaget and Vygotsky are beginning to replace those of learning theorists in educational thought and practice.

Along with Piaget's and Vygotsky's psychological theories about children's conceptual development, a third psychological theory emerged: attachment theory. Attachment theory, which focused on understanding children's social and emotional development, originated in the work of John Bowlby, a British psychiatrist, and Mary Ainsworth, a Canadian developmental psychologist. The view of human nature and development described by their research bears striking similarities to the views contained in the theories of Piaget and Vygotsky.

In order to make sense of their research observations, Bowlby and Ainsworth, like Piaget and Vygotsky, found it necessary to abandon the view of the infant as a passive recipient of stimuli and of development as an individual rather than a social process. All three theoretical perspectives, although not entirely consistent, present a reasonably coherent picture of children as active constructors of meaning, as needing a social context for learning and healthy development, and as being intrinsically motivated to learn about their social and physical world. All three leave behind the notion of infants as blank slates with voracious appetites for satisfying only themselves, finding instead ample evidence that children are biologically prepared to need and adapt to the social environment into which they are born.

Just as the psychological theories of Piaget and Vygotsky have important implications for classroom teaching, attachment theory has important implications for classroom discipline. However, unlike the theories of Piaget and Vygotsky, attachment theory has not yet become widely known and influential in education theory and practice. Two reasons are likely. First, children's social and emotional development is often seen as less central to education than their cognitive development. Second, most of the early work in attachment theory was focused on understanding infants and very young children, not school-age children.

However, attachment theory's view of children's social and emotional development has profound implications for their lives in our classrooms, not only for their social and emotional development but for their cognitive development.

Attachment theory and research support a very different approach to classroom discipline than the predominant approaches in schools and classrooms today. The more traditional approaches view children as individually responsible for their own behavior, and misbehaving children as willful, lazy, or selfish. Because understanding and adopting the theoretical perspective of attachment theory may require abandoning long-held views of children and their motivations, it is important to understand exactly what makes attachment theory and its supporting research so compelling for classroom practice.

The Origins of Attachment Theory

Around 1940, both John Bowlby and Mary Ainsworth independently became interested in children's attachment to their mothers. Bowlby was struck by the negative effects that were often exhibited by very young children who experienced prolonged separation from their parents. Given the predominant theoretical perspectives of the time, there seemed no reason for these negative effects; the children were being fed and cared for. Ainsworth's focus, however, was on understanding the role that a child's security with his or her mother played in the child's development of exploratory behavior.

Bowlby and another British psychiatrist, James Robertson, began a series of studies to document and more thoroughly explore the responses of young children to separation from their families. In 1950, Ainsworth decided to join Bowlby and Robertson in their studies.

As Bowlby cast about for a theoretical framework, he became impressed with the work of European ethologists studying parent-offspring behavior of various species in naturalistic settings (Bowlby, 1958). Ethologists differed from psychiatrists and psychologists of the time in that their work was guided by Darwin's theory of evolution and its now-familiar tenet explaining the survival of species: when a species is experiencing threat to its survival, the members of the species that survive to reproduce are those whose traits are better adapted to the environment in which they live. Gradually, through the combined processes of differential reproduction and random beneficial mutation, each species comes to possess, as part of its genetic make-up, traits and tendencies suitable to the environment in which it lives. When Bowlby applied this evolutionary framework to his observations of children separated from their families, he began to develop a theory that made sense of his observations.

Bowlby (1969) theorized that during the time the human species was emerging—a time he labeled the "environment of evolutionary adaptiveness"—infants required close and constant care by their mothers. He argued that infants who did not receive such care would have been eaten by predators. Because infants and young children in the environment of evolutionary adaptiveness were dependent on the proximity of their mothers for survival, they would have had biologically built-in mechanisms to maintain this proximity.

Infants cannot maintain proximity to their mothers by following them the way, for example, baby ducklings do, so Bowlby hypothesized that other built-in behaviors such as crying, smiling, cooing, and eventually crawling serve to keep their mothers close. Because human children evolved as dependent on the proximity of their mothers, present-day children would arrive in the world with a predisposition to maintain proximity to their mothers and to depend on this predisposition for their development. This view of children would explain the crying, depression, and eventual detachment that Bowlby and his colleagues observed in infants and young children who, although otherwise well cared for, were deprived of proximity to their mothers.

As Bowlby continued his studies of the effects of separation from the mother on infants and young children, Ainsworth returned to her original interest: the role of the child's security with the mother in supporting exploration behavior. She went to Uganda to make field observations of mothers and infants. In recalling this period of her work, Ainsworth notes that what struck her was how active the babies were in obtaining caregiving.

> In seeing these babies on numerous occasions as they interacted with their mothers within the home, I think the thing that struck me most was how *active* babies are and how much it is *they* who take the initiative. They are not passive little things to whom you do things: in fact, in many ways they are the initiators of what happens to them. The picture that you got in those days from the literature was one of a passive infant who merely reacted to whatever the environment did to him, and that was the notion with which I first arrived in Uganda (Ainsworth and Marvin, 1995, pp. 5–6; emphasis in the original).

Ainsworth's observations in Uganda changed not only her view of the degree to which infants are active contributors to their own development but her view of the goal or cause of the ties infants develop to their mothers. The prevailing view was that an infant's tie to his or her mother was based on the pleasure or reinforcement the infant received from being fed. What struck Ainsworth in the course of her observations of Ganda (a tribe in Uganda) mothers and children was the truth of Bowlby's hypothesis that the need for proximity, not the need to be fed, was the "prime mover" of the ties infants develop to their mothers.

> Another common belief that I had learned from reading Freud, as well as various other writers, was that what underlies the baby's tie to his mother is the fact that it is she who feeds him—the infant's pleasure in being fed gives preeminence to the figure of the food provider and becomes the basis for forming an attachment bond. It took the writings of Bowlby . . . to open up people's minds to the notion that other mechanisms might in fact be responsible. My observations in Uganda gave me first-hand evidence that what I had been taught could not be supported—that feeding could *not* be properly conceived as being the "prime mover" of attachment bonds (Ainsworth and Marvin, 1995, p. 6; emphasis in the original).

In addition to being influenced by Bowlby's unconventional theory regarding the origin of a child's tie to his or her mother, Ainsworth was originally influenced by another unconventional thinker, William Blatz, her professor at the University of Toronto. Whereas Bowlby focused on the mother's role as protector from harm or predation, Blatz focused on the mother's role in providing support for her infant's exploration and cognitive development.

> I first encountered Blatz's thinking—which was brand new, quite original as far as I know, and certainly not like anything that Freud wrote—in a course that I took from him in my fourth undergraduate year, and it was his notion of this nice "back-and-forthing" of the baby, the idea of building a secure base from which one can explore, that struck me most and attracted me to his thinking. He believed that, given a background of feeling secure, the infant would interest himself in what goes on around him and want to move out to explore his world. And, should such exploration get him into more than the infant was ready to cope with, it was crucially important that the parent be accessible—that the baby be able to retreat to his "secure base" for comfort and be, as it were, "recharged" before going off again on his own (Ainsworth and Marvin, 1995, pp. 3–4).

Ainsworth's observations of Ganda mothers and their infants convinced her of several things: (1) infants differ substantially in their sense of security; (2) an individual infant's level of security is dependent on the child's relationship with his or her mother; (3) an infant's sense of security arises out of repeated experiences with a mother who is sensitive to his or her needs; (4) infants are hugely active in maintaining a close relationship with their mothers; and (5) the most important function of the mother-child relationship is to provide a safe or secure base from which the infant can explore the world (Ainsworth, 1964; Ainsworth, 1967; Main, 1999). She was also convinced that the security of an infant's attachment to his or her mother would have long-lasting effects on the development of the infant's personality.

Upon returning to the United States, Ainsworth conducted further research into the development and role of the attachment bond between infants and their caregivers. In their homes, she observed the ways in which mothers and their infants interacted during the infants' first year of life. When the infants were twelve months old, she observed them in a somewhat stressful laboratory setting, involving two successive separations of the mother and child and the entry of a stranger. Although Ainsworth expected and found all the infants to be strongly attached to their mothers, the nature of the infants' behavior, and thus the quality of their attachment, differed remarkably. As with the Ganda infants, these differences were found to relate to the responsiveness of their mothers over the preceding year in the home (Ainsworth, Blehar, Waters, and Wall, 1978).

Twelve-month-olds with a history of sensitively responsive caregiving had appeared relaxed and happy in their home settings. In the laboratory setting, they appeared comfortable so long as their mothers were present.

They explored the toys and interacted with their mothers. Some cried when their mothers left for the first time, and nearly all cried when she left the second time. However, all were happy to see their mothers return, immediately sought physical or psychological contact, were quickly soothed by her presence, and soon resumed their exploration and play. As Ainsworth had seen in Ganda infants, these twelve-month-olds appeared to use their mothers as a "secure base," allowing them to explore in an unfamiliar setting and to achieve calm. Ainsworth described them as having a "*secure* attachment relationship." Fifty-seven percent of the infants in this study were found to be securely attached.

Twelve-month-olds with a history of insensitive caregiving that seemed inept but not rejecting—sometimes warm and sensitive, sometimes ignoring, sometimes intrusive or overcontrolling—appeared anxious in their home settings. In the laboratory situation, they were continuously uneasy. From the very beginning, they clung to their mothers, cried inconsolably when their mothers left, were difficult to soothe, and showed little interest in the objects in the room. They frequently displayed anger toward their mother on her return but sought to be near her (Hesse and Main, 1999). They were described as having an "insecure *anxious* or *ambivalent* attachment relationship." In Ainsworth's sample, 13 percent of infants fit this classification.

Another group of twelve-month-olds whose mothers had been generally insensitive to their infants' signals and rejected their bids for contact or closeness, exhibited high levels of anxiety and anger in their home settings. In the laboratory situation, they seemed almost to avoid their mothers and showed no obvious emotion when their mothers left (although in later studies it was found that their heart rate increased [Sroufe and Waters, 1977, as cited in Hesse and Main, 1999]). Although these infants appeared preoccupied with the toys, their play was superficial. They showed no joy upon their mother's return, actively avoided her, and if picked up struggled to get out of the mother's arms. Ainsworth described these children as having an "insecure *avoidant* attachment relationship" (Ainsworth and others, 1978; Hesse and Main, 1999; Sroufe, 1996). Seventeen percent of the infants in the study fit this classification.

Across hundreds of studies, 85 to 90 percent of infants could be classified into one of the three categories: secure, anxious, or avoidant (Sroufe, 1996; van IJzendoorn, Schuengel, and Bakermans-Kranenburg, 1999). Mary Main and Judith Solomon (1986) discovered that most of those infants who could not be classified into one of Ainsworth's three categories fit a third insecure pattern, which they labeled "disorganized." Those infants exhibited a variety of behaviors, most of which could be described as in some way dysfunctional or disorganized. Some of these disorganized infants were found to have mothers who were frightening to them—abusive, anxious, or helpless. The disorganized infants might display contradictory behavior patterns, reflecting their impossible position of being adapted to seek the mother for comfort but finding her anything but comforting (Hesse and Main, 1999). For example, such children moved away from the mother while crying for comfort or, when frightened, they failed to seek their mother's protection, instead falling motionless on the floor (Hesse and Main, 1999; Main and Solomon, 1990). The disorganized attachment pattern is found in 10 to 15 percent of mother-infant dyads in low-risk North American populations and in about 25 percent of dyads in high-risk–low-income populations (Lyons-Ruth and Jacobvitz, 1999; van IJzendoorn and others, 1999). In one study (Lyons-Ruth, Repacholi, McLeod, and Silva, 1991) 84 percent of infants with a known history of maltreatment were classified as having an insecure disorganized attachment relationship. In another study (Manassis, Bradley, Goldberg, Hood, and Swinson, 1994, as cited in Hesse and Main, 1999), 64 percent of infants of mothers suffering from anxiety disorders were found to have a disorganized attachment relationship (see Table A.1).

Whatever the label, Bowlby and Ainsworth had proposed that the nature or quality of a child's attachment to his or her primary caregiver, usually the child's mother, would shape the child's future relationships with others, his or her self-concept, and the ability to explore and learn about the world (Ainsworth and others, 1978; Bowlby, 1969, 1973). Basically, they believed that a secure attachment relationship provided the foundation for later psychological health and competence. A child with a history of responsive and sensitive parenting would develop a belief system, or "working model," of himself or herself as worthy of care and of others as trustworthy to provide care. These children would be able to use their parents as a secure base to explore the world, regulate their emotions, and master the skills needed to survive and become successful members of their community.

Conversely, a child with a history of unresponsive, inconsistent, rejecting, or frightening care would develop a concept of himself or herself as unworthy of care, would believe that others cannot be trusted to provide care, and would find it difficult to use his or her parent as a secure base. Among this group, those with parents who were inconsistent in their caregiving would be likely to become overly dependent on their parents, and those with aloof or rejecting parents would try to cope as much as possible on their own. Likewise, a child with a history of maltreatment or one whose caregiver was too anxious or helpless or frightened to provide safety, would view the world as an unsafe place and seek protection outside the primary attachment relationship. In Bowlby and Ainsworth's view, the negative self-concept, lack of trust in others, and excessive dependence or premature self-reliance characteristic of insecurely attached children would seriously limit their ability to form supportive relationships with others and to successfully use others to acquire the skills and knowledge needed for a successful life.

The Research Base for Attachment Theory

Attachment theory research has looked at a wide variety of outcomes and, in study after study, predictions based on attachment theory have been confirmed. According to attachment theory, attachment relationships have the potential for having both immediate and long-term effects on development, influencing, for example, children's self-concepts, their relationships with their peers and teachers, and, eventually, their relationships with their spouses and their own children. Correspondingly, research on the nature and effects of the attachment relationship has examined its effects not only in infancy but in early and middle childhood, adolescence, and even into adulthood (George and Solomon, 1989; Lyons-Ruth and Jacobvitz, 1999; Main, Kaplan, and Cassidy, 1985; Sroufe, 1996; Weinfield, Sroufe, Egeland, and Carlson, 1999).

Most attachment research has focused on early parent-child relationships, and a few of these studies are cited in the paragraphs to follow. However, an increasing number of studies are looking at the implications of the attachment bond in relationships beyond the home. The studies that are most relevant to a school or classroom setting are noted here.

Attachment Outcomes in Parent-Child Relationships

In a number of studies, toddlers with histories of secure attachment relationships have been found to be more cooperative with and obedient to their parent (Londerville and Main, 1981; Stayton, Hogan, and Ainsworth, 1971) and more socially and empathetically responsive to a stranger (Main and Weston, 1981). Two-year-olds with a history of secure attachment relationships worked more smoothly and successfully with their mothers to solve novel problems. Their mothers offered higher-quality support, and the children seemed to enjoy the joint problem solving. The children with histories of insecure attachment were not only less successful but their relationships with their mothers appeared more conflictual (Matas, Arend, and Sroufe, 1978).

Table A.1.
Characteristics Related to Attachment History
(in Low-Risk North American Populations)

Note: *Information in this table is compiled from several sources: Ainsworth and others, 1978; Hesse and Main, 1999; Main and Solomon, 1990; Sroufe, 1996; van IJzendoorn and others, 1999.*

Attachment Type	Secure	*Insecure* Anxious	*Insecure* Avoidant	*Insecure* Disorganized
Percentage	62%	9%	15%	15%
Home Behavior	• Appeared relaxed and happy	• Exhibited considerable anxiety	• Exhibited high levels of anger and anxiety	• No data
Strange-Situation Behavior	• Appeared relaxed upon entry	• Appeared wary and clingy	• Appeared calm and relatively uninterested in the mother	• Displayed a diverse array of inexplicable, odd, or overtly conflicted behaviors (e.g., approaching the mother while also turning away from her)
	• Able to use the mother as a secure base to explore toys	• Unable to use the mother as a secure base to explore toys; interacted with toys only through the mother	• Played with toys but the play had a superficial quality	
	• Usually cried when the mother left	• Became extremely upset when the mother left	• Did not visibly object to the mother's departure	

Attachment Type	Secure	*Insecure* Anxious	*Insecure* Avoidant	*Insecure* Disorganized
	• Happy to see the mother return, immediately sought contact, and readily comforted by her	• When the mother returned, difficult to console; appeared angry, sometimes even striking her	• Actively ignored or avoided the mother when she returned	
Likely Later Childhood Behavior	• Confident and cooperative	• Clingy and passive *or* • Hyperactive and impulsive	• Angry, defiant *or* • Withdrawn	• Extremely angry and aggressive with little or no empathy *or* • Detached, frightened, and withdrawn
	• Good peer relationships	• Tendency to be a victim	• Aggressive, a bully	• Extremely aggressive *or* A loner
	• Resilient and able to withstand stress	• Easily upset		• With parents often inappropriately adult-like and controlling, sometimes in an angry, punitive way and sometimes in a way that appears sweet and caregiving

Dutch researchers Adriana Bus and Marinus van IJzendoorn (1988) observed one-and-a-half-year-olds, three-and-a-half-year-olds, and five-and-a-half-year-olds with their mothers as together they watched *Sesame Street,* read a picture book, and went through an alphabet book. Not only were the interactions more positive for the children with a history of secure attachment but the securely attached children were more attentive and less easily distracted. In a separate study with three-year-olds, these same researchers found that insecurely attached children were less engaged when their mothers read to them than were securely attached children. The greater the insecurity, the more the children were inattentive and the more the discussion digressed from the story. The less secure the attachment, the harder it seemed for the children to get the message of the text (Bus and van IJzendoorn, 1995).

In sum, as predicted by attachment theory, children with secure attachment relationships have been found to be more cooperative with their parents and others and better able to use their parents to learn and solve problems.

Attachment Outcomes in School and Other Nonfamilial Contexts

In nonfamilial contexts (day care, school, and summer camp), security of attachment has been found to be related to children's personal characteristics as well as to their relationships with peers and teachers. For example, four- and five-year-olds with a history of secure attachment were found to be more positive and cooperative in their peer interactions, more cooperative with their teachers, and better liked by both peers and teachers. Preschool children with a history of insecure attachment, on the other hand, demonstrated poorer social skills, had lower impulse control, and were more dependent on their teachers than securely attached children. Those with a history of insecure-avoidant attachment were also more aggressive with their peers and less compliant with their teachers (Cohn, 1990; Erickson, Sroufe, and Egeland, 1985; Howes and Hamilton, 1992; Pianta and Nimetz, 1991; Pianta, Nimetz, and Bennett, 1997; Sroufe, 1983, 1988, 1996; Sroufe and Fleeson, 1986).

Across the school years, children with histories of secure attachment were found to be resilient, self-confident, independent, and socially competent. They were more likely to form close friendships and function well in a group. In adolescence, those with secure histories were more likely to engage in challenging activities in which there was some risk of self-exposure (Elicker, Englund, and Sroufe, 1992; Sroufe, Carlson, and Shulman, 1993; Urban, Carlson, Egeland, and Sroufe, 1991).

School-age children with a history of insecurity were found to be more dependent, less resilient, and less socially skilled than secure children. Those with histories of avoidant insecurity (children who had consistently experienced parental rejection or intrusive control) and those who were disorganized in their attachment relationship (children whose parents were abusive or in some other way frightening) tended to be aggressive and defiant (Carlson, 1998; Lyons-Ruth and Jacobvitz, 1999; Weinfield, Sroufe, Egeland, and Carlson, 1999).

The most extensive studies of the behavior of children with known attachment histories in a school setting were conducted by Alan Sroufe and his colleagues (Erickson and others, 1985; Kestenbaum, Farber, and Sroufe, 1989; Sroufe and Fleeson, 1986; Sroufe, 1983, 1988, 1996; Weinfield and others, 1999). These studies focus on preschool children from a high-poverty sample and provide rich detail about the behavior in a school setting of children with differing attachment histories. Because by preschool many of children's strategies and behaviors for coping and interacting appear to have emerged, we can learn much about the behavior of older children by a careful read of Sroufe's studies of children in nursery school.

In Sroufe's studies, children with histories of secure attachment were found to have high self-esteem and to be resilient and flexible. Their relationships with their peers were generally pleasant and cooperative. When working in partners, they were nurturant with less able partners and self-assertive with aggressive partners. They generally complied with their teacher's directions, and when they sought their teacher's attention, it was usually for needed help or to share a discovery or accomplishment. Their teachers liked them and held high expectations for them.

Within this same group, children with histories of insecure attachment presented quite a different picture. They tended to have low self-esteem and to be rated by their teachers as being less flexible and resourceful. Insecurely attached children, whether avoidant or anxious, were considerably more dependent on their teachers than securely attached children. Of special significance is the fact that insecurely attached children did not spend more time with their teachers than securely attached children, but the nature of their contact was very different.

Those with an insecure-anxious history tended to be more direct in their bids for teacher attention. They tended to "wear their hearts on their sleeves" and to actively seek help with self-management and with the management of social situations. They were clingy and directly approached their teachers seeking physical contact. Children who had a history of insecure-avoidant attachment were more indirect in their approaches to their teachers. They explicitly did not seek help when they were upset or disappointed "but drew near the teachers (often in subtle and barely noticeable ways) during quiet times" (Sroufe, 1996, p. 228).

Children with histories of insecure attachment, whether anxious or avoidant, received much more control from their teachers, and the teachers showed little expectation that they would comply with their directives. With the secure group, "teachers turned and went about their business after giving a directive." Directives to children with histories of insecure attachment "often were repeated and intensified even before the child had time to comply" (Sroufe, 1988, p. 21).

Because children with a history of insecure-avoidant attachment tended to be more aloof, disruptive, controlling, aggressive, and mean than securely attached children, teachers, understandably, tended to become angry with them. However, an angry response is likely to perpetuate such children's conflictual approach to relationships and to confirm their belief that others cannot be trusted to provide care.

Children with histories of anxious insecurity, usually those whose caregivers were inconsistently responsive, tended to be whiny and obvious in their constant bids for help, affection, and attention. Teachers were found to be highly nurturing to such children but to lower their demands for mature behavior. Again, this is an understandable response but one likely to confirm the low self-concept of these students and to perpetuate their underachievement.

Insecurely attached children also had more difficult peer relationships. When working in partners, those with avoidant histories were often emotionally distant from or hostile toward other children. They frequently engaged in unprovoked aggression, mistreating or dominating the other child, particularly when partnered with a child with an insecure-anxious history. Avoidant children were the only children observed to respond to another's distress in ways that would actually increase the distress, for example by taunting, hitting, or laughing at a hurt child. Those with anxious histories were socially oriented but tended to be impulsive, immature, and easily frustrated, or passive, weak, and helpless. They had difficulty handling the give and take of peer relationships, and although securely attached children tended to protect them, avoidantly attached children tended to exploit them.[1]

Attachment Theory and Learning

Just as Bowlby and Ainsworth predicted, the nature of children's attachment relationships with their parents or primary caregivers has far-reaching effects on children's overall development, including how well they are able to secure and use their teachers' help and how well they adapt to the demands of school life.

Research about the role of children's attachment relationships provides a new and expanded meaning for the phrase "coming to school ready to learn." It's clear from attachment theory research that school readiness is not simply a matter of having heard lots of stories and being familiar with numbers and letters. There are additional important ingredients for school success that some children will not have prior to coming to school: the ability to regulate their emotions and behavior, to form trusting relationships with others, and to seek and accept needed support. These abilities are so important to children's school and life success that they have been called "emotional intelligence" (Goleman, 1995). They are honed in children's relationships with their primary caregivers and are generally lacking in children with histories of insecure attachment relationships.

Especially troubling is the finding that the children who lack the emotional and social qualities to form positive relationships with others are also less likely to have acquired from their parents or caregivers the literacy, numeracy, and problem-solving skills needed for academic success. Children with a history of insecure attachment will have three huge deficits to overcome when they enter school: (1) they will have little ability to regulate their own behavior and emotions; (2) they will find it difficult to trust their teachers enough to use them as a secure base for learning; and (3) they will have acquired fewer skills and less general knowledge on which to build their school learning. For those of us called upon to provide the extra help these children need, knowing why it is needed may make it easier to provide.

Applying Attachment Theory to Classroom Practice

Because we are children's caregivers while they are in our classrooms, attachment theory's attention to caregiver-child relationships can help us understand and work with all of our students, even those who have not yet developed a positive model of themselves or of relationships with caregivers. In addition, in comparison with other classroom management systems, attachment theory offers us a less controlling, more collaborative, and more enjoyable way of working with children.

Making the Most of Biology

Most classroom management systems focus on helping teachers control students through a series of consequences designed to teach them that behaving well will bring rewards and misbehaving will have unpleasant results. When dealing with misbehavior, whether the misbehaving child is generally cooperative or generally defiant, we are advised to take a mistrustful stance. We assume children will not stop their misbehavior unless they experience unpleasant consequences. Likewise, if we want to encourage children to engage in desirable behaviors, we are advised to take the same mistrustful stance—that children will do as we ask only if we offer them rewards or praise.

Attachment theory presents us with a different view of children and of socialization. It is part of children's evolutionary endowment to seek nurturing relationships with their caregivers, and children's development and socialization are a product of that biologically necessary relationship. Disciplining or socializing a child is less a process of *making* a child do what he or she would not otherwise do and more a process of *helping* a child do what he or she biologically needs and wants to do.

According to attachment theory, children's development is accomplished in collaboration with the guidance and support of their caregivers. As their caregivers respond with reasonable sensitivity and consistency, children gradually develop basic trust in themselves, in their caregivers, and in relationships in general. Gradually, with maturation and with support from their caregivers, children learn to regulate their emotions and their behavior. Coping, development, and socialization are collaborative processes. The capacity for empathy and the disposition to be cooperative and prosocial emerge out of children's experiences of collaboration with their caregivers.

In the school setting, the teacher is the caregiver. Research indicates that the qualities of the adult-child relationship leading to positive child outcomes are the same whether the adult caregiver is a parent or a teacher. Children learn best and develop positive self-concepts and cooperative, friendly, caring relationships with others when their caregivers respond sensitively to their needs, offer appropriate assistance, convey unconditional acceptance and emotional warmth, and provide appropriate structures and limits (Pianta, 1999). From the perspective of attachment theory, building trusting, supportive, collaborative relationships with children should be at the heart of our approach to discipline and teaching.

Building such relationships will be relatively easy with the majority of students who enter our classrooms. Most children will have had a history of responsive and sensitive caregiving, and they will enter our classrooms ready to form cooperative relationships with us. They assume our goodwill and we, in turn, can assume theirs.[2]

This is not to say, however, that attachment theory represents a laissez-faire approach to classroom management. In fact, it is the caregiver's role—a necessary condition for successful development—to exercise reasonable authority and control. According to attachment theory, children, in their immaturity, need adults to be responsible for knowing how children need to behave and what they need to learn, and for providing the support and encouragement they need to be successful. The careful exercise of adult guidance and authority are as essential for children's successful development as the clear communication of adult care and commitment. As teachers, we need to provide guidance, support, and limits, as well as love and approval in order for children to succeed and thrive.

Teaching from the perspective of attachment theory—teaching with the goal of forming a collaborative partnership with our students—can be easier and much more pleasant than trying to orchestrate each child's behavior through a prescribed application of rewards and punishments. Instead of being a system for policing children, discipline begins with building a personal relationship with each child in our care and, through that relationship, coming to know our students well enough to adjust our demands and support to the needs of each child. We can expect children with a history of secure attachment relationships to actively seek our help when they need it and to comply with our reasonable requests if they understand them and have the required skills. When they do not comply, we can expect that there is a reason and rely on them to help us find it.

Working with Insecurely Attached Children

What about the students who do not seem to want a collaborative relationship with us—those who seem to constantly seek our attention or who seem defiant and aggressive? In general, these are the children who make teaching difficult and who receive the bulk of reprimands and negative consequences in most classrooms. These are the children whom we sometimes grow to resent and who are likely to drain us emotionally. It is with these children that attachment theory can be most helpful.

Not only will these children be mistrustful, they will have been less able or unable to use their caregivers to help them accomplish the developmental tasks of childhood. Thus they will be less able than securely attached children to, for example, balance their need for autonomy with their need for adult help and guidance, regulate their emotions, or monitor their own behavior. These children will enter the classroom with low social and emotional skills, low self-esteem, little or no trust that teachers can be relied on to care for them, and a belief that their survival depends on their ability to manipulate and coerce others. They are likely to be anxious and passive or angry and aggressive as they struggle to make their way in the world of school. Initially, they will view our efforts to teach, guide, and direct them as efforts to control or coerce them. They will not assume our goodwill, although they will want—desperately, in some cases—a caring relationship with us. Knowing this about insecurely attached children can help us take a particularly focused approach to working with them. From the perspective of attachment theory, neither a discipline system based on rewards and punishments nor one that stresses the application of logical and natural consequences will be helpful in motivating these students to *want* to be cooperative and prosocial.

The best we can expect from a system of rewards and punishments is temporary control. We can never expect to change children's motivation in this way. From the perspective of attachment theory, if we try to teach children to want to be cooperative and prosocial by rewarding their good behavior and ignoring or punishing their unacceptable behavior, we only confirm their view of relationships as coercive and encourage their tendency to be self-focused. If we become angry and withdraw our affection, we will further alienate them and reinforce their negative view of themselves and relationships.

Nor will it be useful to allow or cause insecurely attached children to experience the "natural" or "logical" consequences of their behavior, as is so often recommended by approaches to classroom management based in the humanistic theory of Rudolph Dreikurs (for example, Curwin and Mendler, 1988; Dreikurs, Grunwald, and Pepper, 1982; Nelsen, Lott, and Glenn, 1993).

Many humanistically orientated educators—William Glasser (1969), Thomas Gordon (1974), and Carl Rogers (1969), for example—begin, as attachment theorists do, with trust in children and an emphasis on the importance of respectful human relationships in teaching and discipline. But because they see the relationship between teacher or parent and child as one of equals, they stress allowing children the space or freedom to solve their own problems. In the writings of Rudolph Dreikurs, this focus on equality leads to holding children solely responsible for their successes and failures. Whereas attachment theory views collaboration between the adult and child as necessary to the child's success, Dreikurs views children as individually capable of controlling their behavior and thus capable of choosing appropriate behaviors *if they want to.*

Dreikurs and his followers emphasize getting children to accept responsibility for themselves by "teaching" them that their bad choices will result in negative consequences for them: children who forget their lunch money go without lunch; children who fail to do their homework spend recess doing it; children who allow their attention to wander during a reading lesson lose their turn to read; children who disrupt the class are subjected to the disapproval of their peers. Such consequences isolate rather than integrate children and do nothing to build their motivation toward prosocial behavior.

What insecurely attached children need above all is the experience of a secure and nurturing relationship with an adult caregiver. When children enter our classrooms without having experienced such a relationship, they will not believe that we can be trusted to provide for their needs, and they will not believe that they are really deserving of our care. Until insecurely attached children experience a trusting relationship and so can alter their working models of themselves and relationships, they will resist our efforts to help them as much as our efforts to control them.

Because insecurely attached children have not had sufficient guidance and support from their primary caretakers, their capacities to manage and monitor their emotions and behaviors will be poorly developed. We will need to control their harmful behavior and teach them the social and emotional skills they did not learn in early childhood. But the more such students learn to trust us, the more willing they will be to open themselves up to the risks involved in trying to learn, with our help, both the academic curriculum and the important social and emotional understandings and skills that they failed to learn in infancy and early childhood and that they will need to become part of a caring and collaborative classroom community.

Unless we understand the perspective of these students, it can be difficult to strike the right balance in our efforts to guide, support, and control them. As we saw earlier, studies of student-teacher relationships have found that insecurely attached children are more likely than securely attached children to be disliked and inappropriately treated *by their teachers*.

Because insecurely attached children have not developed a sense of trust but still have a need to belong and to feel connected to others, they struggle to maintain relationships in inappropriate ways. Because they have not acquired the necessary skills to monitor and manage their emotions and behavior, and because we cannot rely on them to seek our help when they need it, we will have to assume more responsibility for their behavior and their success in the classroom. To help these children meet their basic psychological needs in the classroom, we will have to carefully structure the environment to match as much as possible their limited social, emotional, and cognitive capacities. At the same time, we will have to help them increase their underdeveloped understandings and skills.

Understanding that the misbehavior of insecurely attached children is likely the result of their misunderstanding of themselves and the nature of relationships, as well as their relative lack of social and emotional understanding and skills rather than an insatiable appetite for attention or power, can help us better tailor our responses to meet their needs. Although we will frequently need to control their behavior, if we let them know that we value them unconditionally, that we can be relied upon to provide help, and that we have confidence that they can succeed, they will gradually come to trust us. It will take time, but it will happen—in large part because down deep the children themselves want a trusting relationship with us. They want to be part of the classroom community. They want to learn, and they want to be liked and respected.

A number of studies have demonstrated that teachers can and do form supportive and sensitive relationships with children with histories of insecure attachment (Howes and Hamilton, 1992; Howes, 1999; Pianta, 1999). In Martin Haberman's study, in 1995, of teachers of children in poverty, he observed that the successful teachers were those who were able to build trusting relationships with their students. These teachers did not rely on punishment and extrinsic rewards for control, which is the prevalent practice in high-poverty schools. Instead, they relied on their relationships with students and their ability to excite children about learning. Research into the conditions supporting resiliency found that adolescents who succeeded despite living in highly adverse circumstances frequently credited a warm, supportive, adult relationship, usually with a teacher, as crucial to their success (Benard, 1993; Werner and Smith, 1989).

How one manages to form trusting relationships with insecurely attached children and to balance the needs of the class and the needs of individual children will vary with the different options available across different educational settings. Once we understand that even resistant and chronically misbehaving children are by nature motivated to learn and to want a close relationship with us, it is easier to be more sympathetic to them, even while their troublesome behavior is difficult to manage. Attachment theory gives us reason to hold out for positive relationships with all of our children.

Summary

Attachment theory is well grounded in research and presents a different view of children and socialization than the dominant views that have shaped most approaches to classroom discipline. Attachment theory sees children's motivations as rational and largely governed by the powerful belief systems or the working models of relationships that children develop based on the quality of their relationships with their caregivers, usually their mothers, during infancy and early childhood.

Children are predisposed by their very biology to want to learn and to seek nurturing relationships with their caregivers. When children's primary caregivers are sensitive to their needs, children develop trust in their caregivers, form secure attachment relationships, and come to see themselves as worthy of care and to see relationships as cooperative in nature. When these children enter school, they assume the goodwill of their teachers and seek a collaborative, nurturing relationship with them. Although they will need help learning to manage the complex worlds of the school and classroom, they will not need rewards and punishments to get them to want to comply with their teachers' reasonable requests. If their teachers are able to sensitively respond to their needs, providing appropriate support and guidance, they will learn and thrive.

Some parents or caregivers, for a wide variety of reasons, are unable to respond sensitively to their children's needs. This will be particularly likely when parents are under high stress and have little social support. When parents cannot respond sensitively to their children, the children will still seek to maintain nurturing relationships with them, but these relationships will be built on mistrust. When these children enter school, they will not trust their teachers or their peers, they will have generally poor social and emotional skills, and they will believe that relationships are coercive in nature. These children will sometimes be whiny, petulant, and demanding, sometimes aloof and withdrawn, and sometimes aggressive and domineering. Although rewards and punishments may exert some control of these children's behavior, manipulation by rewards and punishments will also confirm their belief that relationships are coercive. Furthermore, these external motivators will keep them from experiencing the intrinsic value of being cooperative and prosocial.

From the perspective of attachment theory, to develop a healthy personality, insecurely attached children need to change their beliefs about themselves and about the nature of relationships. As teachers, we can help these children change their debilitating beliefs by developing a consistently nurturing relationship with them, one that confirms their worth, supports their learning and development, and is sensitive to their unique needs and talents.

Research in attachment theory demonstrates that, over time, teachers can successfully develop mutually trusting relationships with children who have a history of insecure attachment. Attachment theory provides support for our efforts by helping us better understand children and their needs.

The chapters in this book show attachment theory in practice. They provide examples of one teacher's efforts to apply attachment theory in her classroom and include her struggles, her failures, and her successes. I hope these examples of practice and this more academic description of the origins of attachment theory and its supporting research will contribute to your ongoing construction of what children need and how we, as teachers, can meet those needs.

NOTES

1. At the time this study was done, the insecure/disorganized classification had not yet been delineated.
2. This does not mean that *every* securely attached child will automatically adjust to our classroom and form a trusting relationship with us. Children with extremely active, assertive, or shy temperaments need our recognition of and adjustment to their individual needs. Learning strengths can also play a part in children's comfort in our classrooms. And in some cases, a teacher and child's cultural or class differences can interfere with the establishment of trusting relationships. See, for example, the discussion by Howard Gardner (1983) of the demands of responding to multiple intelligences, Nel Noddings's discussion (1992) of the need to adjust to the interests and talents of individual students, Sonia Nieto's descriptions (1999) of teachers' struggles to adjust to the cultural and personal uniqueness of their students, and Rimm-Kaufman, Cox, Saluja, Pianta, Bradley, and Payne's (2002) discussion of the effects of child temperament and teacher sensitivity on children's school success.

APPENDIX 2
ANNOTATED LIST OF RESOURCES

Here is a highly selective and by no means exhaustive list of resources related to building community, fostering caring relationships, and personalizing instruction to meet the unique needs of all students. Several of the listed publications and Web sites provide additional resources.

Listed first are the resources Laura used as she implemented the Child Development Project (CDP) and worked to build a caring classroom community:

Among Friends by Joan Dalton and Marilyn Watson (Oakland, CA: Developmental Studies Center, 1997). Describes, through classroom vignettes and conversations with teachers across the country, the CDP and many teacher-tested ideas for creating classrooms that support both caring and learning.

At Home in Our Schools (Developmental Studies Center, 1994). A practical set of guidelines for designing and implementing inclusive, noncompetitive schoolwide activities and parent involvement that support the academic and ethical values of the total school community.

Blueprints for a Collaborative Classroom (Developmental Studies Center, 1997). Provides practical guidelines for orchestrating collaborative learning across the curriculum and 250 suggestions for partner and small-group activities that develop students' social and emotional skills and their commitment to learning and caring.

Number Power by Laurel Robertson, Shaila Regan, Susie Alldredge, Julie Contestable, Marji Freeman, Susan Urquhart-Brown, and Carol Westrich (Developmental Studies Center, 1993–1997). A set of nine grade-level (K–6) volumes of supplemental math replacement units that foster students' social and mathematical development through collaborative, hands-on lessons. Includes reproducibles.

Our Classroom by Chick Moorman and Dee Dishon (Merrill, MI: Institute for Personal Power, 1986). Chock full of ideas for building unity and community and for fostering student autonomy and responsibility. (Available at www.chickmoorman.com/books.html)

Reading for Real (Developmental Studies Center, 1998). A grade 4–8 literature-based reading program with the same goals as *Reading, Thinking & Caring.* Both programs structure collaborative learning experiences and integrate writing, speaking, and listening into the reading program. Teaching units for over 180 classic, contemporary, and multicultural titles are available.

Reading, Thinking & Caring (Developmental Studies Center, 1998). A K–3 literature-based reading program designed to build students' empathy and moral understanding, as well as their love of reading and their ability to think deeply and critically.

The Second Cooperative Sports and Games Book by Terry Orlick (New York: Random House, 1982). Provides the rationale for engaging children in cooperative games and is full of ideas for fun cooperative activities, many from other countries and cultures.

SIPPS: Systematic Instruction in Phoneme Awareness, Phonics, and Sight Words (three levels) by John Shefelbine and Katherine Newman (Oakland, CA: Developmental Studies Center, 2000). A prepublication version of this phonics program that Laura turned to when she discovered her students having to decode words phonetically. It involves short systematic lessons in phonics, sight words, and polysyllabic decoding, along with daily individualized reading.

That's My Buddy! (Developmental Studies Center, 1997). Provides, in addition to student-tested buddy activities, the rationale for cross-grade learning and caring experiences and guidelines for ways to get a buddies program started and help students receive maximum benefit.

Ways We Want Our Class To Be (Developmental Studies Center, 1996). A short handbook that provides tips on getting started, establishing ground rules, building consensus, and facilitating class meetings, as well as guidelines for fourteen specific class meetings to involve students in planning, assessing, and problem solving in all aspects of the classroom and school community.

Next are additional materials that focus on the practical aspects of building and managing a caring classroom community:

Because We Can Change the World: A Practical Guide to Building Cooperative, Inclusive Classroom Communities by Mara Sapon-Shevin (Boston: Allyn & Bacon, 1998). Written by a leader in the fields of cooperative learning and inclusive education and full of practical ideas for working with diverse learners to build classroom communities imbued with the spirit of respect and care.

The Caring Teacher's Guide to Discipline, 2nd ed., by Marilyn Gootman (San Francisco, Corwin Press, 2001). Provides an experienced teacher-educator's ideas for a sound and practical approach to classroom discipline with a caring stance.

Creating a Caring Classroom by Nancy Letts (New York: Scholastic, 1999). Lots of easy and practical ideas for increasing students' sense of belonging and community.

Creative Conflict Resolution by William J. Kriedler (Santa Monica, CA: Goodyear Publishing Company, 1984). More than two hundred activities for keeping peace in the classroom and teaching students conflict resolution skills.

The First Six Weeks of School by Paula Denton and Roxanne Kriete (Greenfield, ME: The Northeast Foundation for Children, 2000). Many wonderful strategies for building a climate of caring and respect and for supporting the growth of students' responsible autonomy.

Homeside Activities (Developmental Studies Center, 1995–1997). A set of seven grade-level (K–6) books, each containing eighteen activities in English and Spanish designed to help build a home-school partnership.

Life in a Crowded Place by Ralph Peterson (Crystal Lake, IL: Heineman, 1992). Provides a careful analysis of the many aspects of community with lots of practical suggestions for how to create a learning community around the values of care and respect.

Moral Classrooms, Moral Children by Rheta DeVries and Betty Zan (New York: Teachers College Press, 1994). A detailed view, drawn from Piaget's view of discipline as cooperation, of how to achieve in the preschool classroom the kind of respectful, cooperative climate that will support the growth of children's moral autonomy.

The Morning Meeting Book by Roxanne Kriete (Greenfield, ME: The Northeast Foundation for Children, 2002). A powerful rationale with informative and detailed guidelines for beginning every day with a community-building meeting.

Partnership Education in Action: A Companion to Tomorrow's Children edited by Dierdre Bucciarelli and Sarah Pirtle (Tuscon: Center for Partnership Studies, 2001). A collection of articles providing practical suggestions for implementing the pedagogy and curriculum of a partnership approach to education in elementary through high school and for restructuring the overall structure of the school to foster collaboration rather than coercion and domination.

Talk It Out: Conflict Resolution in the Elementary Classroom by Barbara Porro (Alexandria, VA: Association for Supervision and Curriculum Development, 1996). A down-to-earth, easily usable approach to helping children solve problems fairly.

Through Other Eyes by Joan Skolnick, Nancy Dulberg, and Thea Maestre (Toronto: Pippin, 1999). A unique approach to the social studies curriculum focused on building cultural awareness, empathy, and perspective taking.

Tribes by Jeanne Gibbs (Windsor, CA: Center Source Systems, LLC, 2001). Written by a pioneer in the fields of cooperative learning and social development and full of interesting and enjoyable activities for building classroom and school community.

White Teacher by Vivian Paley (Cambridge, MA: Harvard University Press, 1979/2000). A kindergarten teacher talks honestly and vividly about her struggle to overcome deep and unexamined beliefs about other ethnic groups and to understand the role of ethnicity in the classroom.

The following books and articles provide authoritative summaries of the educational theory and research related to major aspects of building caring relationships with all students:

The Challenge to Care in Schools by Nel Noddings (New York: Teachers College Press, 1992). A powerful and carefully reasoned argument for redesigning schools around themes of care, envisioning ways for schools to meet the diverse needs of all our children and outlining practical steps toward this vision at every educational level.

Developing Democratic Character in the Young edited by Roger Sodor, John I. Goodlad, and Timothy McMannon (San Francisco: Jossey-Bass, 2001). A unique blending of character education and education for democratic citizenship. Goodlad defines the concept of democratic character, and several leading educators outline the school's role in its development, resulting in a wide-ranging discussion of goals, possibilities, core concepts, and practical steps.

Enhancing Relationships by Robert Pianta (Washington, DC: American Psychological Association, 1999). Particularly useful for school psychologists and written by a former school psychologist. This book applies attachment theory to understanding the role of teacher-student relationships in student success and discusses ways to support struggling and demoralized teachers.

Teaching with Love by Lisa Goldstein (New York: Peter Lang, 1997). A description by one caring teacher of her struggle to understand what it means to teach with love and her reflections on her struggle to do so.

A Matter of Trust: Connecting Teachers and Learners in the Early Childhood Classroom by Carollee Howes and Sharon Ritchie (New York: Teachers College Press, 2002). Uses attachment theory, research in child development, and vignettes from classrooms serving children living in difficult circumstances to describe a supportive, noncoercive approach to classroom management and to demonstrate the power of positive teacher-child relations and the importance of the social-emotional climate of the classroom.

Tomorrow's Children: A Blueprint for Partnership Education in the 21st Century by Riane Eisler (Boulder, CO: Westview Press, 2000). A persuasive argument, well documented in evolutionary science and cultural history, for sweeping changes in the content and the process of education—changes that stress a cooperative, equalitarian, and inclusive approach to life and learning rather than one based in domination, hierarchy, and exclusion.

Beyond Discipline by Alfie Kohn (Alexandria, VA: Association for Supervision and Curriculum Development, 1996). Cites years of well-documented research in motivation and learning and presents a strong case against discipline, both traditional discipline based on rewards and punishments and the "new disciplines" based on logical consequences, arguing instead for a focus on building community.

Cultural Conflict and Struggle by Patricia Ruggiano Schmidt (New York: Peter Lang, 1998). Documents the many difficulties faced by two culturally diverse, second-language learners throughout their kindergarten year, outlines helpful ways for schools to meet the needs of culturally diverse learners, and describes the teacher's efforts to adopt more culturally sensitive teaching practices and to rally her fellow teachers to join her.

Frames of Mind by Howard Gardner (New York: Basic Books, 1993). Introduces the theory of multiple intelligences and provides support and guidance for personalizing academic learning experiences.

The Light in Their Eyes by Sonia Nieto (New York: Teachers College Press, 1999). Draws on a wide body of research and the personal narratives of teachers and outlines ways that schools and classrooms can be transformed to meet the needs of all students.

Emotional Intelligence by Daniel Goleman (New York: Bantam Books, 1997). The book that brought to public attention the importance of social and emotional skills in school and life success.

The Competitive Ethos and Democratic Education by John Nicholls (Cambridge, MA: Harvard University Press, 1989). A well-researched and thoughtful analysis of the harmful effects of competition on children's learning and development.

Time to Teach and Time to Learn: Changing the Pace of School by Chip Wood (Greenfield, MA: Northeast Foundation for Children, Inc., 1999). A beautifully written and powerfully argued case for creating personalized learning environments in our schools and for addressing social and ethical as well as academic learning. The three chapters that follow a teacher and two students (a seventh-grade girl and a first-grade boy) through a school day are particularly eye-opening, and the concrete suggestions for creating more caring learning communities are insightful as well as practical.

Following are publications describing school programs focused on social, emotional, and moral development:

Becoming Good American Schools by Jeannie Oakes, Karen Hunter Quartz, Steve Ryan, and Martin Lipton (San Francisco: Jossey-Bass, 2000). Tells the difficult but inspiring stories of fifteen middle schools as they struggled to become more just, caring, academically rigorous, and committed to diversity.

Caring Classrooms/Intelligent Schools edited by Jonathan Cohen (New York: Teachers College Press, 2001). Outlines core concepts and educational practices involved in education for social and emotional development and describes in depth several elementary SEL programs.

Educating Hearts and Minds by Catherine Lewis (Cambridge University Press, 1985). Uses the voices of Japanese teachers and vivid examples from Japanese classrooms to show how teachers can focus on the development of the whole child, thus helping children build caring and responsible attitudes and develop their understanding of academic content.

Educating Minds and Hearts by Jonathan Cohen (New York: Teachers College Press, 1999). Provides an overview of the history of social and emotional learning in schools, with several leading figures in the field describing SEL programs for middle schools.

Promoting Social and Emotional Learning by Maurice Elias, Joe Zins, Roger Weissberg, Karen Frey, Mark Greenberg, Norris Haynes, Rachael Kessler, Mary Schwab-Stone, and Timothy Shriver (Alexandria, VA: Association for Supervision and Curriculum Development, 1997). Looks at preschool through high school, with leading figures in the field of social and emotional learning describing essential emotional and social skills, providing guidelines for program development, and describing exemplary programs.

Safe and Sound, written and published by the Collaborative for Academic, Social, and Emotional Learning (CASEL), 2002. Provides a brief background on the theory and research related to social and emotional learning and an extensive, *Consumer Reports*-style review of eighty-one SEL programs.

School Power by James Comer (New York: Free Press, 1995). Describes the first school reform program to address all aspects of children's development and to recognize that if teachers are to meet the needs of all their students, they will need help not only from families but from social and mental health workers.

The Soul of Education: Helping Students Find Connection, Compassion, and Character at School by Rachael Kessler (Alexandria, VA: Association for Supervision and Curriculum Development, 2000). Describes and provides the rationale for Passages—a school-based program to help adolescents meet their needs for belonging and spirituality as they prepare to assume the responsibilities of adult life in a caring democratic community.

Waging Peace in Our Schools by Linda Lantieri and Janet Patti (Boston: Beacon Press, 1998). Describes the rationale, the nuts and bolts, and the successes of Resolving Conflicts Creatively—the well-regarded conflict resolution program developed by Educators for Social Responsibility.

The following are useful organizations and Web sites:

The Character Education Partnership (www.character.org) Dedicated to supporting schools and programs focused on building children's commitment to the core values and virtues essential to a just and caring democratic society. They sponsor an annual conference and a schools-of-character award, and publish materials and a newsletter.

Center for Partnership Studies (www.partnershipway.org) Based on the work of Riane Eisler and offering staff development, coaching, and curriculum materials to support educational approaches characterized by collaboration, empathy, caring, individual respect, and concern for peace and justice.

Center for Social and Emotional Learning (www.csse.net) Headed by Jonathan Cohen and produces books on SEL programs, hosts conferences, and maintains a Web site dedicated to helping parents, administrators, school counselors, and teachers foster students' social and emotional learning. The Web site provides information about child development, connections to other organizations, interviews with experts in the field, and lists of recommended articles and books.

Collaborative for Academic, Social, and Emotional Learning (CASEL) (www.casel.org) Sponsors conferences and helps coordinate information related to social, emotional, and moral learning and development. This organization produced *Safe and Sound,* which can be downloaded from their Web site. The Web site also contains information about conferences and recent publications related to social and emotional learning, which can usually be downloaded directly from the site.

Developmental Studies Center (DSC) (www.devstu.org) Home of the Child Development Project and dedicated to fostering children's social, moral, and intellectual development in school and after-school settings. They publish a wide assortment of print and video materials and provide staff development supportive of their mission. They also produce collegial study packages for several of their programs consisting of a book focused on a particular classroom practice along with videos of the practice in several classrooms and guidelines for organizing a supportive study group. The Web site describes their mission, programs, and materials and provides summaries of their research.

Educators for Social Responsibility (ESR) An organization with a mission to make teaching social responsibility a core practice in education. They publish a newsletter and curriculum materials and provide staff development support focusing on conflict resolution, peace education, and respect for diversity. Their Web site provides free materials, for example, suggestions for helping students understand 9/11 and for guiding them in its aftermath. It also describes staff development programs and materials (Pre-K–12) supportive of their mission.

The Foundation for Educational Renewal (www.pathsoflearning.net) A nonprofit organization dedicated to connecting people concerned with democratic, holistic, student-centered forms of education. They publish the journal *Paths of Learning,* provide links to many like-minded organizations, offer annotated lists of additional readings on topics addressed in *Paths of Learning,* and run an educational clearinghouse.

The George Lucas Foundation (www.glef.org) A site focused on education. The Web site provides information about staff development, promising practices in performance-based assessment, teaching for emotional intelligence, and project-based learning. The site contains interviews with prominent educators, video clips of promising programs, articles by teachers and principals, instructional modules for courses or staff development, curriculum materials, and the opportunity to sign up for their free newsletter.

Northeast Foundation for Children/Responsive Classroom (www.responsiveclassroom.org) Although this organization uses logical consequences as a cornerstone of its approach to classroom discipline, they also have a strong focus on building a caring community that meets students' social and emotional needs. They publish fine materials and provide staff development support. The Web site contains useful articles, lists of publications and workshops, and useful tips from teachers.

Studies in Moral Development and Education (www.moraled.org) Created and maintained by Larry Nucci and containing descriptions of classroom practices supportive of students' moral development, lists of assessments in the moral domain, and reviews of selected articles and books related to moral development.

Teaching Tolerance (www.tolerance.org) Sponsored by the Southern Poverty Law Center and providing lots of resources for teaching the values of tolerance, respect and equity. You can download news articles, get ideas for classroom activities, read reviews of books and resources, send for free curriculum packages, read the newsletter, join in conversations with other teachers focused on teaching tolerance, and find out about grants to support projects focused on teaching tolerance.

UCLA School Mental Health Project (www.smhp.psych.ucla.edu) Provides practical ideas for supporting students' social and emotional health, for example, tips for welcoming new students, as well as research articles on mental health and its impact on academic learning.

Finally, here is a list of the children's literature that Laura mentions:

Amelia's Notebook, Marissa Moss, Pleasant Company Publications, 1999.

Chicken Sunday, Patricia Polacco, Philomel Books, 1992.

Daniel's Duck, Clyde Robert Bulla, Harper Trophy, 1982.

Frog and Toad Are Friends, Arnold Lobel, Harper & Row, 1979.

The Gold Coin, Alma Flor Ada, Atheneum, 1991.

J. T., Jane Wagner, Dell Yearling, 1985.

Martin Luther King, Jr.: A Man Who Changed Things, Carol Green, Children's Press, 1989.

Miss Maggie, Cynthia Rylant, E. P. Dutton, 1983 (out of print).

The Outside Dog, Charlotte Pomerantz, HarperCollins, 1993.

Shoeshine Girl, Clyde Robert Bulla, Thomas Y. Crowell, 1975.

The Stories Julian Tells, Ann Cameron, Pantheon Books, 1981.

REFERENCES

Ainsworth, M.D.S. "Patterns of Attachment Behavior Shown by the Infant in Interaction with His Mother." *Merrill-Palmer Quarterly,* 1964, *10,* 51–58.

Ainsworth, M.D.S. *Infancy in Uganda: Infant Care and the Growth of Love.* Baltimore: Johns Hopkins University Press, 1967.

Ainsworth, M.D.S., Blehar, M. C., Waters, E., and Wall, S. *Patterns of Attachment.* Hillsdale, N.J.: Erlbaum, 1978.

Ainsworth, M.D.S., and Marvin, R. S. "On the Shaping of Attachment Theory and Research: An Interview with Mary D. S. Ainsworth." *Child Development,* 1995, *60,* 1–2, 3–21.

Banks, J. A. "Multicultural Education: Characteristics and Goals." In J. A. Banks and C. A. Banks (eds.), *Multicultural Education: Issues and Perspectives.* Boston: Allyn & Bacon, 1993.

Bateson, M. C. *Composing a Life.* New York: Plume/Penguin, 1990.

Battistich, V., Solomon, D., Watson, M., and Schaps, E. "Caring School Communities." *Educational Psychologist,* 1997, *32*(3), 137–151.

Bayles, E. E., and Hood, B. L. *Growth of American Educational Thought and Practice.* New York: Harper & Row, 1966.

Benard, B. "Fostering Resiliency in Kids." *Educational Leadership,* Nov. 1993, 44–48.

Blatchford, P., Moriarty, V., Edmonds, S., and Martin, C. "Relationships Between Class Size and Teaching: A Multimethod Analysis of English Infant Schools." *American Educational Research Journal,* 2002, *39*(1), 101–132.

Bower, G. H., and Hilgard, E. R. *Theories of Learning.* Englewood Cliffs, N.J.: Prentice Hall, 1981.

Bowlby, J. "The Nature of the Child's Tie to His Mother." *International Journal of Psychoanalysis,* 1958, *39,* 350–373.

Bowlby, J. *Attachment and Loss,* Vol. 1: *Attachment.* New York: Basic Books, 1969.

Bowlby, J. *Attachment and Loss,* Vol. 2: *Separation.* New York: Basic Books, 1973.

Bretherton, I. "Attachment Theory: Retrospect and Prospect." In I. Bretherton and E. Waters (eds.), *Growing Points of Attachment Theory and Research.*

Monographs of the Society for Research in Child Development, 1985, *50*(1–2), no. 209, 3–35.

Bryk, A., and Driscoll, M. *The High School as Community: Contextual Influences and Consequences for Students and Teachers.* Madison, Wis.: National Center on Effective Secondary Schools, University of Wisconsin-Madison, 1988.

Bus, A. G., and van IJzendoorn, M. H. "Mother-Child Interactions, Attachment, and Emergent Literacy: A Cross-Sectional Study." *Child Development,* 1988, *59,* 1262–1272.

Bus, A. G., and van IJzendoorn, M. H. "Mothers Reading to Their 3-Year-Olds: The Role of Mother-Child Attachment Security in Becoming Literate." *Reading Research Quarterly,* 1995, *30,* 998–1015.

Carlson, E. A. "A Prospective Longitudinal Study of Attachment Disorganization/Disorientation." *Child Development,* 1998, *69,* 1107–1128.

Cassidy, J. "Emotion Regulation: Influences of Attachment Relationships." In N. Fox (ed.), *The Development of Emotion Regulation: Biological and Behavioral Considerations.* Monographs of the Society for Research in Child Development, 1994, *59*(2–3), no. 240, 228–249.

Cassidy, J., and Shaver, P. R. (eds.). *Handbook of Attachment: Theory, Research, and Clinical Applications.* New York: Guilford Press, 1999.

Cohn, D. A. "Child-Mother Attachment of Six-Year-Olds and Social Competence at School." *Child Development,* 1990, *61,* 152–162.

Cortes, C. E. "The Education of Language Minority Students: A Contextual Interaction Model." In *Beyond Language: Social and Cultural Factors in Schooling Language Minority Students.* Los Angeles: Office of Bilingual Education, California State Department of Education, Evaluation, Dissemination, and Assessment Center, 1986.

Cortes, C. E. *The Children Are Watching.* New York: Teachers College Press, 2000.

Crockenberg, S. "Infant Irritability, Mother Responsiveness, and Social Support Influences on the Security of Infant-Mother Attachment." *Child Development,* 1981, *52,* 857–865.

Curwin, R. L., and Mendler, A. N. *Discipline with Dignity.* Alexandria, Va.: Association for Supervision and Curriculum Development, 1988.

Dalton, J., and Watson, M. *Among Friends: Classrooms Where Caring and Learning Prevail.* Oakland, Calif.: Developmental Studies Center, 1997.

deCharms, R. *Personal Causation.* New York: Academic Press, 1968.

deCharms, R. *Enhancing Motivation: Change in the Classroom.* New York: Irvington, 1976.

Deci, E. L., and Ryan, R. M. *Intrinsic Motivation and Self-Determination in Human Behavior.* New York: Plenum Press, 1985.

Delpit, L. *Other People's Children: Cultural Conflict in the Classroom.* New York: The New Press, 1995.

Dewey, J. *Experience and Education.* New York: Collier Books, 1958. (Originally published 1939.)

Dewey, J. *Democracy and Education: An Introduction to the Philosophy of Education.* New York: Free Press, 1966. (Originally published 1916.)

Dewey, J. *Moral Principles in Education.* Carbondale: Southern Illinois University Press, 1975. (Originally published 1909.)

Dreikurs, R., and Cassel, P. *Discipline Without Tears.* New York: Hawthorn Books, 1972.

Dreikurs, R., Grunwald, B. B., and Pepper, F. C. *Maintaining Sanity in the Classroom: Classroom Management Techniques.* New York: HarperCollins, 1982.

Elicker, J., Englund, M., and Sroufe, L. A. *Predicting Peer Competence and Peer Relationships in Childhood from Early Parent-Child Relationships: Modes of Linkage.* Hillsdale, N.J.: Erlbaum, 1992.

Erickson, M. F., Sroufe, L. A., and Egeland, B. *The Relationship Between Quality of Attachment and Behavior Problems in Preschool in a High-Risk Sample.* Monographs of the Society for Research in Child Development, 1985, *50,* 147–193.

Erikson, E. *Childhood and Society.* New York: W. W. Norton, 1963. (Originally published 1950.)

Flinders, D. J., and Noddings, N. *Multiyear Teaching: The Case for Continuity.* Bloomington, Ind.: Phi Delta Kappa, 2001.

Freud, S. *Civilization and Its Discontents.* New York: W. W. Norton, 1961. (Originally published 1930.)

Gardner, H. *Frames of Mind: The Theory of Multiple Intelligences.* New York: Basic Books, 1983.

George, C., and Solomon, J. "Internal Working Models of Caregiving and Security of Attachment at Age Six." *Infant Mental Health Journal,* 1989, *10,* 222–237.

Gilligan, C. *In a Different Voice: Psychological Theory and Women's Development.* Cambridge, Mass.: Harvard University Press, 1982.

Glasser, W. *Schools Without Failure.* New York: Harper & Row, 1969.

Goldstein, L. S. *Teaching with Love: A Feminist Approach to Early Childhood Education.* New York: Peter Lang, 1997.

Goleman, D. *Emotional Intelligence.* New York: Bantam Books, 1995.

Goodenow, C., and Grady, K. E. "The Relationship of School Belonging and Friends' Values to Academic Motivation Among Urban Adolescent Students." *Journal of Experimental Education,* 1993, 62(1), 60–71.

Gordon, T. *Teacher Effectiveness Training.* New York: Wyden, 1974.

Haberman, M. *Star Teachers of Children In Poverty.* West Lafaytte, Ind.: Kappa Delta Pi, 1995.

Heath, S. B. *Ways with Words.* New York: Cambridge University Press, 1983.

Hesse, E., and Main, M. "Second-Generation Effects of Unresolved Trauma in Non-Maltreating Parents: Dissociated, Frightened and Threatening Parental Behavior." In D. Diamond and S. J. Blatt (eds.), *Psychoanalytic Theory and Attachment Research*, Vol. 1: *Theoretical Considerations. Psychoanalytic Inquiry*, 1999, *19*.

Hesse, E., and Main, M. "Disorganization Infant, Child, and Adult Attachment: Collapse in Behavioral and Attentional Strategies." *Journal of the American Psychoanalytic Association*, 2000, *48*(4), 1097–1127.

Hoffman, M. L. "Empathy: Its Development and Prosocial Implications." In C. B. Keasey (ed.), *Nebraska Symposium on Motivation*, Vol. 25. Lincoln: University of Nebraska Press, 1978.

Hoffman, M. L. *Empathy and Moral Development: Implications for Caring and Justice*. Cambridge: Cambridge University Press, 2000.

Howes, C. *Attachment Relationships in the Context of Multiple Caregivers*. In J. Cassidy and P. R. Shaver (eds.), Handbook of Attachment Theory, Research, and Clinical Applications. New York: Guilford, 1999.

Howes, C., and Hamilton, C. "Children's Relationships with Child Care Teachers: Stability and Concordance with Parental Attachments." *Child Development*, 1992, *63*, 867–878.

Johnson, D. W., and Johnson, R. *Cooperation and Competition: Theory and Research*. Edina, Minn.: Interaction Books, 1989.

Johnson, R. T. *Hands Off: The Disappearance of Touch in the Care of Children*. New York: Peter Lang, 2000.

Karier, C. J. *The Individual, Society, and Education: A History of American Educational Ideas*. Urbana: University of Illinois Press, 1986.

Kestenbaum, R., Farber, E., and Sroufe, L. A. "Individual Differences in Empathy Among Preschoolers: Concurrent and Predictive Validity." In N. Eisenberg (ed.), *Empathy and Related Emotional Responses*. New Directions for Child Development, no. 44. San Francisco: Jossey-Bass, 1989.

Koestner, R., Ryan, R. M., Bernieri, F., and Holt, K. "Setting Limits on Children's Behavior: The Differential Effects of Controlling vs. Informational Styles on Intrinsic Motivation and Creativity." *Journal of Personality*, 1984, *52*, 233–248.

Kohlberg, L. "Stage and Sequence: The Cognitive-Developmental Approach to Socialization." In D. Goslin (ed.), *Handbook of Socialization Theory and Research*. Chicago: Rand McNally, 1969.

Kohn, A. *No Contest: The Case Against Competition*. (Rev. ed.) Boston: Houghton Mifflin, 1992.

Kohn, A. *Punished by Rewards: The Trouble with Gold Stars, Incentive Plans, A's, Praise, and Other Bribes*. Boston: Houghton Mifflin, 1993.

Kohn, A. *Beyond Discipline: From Compliance to Community*. Alexandria, Va.: ASCD, 1996.

Londerville, S., and Main, M. "Security of Attachment, Compliance, and Maternal Training Methods in the Second Year of Life." *Developmental Psychology,* 1981, *17,* 289–299.

Lyons-Ruth, K. "Attachment Relationships Among Children with Aggressive Behavior Problems: The Role of Disorganized Early Attachment Patterns." *Journal of Consulting and Clinical Psychology,* 1996, *64,* 64–73.

Lyons-Ruth, K., and Jacobvitz, D. "Attachment Disorganization: Unresolved Loss, Relational Violence, and Lapses in Behavioral and Attentional Strategies." In J. Cassidy and P. R. Shaver (eds.), *Handbook of Attachment: Theory, Research, and Clinical Applications.* New York: Guilford Press, 1999.

Lyons-Ruth, K., Repacholi, B., McLeod, S., and Silva, E. "Disorganized Attachment Behavior in Infancy: Short-Term Stability, Maternal and Infant Correlates, and Risk-Related Subtypes." *Developmental and Psychopathology,* 1991, *3,* 377–396.

Maehr, M. L., and Midgley, C. *Transforming School Cultures.* Boulder, Colo.: Westview Press, 1996.

Main, M. "Mary D. Salter Ainsworth: Tribute and Portrait." *Psychoanalytic Inquiry,* 1999, *19,* 682–736.

Main, M., Kaplan, N., and Cassidy, J. "Security in Infancy, Childhood, and Adulthood: A Move to the Level of Representation." In I. Bretherton and E. Waters (eds.), *Growing Points of Attachment Theory and Research.* Monographs of the Society for Research in Child Development, 1985, *50*(1–2), no. 209, 66–104.

Main, M., and Solomon, J. "Discovery of a New, Insecure-Disorganized/Disoriented Attachment Pattern." In T. B. Brazelton and M. W. Yogman (eds.), *Affective Development in Infancy.* Norwood, N.J.: Ablex, 1986.

Main, M., and Solomon, J. "Procedures for Identifying Infants as Disorganized/Disoriented During the Ainsworth Strange Situation." In M. T. Greenberg, D. Cicchetti, and E. M. Cummings (eds.), *Attachment in the Preschool Years: Theory, Research, and Intervention.* Chicago: University of Chicago Press, 1990.

Main, M., and Weston, D. "The Quality of the Toddler's Relationship to Mother and to Father: Related to Conflict Behavior and the Readiness to Establish New Relationships." *Child Development,* 1981, *52,* 932–940.

Maslow, A. *Motivation and Personality.* London: Cambridge University Press, 1970. (Originally published 1954.)

Matas, L. M., Arend, R. A., and Sroufe, L. A. "Continuity of Adaptation in the Second Year: The Relationship between Quality of Attachment and Later Competence." *Child Development,* 1978, *49,* 547–556.

Nelsen, J., Lott, L., and Glenn, H. S. *Positive Discipline in the Classroom.* Rocklin, Calif.: Prima, 1993.

Nicholls, J. G. *The Competitive Ethos and Democratic Education.* Boston: Harvard University Press, 1989.

Nieto, S. *Affirming Diversity: The Sociopolitical Context of Multicultural Education.* New York: Longman, 1992.

Nieto, S. *The Light in Their Eyes: Creating Multicultural Learning Communities.* New York: Teachers College Press, 1999.

Noddings, N. *Caring: A Feminine Approach to Ethics and Moral Education.* Berkeley: University of California Press, 1984.

Noddings, N. "An Ethic of Caring and Its Implications for Instructional Arrangements." *American Journal of Education,* 1988, *96,* 215–230.

Noddings, N. *The Challenge to Care in Schools: An Alternative Approach to Education.* New York: Teachers College Press, 1992.

Noddings, N. "Conversation As Moral Education." *Journal of Moral Education,* 1994, *23,* 107–117.

Noddings, N. "Character Education and Community." In A. Molner (ed.), *The Construction of Children's Character.* National Society for the Study of Education. Chicago: University of Chicago Press, 1997.

Noddings, N. *Educating Moral People: A Caring Alternative to Character Education.* New York: Teachers College Press, 2002.

Nucci, L. P., and Turiel, E. "Social Interactions and the Development of Social Concepts in Preschool Children." *Child Development,* 1978, *49,* 400–407.

Nye, B., Hedges, L. V., and Konstantopoulos, S. "The Effects of Small Classes on Academic Achievement: The Results of the Tennessee Class Size Experiment." *American Educational Research Journal,* 2000, *37*(1), 123–151.

Orlick, T. *The Second Cooperative Sports & Games Book.* New York: Pantheon Books, 1982.

Osterman, K. F. "Students' Need for Belonging in the School Community." *Review of Educational Research,* 2000, *70*(3), 323–367.

Piaget, J. *The Origins of Intelligence in Children.* New York: International Universities Press, 1952.

Piaget, J. *The Moral Judgment of the Child.* New York: Free Press, 1965. (Originally published 1932.)

Pianta, R. C. *Enhancing Relationships Between Children and Teachers.* Washington, D.C.: American Psychological Association, 1999.

Pianta, R. C., and Nimetz, S. L. "Relationships Between Teachers and Children: Associations with Behavior at Home and in the Classroom." *Journal of Applied Developmental Psychology,* 1991, *12,* 379–393.

Pianta, R. C., Nimetz, S. L., and Bennett, E. "Mother-Child Relationships, Teacher-Child Relationships and Adjustment in Preschool and Kindergarten." *Early Childhood Research Quarterly,* 1997, *12,* 263–280.

Rimm-Kaufman, S. E., Early, D., Cox, M., Sakuja, G., Pianta, R., Bradley. R., and Payne, C. "Early Behavioral Attributes and Teachers' Sensitivity as

Predictors of Competent Behavior in the Kindegarten Classroom." *Journal of Applied Developmentsl Psychology*, 2002, *23*, 451–470.

Rodriguez, L. J. *It Doesn't Have to Be This Way: A Barrio Story.* San Francisco: Children's Book Press, 1999.

Rogers, C. *Freedom to Learn.* Columbus, Ohio: Charles E. Merrill, 1969.

Ryan, R. M., and Deci, E. L. "Self-Determination Theory and the Facilitation of Intrinsic Motivation, Social Development, and Well-Being." *American Psychologist,* 2000, *55,* 68–78.

Schmidt, P. R. *Cultural Conflict and Struggle: Literacy Learning in a Kindergarten Program.* New York: Peter Lang, 1998.

Shefelbine, J., and Newman, K. K. *SIPPS: Systematic Instruction in Phoneme Awareness, Phonics, and Sight Words.* Oakland, Calif.: Developmental Studies Center, 2000.

Sheldon, K. M., Elliot, A. J., Kim, Y., and Kasser, T. "What Is Satisfying About Satisfying Events? Testing 10 Candidate Psychological Needs." *Journal of Personality and Social Psychology,* 2001, *80*(2), 325–339.

Solomon, D., Battistitch, V., Kim, D., and Watson, M. "Teacher Practices Associated with Students' Sense of the Classroom as Community." *Social Psychology of Education,* 1997, *1637*, 235–267.

Solomon, D., Battistitch, V., Watson, M., Schaps, E,, and Lewis, C. "A Six-District Study of Educational Change: Direct and Mediated Effects of the Child Development Project." *Social Psychology of Education,* 2000, *4,* 3–51.

Solomon, D., Watson, M., and Battistitch, V. "Teaching and Schooling Effects on Moral/Prosocial Development." In V. Richardson (ed.), *Handbook of Research on Teaching* (4th ed.). Washington, D. C.: American Educational Research Association, 2001.

Sroufe, L. A. "Infant-Caregiver Attachment and Patterns of Adaptation in Preschool: The Roots of Maladaptation and Competence." In M. Perlmutter (ed.), *Minnesota Symposia on Child Psychology,* no. 16, Hillsdale, N.J.: Erlbaum, 1983, 41–83.

Sroufe, L. A. "The Role of Infant-Caregiver Attachment in Development." In J. Belsky and T. Nezworski (eds.), *Clinical Implications of Attachment.* Hillsdale, N.J.: Erlbaum, 1988.

Sroufe, L. A. *Emotional Development: The Organization of Emotional Life in the Early Years.* Cambridge: Cambridge University Press, 1996.

Sroufe, L. A., Carlson, E., and Shulman, S. "Individuals in Relationship: Development from Infancy Through Adolescence." In O. C. Funder, R. Park, C. Tomlinson-Keesey, and K. Widaman (eds.), *Studying Lives Through Time: Approaches to Personality and Development.* Washington, D.C.: American Psychological Association, 1993.

Sroufe, L. A., and Fleeson, J. "Attachment and the Construction of Relationships." In W. Hartup and Z. Rubin (eds.), *Relationships and Development.* Hillsdale, N.J.: Erlbaum, 1986.

Sroufe, L. A., and Waters, E. "Attachment as an Organizational Construct." *Child Development,* 1977, *48,* 1184–1199.

Sroufe, L. A., and Waters, E. "Heart Rate as a Convergent Measure in Clinical and Developmental Reaearch." *Merrill-Palmer Quarterly,* 1977, *23,* 3–27.

Stanne, M. B., Johnson, D. W., and Johnson, R. "Does Competition Enhance or Inhibit Motor Performance? A Meta-Analysis." *Psychological Bulletin,* 1999, *125,* 133–154.

Stayton, D. J., Hogan, R., and Ainsworth, M.D.S. "Infant Obedience and Maternal Behavior: The Origins of Socialization Reconsidered." *Child Development,* 1971, *42,* 1057–1069.

Steinberg, L., Brown, B. B., and Dornbusch, S. M. "Ethnicity and Adolescent Achievement." *American Educator,* Summer 1996, 28–48.

Urban, J., Carlson, E., Egeland, B., and Sroufe, L. A. "Patterns of Individual Adaptation Across Childhood." *Development and Psychopathology,* 1991, *3,* 445–460.

van IJzendoorn, M. H., and Sagi, A. "Cross-Cultural Patterns of Attachment: Universal and Contextual Dimensions." In J. Cassidy and P. R. Shaver (eds.), *Handbook of Attachment: Theory, Research, and Clinical Applications.* New York: Guilford Press, 1999.

van IJzendoorn, M. H., Schuengel, D., and Bakermans-Kranenburg, M. J. "Disorganized Attachment in Early Childhood: Meta-Analysis of Precursors, Concomitants, and Sequelae." *Development and Psychopathology,* 1999, *11,* 225–249.

Vygotsky, L. *Thought and Language.* Cambridge: MIT Press, 1968.

Watson, J. B. *Behaviorism.* Chicago: University of Chicago Press, 1930.

Weinfield, N. S., Sroufe, L. A., Egeland, B., and Carlson, E. A. "The Nature of Individual Differences in Infant-Caregiver Attachment." In J. Cassidy and P. R. Shaver (eds.), *Handbook of Attachment: Theory, Research, and Clinical Applications.* New York: Guilford Press, 1999.

Wentzel, K. R., and Caldwell, K. "Friendships, Peer Acceptance, and Group Membership: Relations to Academic Achievement in Middle School." *Child Development,* 1997, *68*(6), 1198–1209.

Werner, E., and Smith, R. *Vulnerable But Invincible: A Longitudinal Study of Resilient Children and Youth.* New York: Adams, Bannister, and Cox, 1989.

White, R. W. "Motivation Reconsidered: The Concept of Competence." *Psychological Review,* 1959, *66,* 297–333.

Wood, D., Bruner, J. S., and Ross, G. "The Role of Tutoring in Problem Solving." *Journal of Child Psychology and Psychiatry,* 1976, *17*(2), 89–100.

ABOUT THE AUTHORS

Marilyn Watson recently retired from Developmental Studies Center (DSC) to write this book and to move closer to her grandchildren. While at DSC, she served as program director of the Child Development Project—the center's award-winning school-change initiative focused on helping schools foster students' social and moral as well as intellectual development. She also directed the center's work in preservice education, literature, and literacy. Prior to her work at DSC, she was a preschool teacher, a faculty member in the education department at Mills College, and the director of the Mills College Children's School. She has also taught at Wayne State University, the University of California at Berkeley, and the University of Fribourg, Switzerland. She has authored or coauthored over forty articles related to children's social and moral development and coauthored two books: *Among Friends: Classrooms Where Caring and Learning Prevail* with Joan Dalton (1997, Developmental Studies Center) and *Company in Your Classroom: Building a Learning Relationship With Your Student Teacher* with Amy Schoenblum (2000). She served on the Association of Teacher Educators (ATE) National Commission on Character Education and is currently chair of the advisory panel of the Character Education Partnership's teacher education project.

Laura Ecken is a veteran teacher of sixteen years and is currently the science resource teacher at Cane Run elementary school in Louisville, Kentucky. The mother of five children, she started her professional life as a dental hygienist. While volunteering in her children's classrooms, she became interested in teaching and returned to school to obtain a Master of Arts in Teaching degree from Spalding University. Laura taught second through fourth grades and multi-aged primary students at Hazelwood elementary school for thirteen years. In addition to working with the Child Development Project, she has participated in the Louisville Advantage class, sponsored by the National Writing Project, and has done staff development for the Child Development Project, Kentucky's Ungraded Primary Program, and the Four Block Reading Model.

Index

A

B

E

F

G

Q

R

S

T

U

V

W

Y

Z

Other Books of Interest

What to Look for in a Classroom: . . . and Other Essays

Alfie Kohn

$18.00 Paperback
ISBN: 0-7879-5283-4

"Here at last is an honest, compassionate educator with his head screwed on right, whose ideas deserve to be put into general practice." —The New York Times Book Review

"Of the dozens of 'experts' on what's *wrong (and right) in U.S. schools, only a handful are truly worth reading; Kohn has long been one of the soundest."* —Booklist

From self-esteem to school uniforms, from grade inflation to character education, Alfie Kohn raises provocative questions about the status quo in this collection of incisive essays—challenging us to reconsider some of our most basic assumptions about children and education. Whether he is explaining why cooperative learning can be so threatening or why detracking is so fiercely opposed, Kohn offers a fresh, informed, and frequently disconcerting perspective on the major issues in education.

[Prices subject to change]

Other Books of Interest

Shaping School Culture: The Heart of Leadership

Terrence E. Deal
and Kent D. Peterson

$21.00 Paperback
ISBN: 0-7879-6243-0

"*No guidebook presents a better, more approachable path toward understanding and building a school culture than this one. I wish I had had* Shaping School Culture *beside me during my own turbulent years as a school principal!*" —Roland S. Barth, author of *Improving Schools from Within* and *Learning by Heart*

In this paperback edition of their classic book, Deal and Peterson draw from over twenty years of research and work to show how leaders can harness the power of school culture to build a lively, cooperative spirit and a sense of school identity. They describe the critical elements of culture—the purposes, traditions, norms, and values that guide and glue the community together—and show how a positive culture can make school reforms work.

[Prices subject to change]

Other Books of Interest

Holding Sacred Ground: Essays on Leadership, Courage, and Endurance in Our Schools

Carl D. Glickman

$27.00 Hardcover
ISBN: 0-7879-5671-6

"A very important book: lucid, lively, and readable . . . a work of courage and care. It's Carl to the core. I only wish that I had this book before I started so many school and community initiatives." —Deborah Meier, co-principal of The Mission Hill School, Boston and founder of a network of schools in East Harlem, New York

In twenty-two inspirational essays, Carl Glickman lays out the distinct characteristics of powerful schools, and examines the leadership priorities and practices that enable these schools to thrive and endure for generations. In the face of testing mandates, reduced funding, teacher shortages, and other challenges, it's easy for educators to lose sight of their ideals for equity and excellence in schooling. This book shows how some schools manage to hold onto the "sacred ground" by offering strategies for improving leadership, teaching, curriculum, student achievement, and collective action; in sum, the practical wisdom to weather the unpredictable obstacles ahead.

[Prices subject to change]

CPSIA information can be obtained at www.ICGtesting.com
Printed in the USA
BVOW040648241212

308751BV00005B/89/P

9 780787 966508